SHOAH
The Paradigmatic Genocide

SHOAH,
The Paradigmatic Genocide

Essays in Exegesis and Eisegesis

Zev Garber

Studies in the Shoah

Volume VIII

University Press of America
Lanham • New York • London

Copyright © 1994 by
University Press of America,® Inc.
4720 Boston Way
Lanham, Maryland 20706

3 Henrietta Street
London WC2E 8LU England

Library of Congress Cataloging-in-Publication Data

Garber, Zev.
Shoah : the paradigmatic genocide : essays in exegesis and
eisegesis / Zev Garber.
p.   cm. — (Studies in the Shoah ; v. 8)
Includes bibliographical references and index.
1. Holocaust, Jewish (1939-1945)—Historiography.   2. Holocaust
(Jewish theology)   I. Title.   II. Series.
D804.3.G38   1994   940.53'18'072—dc20   94–27782 CIP

ISBN 0–8191–9658–4 (cloth : alk. paper)
ISBN 0–8191–9659–2 (pbk. : alk. paper)

To Susan

CONTENTS

ACKNOWLEDGEMENTS

This book is a mosiac of thought, stimulated but not limited by the Dual Torah of the Sinai Mosaic faith, reflecting on the cyanide of the Jewish people in our time, the Shoah. Before national and international conferences of scholars, I presented my exegetical and eisegetical thinking, which has been refined in chapter setting. A number of chapters has appeared in earlier versions or as is elsewhere:

Chapter 2 in Zev Garber, Alan L. Berger and Richard Libowitz, eds., *Methodology in the Academic Teaching of the Holocaust* (Lanham: University Press of America, 1988), and in Gideon Shimoni, ed. *The Holocaust in University Teaching* (Oxford/New York/Seoul/Tokyo: Pergamon, 1991); reprinted with permission. Chapter 3 in *Modern Judaism*, vol. 9, no. 2 (May 1989): reprinted with permission. Chapter 4 in Alan L. Berger, ed., *Bearing Witness to the Holocaust*, 1939-1989 (Lewiston/ Queenston/Lampeter: The Edward Mellen Press, 1991); reprinted with permission. Chapter 5 in Harry James Cargas, ed., *The Unnecessary Problem of Edith Stein* (Lanham: University Press of America, 1994); reprinted with permission. Chapter 6 in *Shofar*, vol. 12, no. 1 (Fall 1993), by Purdue Research Foundation, West LaFayette, Indiana 47907, and in Franklin H. Littell, Alan L. Berger, and Hubert G. Locke, eds., *What Heve We Learned?* (Lewiston/Queenston/Lampeter: The Edward Mellen Press, 1994); reprinted with permission. Chapter 7 in G. Jan Colijn and Marcia S. Littell, eds., *The Netherlands and Nazi Genocide* (Lewiston/Queenston/ Lampeter: The Edward Mellen Press, 1992); reprinted with permission. Chapter 10 in the *Journal of Ecumenical Studies*, vol. 28, no. 4 (Fall 91). and in *Shofar*, vol. 10, no. 4 (Summer 1992), by Purdue Research Foundation, West Lafayette, Indiana 47907; reprinted with permission.

A number of good people have felt my anguished introspection and has heard my vision on what can and cannot be done in presenting the Shoah as paradigmatic exercise in remembering and doing: Alan L. Berger, Rahel Brenner, Seymour Cain, Steven L. Jacobs, Richard Libowitz, Hubert G. Locke, James Moore and Bruce Zuckerman. For their criticism and support, I am thankful.

I wish to acknowledge the diligent work of my former student and friend, Shahram Siman, a leader in the International Judea Federation, in setting this manuscript for publication. His conscientious devotion and wonderful disposition proved beneficial in bringing this project to completion. He also introduced me to unchartered waters: The importance of teaching Shoah-related issues to the Persian Jewish community. As a result, I write a column on Shoah, among other facets of the Jewish experience, for the Farsi monthly journal, *Chashm Andaaz*.

I am especially grateful and honored that two of the world's great scholars on the Shoah, Franklin H. Littell and Harry James Cargas, have written kind words on my methodology and thought. Language cannot adequately express my debt of gratitude to these two *hasidei ummot ha-olam* for their ecumenical inspiration, encouragement and guidance.

The book is dedicated to my wife, Susan Garber. My partner in life and work, she provided the environment and solace in which I could complete my task. Her presence in every turn, twist and detour enabled me to stay on course in my journey of beginnings - interruptions - endings, parochial and universal. She is an exemplar of the vivid reminder "to thinking people" as the essential starting point in Shoah Studies. This volume is a small token of my appreciation and respect for her, and hopeful blessing for length of days, years of life and well-being, *ad meah ve-esrim*.

Zev Garber

Yom Ha-Shoah
8 April 1994

FOREWORD

by
Franklin H. Littell

Zev Garber is a diligent and creative philosopher of history - a rare academic bird in a season when history is disregarded and the interpretation of history widely despised. He has splendid command of the languages and methodologies of Torah and Midrashim, so that the dialogue with the Book of Books comes alive at his hands.

The burden of the 19th century rests heavily on us yet, and a number of academics still seem to think the sheer accumulation of mountains of data is self-justifying. Professor Garber has moved well beyond this illusion that the human present and future may be fully explicated by the vigorous exercise of human reason. He is not afraid of the mythic and the mysterious, the poetic and the paradoxical.

Professor Garber has no problem with making his contributions to the documentation of the story of the Holocaust, nor with expounding fresh insights in the methodologies of successfully teaching the brute facts. But his rare genius finds its best expression in presenting and interpreting the meaning(s) which are there to be read out in the dialogue with the Book of History.

In inter-acting with the Book of History, we are presently aware of the past, presently aware of the present moment, and presently aware of the future. Along this continuum of awareness, the person who lives in human history - and not in a dream world apart from it - grows and matures with his years.

Professor Garber's essays help us to prevent a premature closure on the story of the Holocaust, and to keep it a continuing warning of the wickedness to which men and women are prone when they lose the human touch and devote their brains and skills to the service of idols like the *Führer* and the *Führerstaat*. His work remind us, as no more accumulation of "facts" ever could, that we were human beings before we acquired those academic degrees, and that - like those technically competent barbarians who created the complex killing machine that was the Nazi Third Reich - we too shall stand naked at the Grand Assize.

Franklin H. Littell
Baylor University

Preface

The Shoah was an extraordinary event. It requires an extraordinary response. That should be plural: it requires extraordinary responses. Just the awesome event was so unique in human history, so must each of our responses be unique to us. Not unique to be different but unique to be creative. There will be no one adequate response to the Holocaust. The best we can hope for is that each of us confront the crisis fully, honestly, to the best of our capabilities to discover in our minds, in our hearts, the significance that the Shoah has for each of us individually and the world collectively.

Zev Garber has had the courage to do that. There are rationalizations which we might take in order not to experience (from our personal distances, of course) the crime of genocide against the Jews *panim b' fanim* or "face to face" to the degree that we can. Whether we say it is too overwhelming, or the past is past, or it should be left to the scholars, the philosophers, the historians, the theologians, whatever the "excuse" these are inadequate. Professor Garber says in his talk at the Berlin International Conference, we must "address the Shoah as living history." However, as he insists, we must do this "in terms of activism and not quietism." To do otherwise would be to betray the dead.

It could also be to betray the living. Hence Garber's continued significant work on teaching the Holocaust. Because of its tremendous importance, the Shoah must not be taught casually. It is not merely another course to be passed, another three credit block to be scheduled, another program to be gotten through. There has never been another subject like it. Furthermore, there are no precedents on which to build. There is no adeqaute vocabulary to desribe certain events of World War II. Therefore guidance by authentic teachers is both welcome and necessary. The second chapter of this volume addresses that need.

Part of the question of teaching and vocabulary is examined in the third chapter on the reason the Holocaust is so called. That our response to the Holocaust is not logical but psychological, as Garber puts it, is exactly right. And again he is correct when he reminds us that in one sense the question is academic because the label will have a life of its own. Even the word "Shoah" he points out is not a perfect word because of its largely passive connotation. Yet the question is not to be easily dismissed as Garber's essay indicates. It has a great bearing on many aspects of the problem including ways in which the Holocaust is unique.

What may be seen as a companion piece is Garber's examination of the dating of the Shoah. And the conclusion at which he arrives is consistent with all that he writes (and lives) regarding activism versus quietism: "Thus on April 12, 1951, the Knesset read first the declaration on *Yom ha-Atzmaut* followed by the declaration on *Yom ha-Shoah*. The order of the readings is important; it suggests that only a relentless commitment to life and hope (Zionist dream and hope) can withstand the pain and grief of remembering the Shoah. The reverse is unthinkable."

Scholarship without imagination can prove sterile. As we read in Chapter Six, mythicizing history is invaluable for those who would understand. Imaginative, even fictional truth, has its own level of integrity and meaning — at least on a par with so called historical truth. In the example he gives us of the martyrs known as the Ninety-Three Maidens he shows us how, in the sense of biblical story telling, the letter of these women "confronts the generations after Auschwitz with the 'living' message of the dead." Again, in his consistency, he insists that "Their act of Kaddish becomes an act of doing not just an exercise in remembering."

Another kind of martyrdom is approached in the essay on Edith Stein. The nature of her death is ambiguous. Did she die as a Jew or as a Christian as far as her murderers were concerned? Jewish and Christian authorities can be found who are convinced on both sides of the issue. Typically, Garber does not duck it but faces it squarely *panim b'fanim*.

As in the piece on Edith Stein, and in fact all of his other chapters, Garber writes from a perspective based in his understanding of Jewish theology. This is certainly true in "Night Encounters" of the interlocation of Shoah in Passover rites (where classical rabbinic thinking is a part of the living service and therefore both Liberty and Law are stresses) and of Amalekphobia as discussed in Chapter Seven.

My point in this little reprise is to remind the reader of the range that this volume covers. Professor Garber did not set out deliberatley to impress us with the scope of his conviction. Each of these is an occasion piece, written for a specific audience or event. Yet together they make a cohesive whole. It is as if he purposely set out to expand the meaning of the term "ecumenical." In common parlance it has to do with intrareligious dialogue—within Christianity. However no religious group exists in isolation even if it wishes to. Garber takes up the wider expanse of Christian-Jewish dialogue which is necessary and all too often absent on anything beyond the superficially social level and he gives it substance in a way that is unique to him.

May we see many more such works from his mind and heart.

Harry James Cargas
Webster University

CHAPTER ONE

Insiders and Outsiders: For Whom Do We Toil?

Insiders and outsiders --- survivors, theologians, academics, activists --- sharply differ on pressing Shoah questions of the day. Christian and Jewish theologians argue, "Never again ... do theology in such a way that its construction remains unaffected, or could remain unaffected, by Auschwitz" (Alice L. and A. Roy Eckardt) and, "Let us offer this fundamental criterion after the Holocaust. No statement, theological or otherwise, should be made that would not be credible in the presence of burning children" (Irving Greenberg). Yet there is tension between the more intellectual, dispassionate academic and the survivors, who are fired by patterns of suspicion that scholars objectify their many years of agony, pain and torment. Many older survivors oppose any dialogue, for example, with Germans or with anyone that implies reconciliation between the German and Jewish peoples. But child survivors and children of survivors concur with scholars in the importance of dialogue to "sensitize" the German people not to "sanitize" proper memory and respect for the Shoah. Also, Christian and Jewish divines differ as to an honorable Kaddish by the living for the dead: The former, not to forget but forgive and the latter, not to forget nor forgive.

My essay examines some of these examples to demonstrate that longstanding bias and pivotal positions must be integrated or put aside if we are to dwell in unity in preserving and presenting the Shoah as living history.

A preliminary draft of "Insiders and Outsiders" was presented at the 22nd Annual Scholars' Conference meeting at the University of Washington, 29 February - 4 March 1992. At the Conference, I and Conference Secretary, Hubert G. Locke (Professor of Public Affairs, Graduate School of Public Affairs, University of Washington), co-founder with Franklin H.

Littell of the Annual Scholars' Conference on the Holocaust and Church Struggle, presented to Professor Littell a re-publication of his **The German Phoenix: Men and Movements in the Church in Germany** *(Studies in the Shoah 2: Lanham: UPA, 1992) in tribute of his 75th year. The honoree has devoted his professional life "to keep the study and teaching of the Shoah interfaith, inter-disciplinary and international." I write in his shadow.*

I. Prolegomenon

Advances in understanding the Shoah, its causes, effects and responses have been dramatic and widely chronicled in the second half of the twentieth century, but the writing has been written in successive waves. The first recounted the horror of the Nazi treatment of Europe's Jews in the historical context of deep rooted prejudices and secular antisemitic behavior. Then came the indictment against the intent and will of strength of the German and Austrian nations, the Church leadership, the French and English and Soviet governments, and the free world, to combat morally the threat of and from Nazism. Also, the question, what about God? Where was the God of promises when millions of innocent Abrahams, Isaacs, Jacobs, Sarahs, Rebeccahs, Leahs and Rachels have gone up in smoke? In short, what is human and divine responsibility after Aushwitz?

The responses, quantitatively few but qualitatively perceptive, cover the gamut of Jewish thought. From Richard Rubenstein's death of God theology, i.e., letting go of traditional Judaism's doctrine of God for a new symbol of God's reality conducive to the lessons learned from the Shoah,[1] to hasidic masters who argue classical Orthodox belief rooted in spontaneous religious experience.[2] Though Elie Wiesel maintains that the Shoah transcends history and the living are neither capable nor worthy of recovering its mystery, still he relates witness-stories. They bear testimony to the depths of Jewish suffering and the dignity of the Jewish dead, while promoting Jewish survival as an unshakable dogma. Emil Fackenheim's 614th Commandment, no posthumous victory to Hitler, suggests that Shoah claims another victim whenever a Jew doubts his/her Jewishness; conversely, when a Jew lives up to Judaism's creeds and deeds, s/he advances *tikkun 'olam* ("repairing the world"). Also, Irving Greenberg's recognition that we live not in ever-present faith but in "moments of faith, moments when Redeemer and vision of Redemption are present, interspersed with times when the flames and smoke of the burning children blot out faith—though it flickers again,"[3] signals that Israel's covenant is no longer obligatory but voluntary.

Peculiar, but not surprising, Jewish belief in a post-Auschwitz age says more about the concerns and fears for a meaningful Jewish present and future than about the Nazi agenda for Judeocide. What connects these theological viewpoints is the Jewish potential and self-accountability in bridging the chasm betweem God and Israel and Israel and the world.

In the 1980s, an old-new problem has erupted: Deal with the denial of facts and the minimization of the Event and emphasize that moral bankruptcy in individuals, institutions, and governments is an early warning sign of genocidal tendencies. Also, reaffirm high moral standards for all nations and races so that the dignity, integrity, and liberty of the human being are ensured.[4]

Workers in the cemetery of the Shoah testify to the stubborn persistence of the Shoah to "the past that weighs like a nightmare on the brain of the living," as French philosopher Jean-Paul Sartre once described history. It is the "deadly weight" of the Shoah—the horrific tradition of state-sponsored victimization and murder, and the unaccountable human, spiritual and material loss that followed in its smoke—that has aroused many to speak out against the Bitberg spirit of "storycide" and to discuss antisemitism (past, present, future) and how the lessons from the Shoah might help prevent future genocide.

However, insiders and outsiders—survivors, theologians, academics, activists—sharply differ on pressing Shoah questions of the day. Christian and Jewish theologians argue, "Never again...do theology in such a way that its construction remains unaffected, or could remain unaffected, by Auschwitz" (Alice L. and A. Roy Eckardt) and, "Let us offer the fundamental criterion after the Holocaust. No statement, theological or otherwise, should be made that would not be credible in the presence of burning children" (Irving Greenberg).

Yet there is tension between the more intellectual, dispassionate academic and the survivor, who is fired by patterns of suspicion that scholars objectify his/her many years of agony, pain and torment. For example, many older survivors oppose any dialogue with Germans or with anything that implies reconciliation between the German and Jewish peoples. But child survivors and children of survivors concur with scholars in the importance of dialogue to "sensitize" the German people not to "sanitize" proper memory and respect for the Shoah. Also, Christian and Jewish divines differ as to an honorable Kaddish by the living for the dead: The former, not to forget but to forgive, and the latter, neither to forget or forgive.

Mark Lidzbarski, the noted orientalist of a bygone age, relates in the story of his youth (**Auf Rauhem Wege**) a tale his grandfather was fond of telling: A man, on meeting a misfit wearing a patched coat asked the wearer if he knew what patch came from the original cloth. The fellow replied that nothing had remained of the original material. Such, noted the grandfather, is the state of religion; patch holds to patch, but no one knows whether any patch is of the original fabric.

Substitute "Shoah" for "religion" and "personal agenda" for "patch" and you have a core problem in the presentation of Shoah today: in clothing the naked dead, we are more concerned in validating the patches than presenting the finished product. What, then, are some of the pivotal positions and bias that must be integrated or set aside if we are to dwell in unity in preserving and presenting the Shoah as living history? The prayer shawl is damaged: Disparate voices hover above it, enter into it, and tear it to shreds. By responding knowlingly "for whom do we toil?" can we restore the garment by threads of compassion, love and justice.

II. No Right Term

At the 1988 Oxford Conference on the Impact of the Holocaust and Genocide on Jews and Christians, my colleague, Professor Bruce Zuckerman (USC), and I presented a paper which investigated the etymology of the term "Holocaust" and its historic background, and contained a section on the implications of the term. We pointed out that a basic meaning of "something wholly burnt up" to an applied meaning of "total destruction" is largely misleading. Pre-Nazi period dictionaries translate the Hebrew for whole-burnt offering, the *'olah* (e.g., I Sam 7:9), by what was considered the most appropriate English equivalent: "Holocaust."

(The term comes via the Latin *holocaustum* from the Greek *'olokaustos*. This , in turn, is a compound composed of *'olos*, an adjective meaning "whole, entire, complete in all its parts" and *kaustos*, another objectival from meaning "burnt, red hot.")

Thus, the employ of a specifically religious term for the genocide of European Jews in World War II, makes the Nazi murderers priestly officiants of divine propiation. Moreover, going far beyond questions of terminological propriety, there are basic psychological attitudes on the conventional *Jewish* view of the Shoah: That the event is unique, limited to Jewish victims of the Nazis, and a fulfillment of the Jews' traditional role as God's people, chosen to suffer for the redemption of mankind. We reject this view , and see the Shoah as one more tragic example of man's inhumanity to man, in which both murderers and victims are ordinary human beings in an extraordinary situation, a secular event without either saints or demons. We fear that the attitudes behind the continued use of the term "The Holocust" may lead to Jews seen as Christ-like sacrificial "lambs of God" or extreme ethnic chauvinism.

The message of the Shoah, then, is in this respect: Its ability to focus attention and its capacity to serve as a touchstone for all who would recognize that man's inhumanity to man is all too human. Having said this, however, we acknowledge the possibility that the heroism and memory of the Six Million *kedoshim* will be lost and oblitrated in seeing Everyman as victim. From Elie Wiesel we learn that not every victim was a Jew but all Jews were victims.

Irving Greenberg points out that Jews were unlike other victims. They were not considered sub-human Aryans, as were the Poles. Jews were seen not as human beings; they were vermin that had to be utterly destroyed. Jews had no choice of resistance or submission as others had; they were murdered for the crime of having been born.

During World War II, the Western powers were careful not to engage in specific Jewish rescue operations lest they flame the grist of antisemitism home-side by singling Jews out for special favors. However, the Nazis did single out the Jews for unique torment and death. Ironically, Holocaust Remembrance Day memorials, which loop together Six Million Jews and millions of other victims of Nazism are continuing (perhaps, unconsciously) this offensive omission.

We must stand vigil against any Bitberg-like attempt to obliterate the Jew as victim or unusual victim among revisionist historians, Third World liberation theologians, and some Church authorities, who argue convent and not covenent at Auschwitz.[5] Destroying the Jewish people and its *raison d'etre*, to paraphrase Emil Fackenheim, is not an accidental byproduct of Nazism but rather its inmost essence.

From a parochial experience comes forth a universal message which constitutes a circle—"the Holocaust circle." Though labeled *sui generis*, the cataclysmic event, the discontinuity in history, we insist that "The Holocaust" is in history and of history. The unspeakable events that befell the murdered Jewish people of Europe must be taken as emblematic and paradigmatic: The true horror inherent in what all people are capable of doing and what all people are capable of suffering.

This brings us to the Hebrew term for the Nazi war against the Jews: "Shoah". This term occurs at least twelve times in the Hebrew Bible.[6] Collectively, the texts in which it is found speak of the destruction of Israel/Judah and Babylon; desolation of nature and the land; and distress and anguish in the realm of personal experience. Unlike "Holocaust" and *Churban*,[7] which connote religious and sacrificial imperatives, "Shoah" suggests devastation and catastrophe in historical and providential categories. The earliest use of the term Shoah in regard to the Jewish murdered of the Second World War is in the booklet, **Shoat Yehudei Polin** ("Devastation of Polish Jewry"), published in Jerusalem in 1940. The awareness and identification of the Zionist leadership and Hebrew writers with the tragic fate of European Jewry enabled the Hebrew word Shoah to be widely used and recognized.

The popularity of the term began in 1942, when the Jewish Agency declared that a Shoah was taking place in Europe; also, before a gathering of his colleagues, the great Hebrew poet, Shaul Tschernichowsky (1875-1943), issued a wake-up call: "The command of the *sha'ah* (hour) is the command of the horrible Shoah that is coming upon us."

In text and context, Shoah conveys feelings associated with the universal phenomenon of mass extermination: Fear, agony, cruelty, violence, and evil. But the phrase does not perfectly describe Nazi Germany's agenda for the Jews: Genocide.

(Raphael Lemkin, a Polish Jew, coined the word "genocide" in response to the murder of most of his family members in Warsaw by the Germans during World War II. Lemkin designed a word to define the murder of a people to be a crime in international law; it is so recognized by the Genocide Convention, adopted by the United Nations in 1949.)

However, Judeocide, too, has its problems. Hitler's wish was the total annihilation of Judaism and *Yiddishkeit* in addition to Jews as a people.

So, we have come full circle. Let it be said that no term of record (Holocaust, Churban, Shoah, and Judeocide) captures the full metahistorical and historical impact of the senseless murder of millions. The right word, if there is one, might lull the memory to rest, and we insist, 50 years after Wannsee, that it must not be laid to rest.

III. Shoah and Remembrance: Christian Responses

Ever since the biblical writer declared, "This is the book of the generations of Adam, on the day that God created Adam (Man) it was in the image of God He created them" (Gen 5:1; see also **Sifra Kedoshim**), Judaism has committed itself and its ethical structure to the interdependence of mankind, and its corollary, man's repsonsibility to one another.

In the post-Auschwitz age this must be reemphasized at every possible moment, if the Jewish people and mankind are to witness the birth of the twenty-first century and beyond.

Christian scholars devoted to dialogue, in search of a common understanding between Jew and Christian and done not at the expense of altruism and egoism but in light of the principle, "Love your neighbor as yourself" (Lev 19:18; Matt 22:38; Mark 12:31; Luke 10:27), are to be encouraged and supported.

Readers of F. Littell's **The Crucifixion of the Jews** (Harper and Row, 1975), C. Thoma's **A Christian Theology of Judaism** (Paulist, 1980), R. Reuther's **Faith and Fraticide: The Theological Roots of Anti-Semitism**

(Seabury, 1974), Paul M. Van Buren's **Discerning the Way** and **A ChristianTheology of the People Israel**, Parts I and II of **A Theology of the Jewish Christian Reality** (Seabury, 1980 and 1983) and A. Roy Eckardt, **Reclaiming The Jesus of History** (Fortress, 1992) will sense that there are four major emphases in a Christian response to the Shoah.

First, the need to expose the anti-Jewish bias of *contra-Judaeos* found at the crossroads of Christian teaching and preaching. By stressing the importance of the study of Judaism on its own terms, Christian scholars are able to assess correctly the positive value of Jewish cult, rite, and law on the nascent Church and on the later history of Christianity.

For example, the Pharisees, unjustly maligned in the New Testament and in the writings of the Church Fathers, have been misunderstood and damned by centuries of Christian laity and scholars.[8] Fortunately, the image has been corrected. George Foote Moore, Reinhold Niebuhr, Jules Isaac, James Parkes, and others, have exposed the Church's prejudicial understanding of pharisaic Rabbinic Judaism as bad theology and poor historical interpretation. This in turn has led to the shameful "teaching of contempt" Christians have projected on the Jews for the past two millennia across all denominational barriers.

Second, whether or not there is a direct link between two thousand years of Christian supersession and the Shoah, Christian culpability in the near total destruction of European Jewry cannot be denied.

The words of Franklin H. Littell are instructive and to the point:

> Certain traditional Christian teachings of alienation and hatred must be eliminated. More important and more difficult by far, some negative teachings deeply rooted in traditional religious and cultural antisemitism must be changed. Although Christian teaching carried a heavy overload of theological antisemitism, consent to mass murder of the Jews—let alone approval of it—was contrary to doctrinal statement, confessions of faith, and the ordination vows of the clergy. The trouble was that under pressure most of the clergy buckled, and the masses of the baptized simply ran with the murderous mob. Poorly trained and poorly led, they were unable to distinguish between Christian verities and Nazi slogans, between Christian spirituality and boundless Nazi enthusiasm (*Geistigkeit*). The correction of bad teaching, therefore, must be paralleled by the recovery of a Christian discipline and style of life

communicating credibility and worthy of the Name.[9]

Continuing in the same vein, and going further, is A. Roy Eckardt. At the Oxford conference, "Remembering for the Future" (Summer, 1988), he found anti-Judaism in the essence of Christian doctrine:

> The resurrection of Jesus remains a primordial and unceasing source of the Christian world's anti-Judaism. How can the resurrection of Jesus be proclaimed as the special saving of God, without the Christian supersessionism (of Judaism) and triumphalism that helped lay the railroad tracks to the murder centres.

For Littell, Eckardt and other like-minded Christian theologians, Nazi Germany lived out 19 centuries of fratricidal teaching and applied this hatred in the murder of Jews. Their response to Christian imperialism is unequivocal rejection and advocacy of full and affirmative Christian support and fraternity with the Jewish people.

Third, essays and books by Eugene Fisher, Krister Stendahl, Paul M. Van Buren, John T. Pawlikowski, Harry James Cargas, *et. al.*, take seriously the Jews as God's ongoing covenantal people whom Christians in their understanding of God's Word in Scriptures and tradition are morally bound to defend and support. Judaism and Christianity, the former seen as "The Chosen People" and the latter defined as "the Chosen Church," are viewed as counter-cultural. Both, to the extent that the community is faithful to its divine calling, are swimming against the stream but knowing full well that their separate but equal efforts will one day help usher in a blissful age of peace and security for all mankind.

Fourth, the impressiveness of recent Christian expression of, on and with the Jewish people in the form of official pronouncements by world church bodies. For example, the Vatican-inspired **Guidelines for Catholic-Jewish Relations** and **Notes on the Correct Way to Present Jews and Judaism in Preaching and Catechesis of the Roman Catholic Church with a Note for the Preparation of the Document** (1985) are an important step in developing Shoah curricula for Catholic schools and catechetical programs. The pamphlets' avowed purpose is to encourage the importance of Jewish sources (Scripture, rabbinics, philosophy, mysticism, Zionism) for Christianity today as in the past. The Christian faithful is challenged to rediscover the Jewish roots of his/her faith which are deep and far reaching, and to live the *imitatio Christi* without antisemitism. When relevant in Christian preaching and catechesis,

Jewish understanding, belief and practice are to be presented without polemics, politics, and paternalism. A study paper, entitled "A Theological Understanding of the Relationship Between Christians and Jews," was commended to the Presbyterian Church for study and reflection by the 199th General Assembly (1987). The paper repudiates Christian "supersessionism" and "teaching of contempt" for the Jews, together with the acts and attitudes which they generate. It also affirms that both the Church and the Jewish people are elected by God for witness to the world and that the election of both are irrevocable.

In 1988, the Secretariat for Catholic-Jewish relations issued a pamphlet, **On the Holocaust** (Washington, D.C.: National Conference of Catholic Bishops, 1988), which contains excerpts of 13 selected statements issued by Pope John Paul II from 1979-1988. Arranged and edited by Eugene J. Fisher, the publication addresses the Catholic world on the meaning of the Shoah and the historic background of antisemitism that is related to it. The goal, in the words of the introduction, is to recall Pope John Paul II's words "to remember 'in particular, the memory of the people whose sons and daughters were intended for total extermination' (Auschwitz, 1979), who were 'exterminated only because they were Jews' (Miami, 1987). From the intensity of his own personal experiences, the Pope is able to articulate both the uniqueness of the Jewish experience of the Shoah, while at the same time revering the memory of all of Nazism's millions of non-Jewish victims."[10]

Here, the Apostolic See alludes to Jewish fears, and by using the term "Shoah," it is sending a clear and strong message to Christendom and the world: Do not rob the Event of its Jewish particularity. Elsewhere, however, the Vatican accentuates Jewish fears: Advertingly, at the mass for the beatification of Edith Stein in Cologne, May 1, 1987[11] ; and inadvertently, the Holy Father's admonition to the Polish people (September 26, 1990): "The (Jewish) people who lived with us for many generations remained with us after the terrible death of many millions of their sons and daughters. Together we wait for the day of judgment and resurrection."

The data, in sum, reveal good news and bad: by teaching about the Shoah, the Church is determined to eliminate from the catechism erroneous (and dangerous) teachings about the Jews, but disappointment in its inability to comprehend traits by which Jews define their greatest tragedy.

True, Poland was a victim of German invasion, but to say, for example, that Poland was the second Jewish fatherland and that Jewish and Polish blood mixed in his *Heilig Blut* under Nazi racism is stretching fact and metaphor. Also, to suggest that Poles and Jews wait the resurrection in the land of Auschwitz, begs the agonizing question: What role did the

Church, state, and people of Poland play when 3.5 million Jews—90% of the Polish Jewish population—were alive. Finally, from time to time, papal homilies teach Israel's infidelity to the "Old Covenant" and the Church's salvific role in the "New Covenant" and this can strain Jewish-Catholic contact.

Still, there is hope in Catholic-Jewish relations in the post-Shoah era. Jews must believe in that. Exposure to the good side of dialogue is essential. Jews need to be reminded that the Church views the encounter with Judaism and the Jewish people, in the words of Clemens Thoma, "not merely one of historic importance but an organic part of Christian unity." Catholics need to be reminded that Judaism sees Christianity as a legitimate monotheistic partner in *tikkun 'olam*, making the world whole and complete in preparation for the messianic period.

All who take seriously the interdependence of Judaism and Christianity need to be reminded.

IV. Historikerstreit: Truth in Scholarship

Responsible and thought-provoking historians who write on the unmerited suffering of the Jew on the road to Auschwitz fall into several schools of thought. Many write on the political, economic, religious, and social factors which led to the savage program of Nazi antisemitism, which included disenfranchisement, ghettoization and extermination. Others concentrate on an important aspect of the program, e.g., "The Final Solution." They record the step-by-step ideology of German National Socialism and portray the calculated murder of Jews: Roundup, shooting, flight to the woods, capture, transportation to camps, and death.

Some compose not a conventional history but a psychological understanding of Jewish victimization during the Nazi period. Here it is argued that the extent to which the process of Hitlerism succeeded depended upon the consensus by majority groups influenced by institutional leadership which viewed the victims as an expandable surplus minority. In other words, the incarceration and destruction of European Jewry during World War II was a function (e.g., Poland) or dysfunction (e.g., Denmark) of state and society to German racial policy.

Who orchestrated the genocide platform of the Nazi program is debated between the "functionalists," who credit major responsibility in the murder of Jews and other innocents to the structure of the Nazi state and the regime's search for policy in meeting events as they unfolded; and the "intentionalists," who argue that Hitler's personal contribution to suffering, tragedy, and genocide of millions was not conditioned by factors beyond his control. He was in total command of his obsessive venomous racial hatred.

A landmark work in the "functionalis-intentionalist" debate is Gerald Fleming, **Hitler and the Final Solution,** (Berkeley: University of California Press, 1984) which was written to combat David Irving's claim that Hitler was not the originator of the plan to exterminate the Jews. Hitler, according to Irving, had wished to make Germany and Europe *Judenfrei*, but he had never entertained the thought of the mass murder of the Jews nor had he ever proclaimed it. This diabolical plan was conceived by Himmler and Hydrich and carried out by the SS and civilian police. Although much has been said and written to show the incorrectness of Irving's thesis, Fleming's book is the first to treat meticulously the ideological origins of Nazi extermination and to set it within the chain of command that began and ended in the pharase, "Es ist der Führers Wunsch."

Drawing on a wide range of documents and sources in a number of languages, including oral testimonies from now-obscure German eyewitnesses, Fleming shows that Hitler personally ordered the execution of the Jews in places removed from German soil, in total secrecy, and in a manner that would camouflage his own direct connection with the annihilation order. Why so? For astute political reasons- for example, Hitler's ordered "euthanasia" killing program (*Gnadentod*) which took the lives of more than ninety thousand people deemed mentally deficient and hopelessly ill, was terminated in August 1941 due to public protest. This taught Hitler an important lesson: Cold-blooded mass-murder was a thankless job and few Germans, even those who wholeheartedly supported *Weltpolitik*, *Lebensraum*, and German *Judenrein* policies, were willing to support it or associate the polity of the Third Reich with it. Consequently, Hitler took all precautions to dissociate publicly the Führer Chancellery from his secret orders to perform genocide.

Each chapter covers a different aspect of the "Führer's wish" and assesses its influence and significance. By presenting documented situations clearly showing that variations of the phrase"It is the Führer's wish" came to be regarded as an authoritative directive from Hitler himself (for example, an early usage of the formula was by Himmler when he ordered the liquidation of the Riga Ghetto in November 1941: "It is my order and also the Führer's wish"), the author demonstrates the nature and extent of Hitler's participation in the *Endlösung*. Persuasively, he reveals why a written annihilation order issued directly by Hitler does not exist and why, in a thorough analysis of Nazi Hitler's imperialistic ideology, it was not necessary.

The importance of Fleming's research cannot be underestimated. It takes one giant step forward in portraying Hitler's criminality and advances our knowledge of his ubiquitous part in the atrocities of the Shoah.

It uncovers the frailty, falsehood, and misdirection by some past-Shoah revisionist writers who in their zeal to re-evaluate Hitler claim that his image is a product of allied war propaganda and unfounded post-war accusations-the real Hitler"was an ordinary, walking , talking human, weighing some 155 pounds, with graying hair, largely false teeth and chronic digestive ailments" (David Irving).

How best to explain "Why the Jews"? is made a more complex by the way the Nazis did things: The secrecy, the unwritten orders, the destruction of records and the euphemistic code names for the extermination of the Jews. The ongoing debate is over just what had happened, why and who should bear responsibility. A stimulant in this discussion is Princeton professor Arno Mayer's **Why Did the Heavens Not Darken? The "Final Solution" in History** (New York: Pantheon Books, 1988). Mayer sees an interconnection of antisemitism and anti-communism in the Nazi ideology and in the "Final Solution." He argues that Hitler's obsession with the war in eastern Europe, home of millions of European Jews and the principal site of their suffering and death, is Nazi Germany's dual purpose for unlimited *Lebensraum* and the liquidation of the Soviet regime. Also, the author connects the destruction of Jews to the European upheaval of the first half of the twentieth century, which included World War II, rooted in the Nazi counterrevolution in Germany, with its inherent drive toward foreign conquest. Further, the spiraling persecution of the Jews is correlated with the changing nature of Nazi Germany's changing fortunes in its desperate all-or-nothing fiery crusade against Bolshevism. In Mayer's view , World War II from a German perspective was the war against Communism, and had the blitzkrieg succeeded in the East, the "Jewish problem" would have been solved by deportation and not massacre.

True, German industrialists exploited Jewish slave labor; Army officers and some Nazi leaders disapproved of any action that would subvert the war effort; and the policy of mass murder of Jews did not actualize until the Fall of 1941, when the German army was bogged down in Russia. Mayer's writing provides a 25-page bibliography and no footnotes, and this lack of substantiated documentation renders unpersuasive his argument that the Nazis began killing masses of Jews as a vent to their frustration against the Russians; the machine gunning and gassing in crude mobile vans behind German lines in Russia were regional antisemitic acts and not the start of a deliberate SS extermination program; and the Jews in death camps, Auschwitz in particular, died of so-called "natural causes" rather than by "unnatural ones"-shooting, hanging, gassing. In essence, by blaming the anti-Bolshevism of many Germans for the start of Judeocide, Mayer is holding a lot more people accountable than those who fixate on Hitler. But the price paid, in my opinion, is nonnegotiable and unspeakable: The denial of Nazi racial ideology, fed by religious and secular antisemitism.

The current controversy among German intellectuals, known as the *Historikerstreit* (the historian's conflict), is not over how much Hitler or how multi-issue was the German World War II policy, but whether the Nazi crimes were unique. Is the *novum*, which we call Shoah/Holocaust, *sui generis*, or is it compatible to other national atrocities? Whither uniqueness, when we think of the 10-12 million human beings done in by Stalinst terror; the killing fields of Cambodia under Pol Pot which claimed an estimated 2-2.5 million men, women, and children in a much shorter time than that of the Shoah; and the other genocides of the 20th century, Armenian, Gypsy, Ugandan, and others. Uniquess, it is argued by some, is not the issue; the killing remains horrific whether or not other regimes committed mass murder. Comparability does not exonerate or mitigate the crime. Similarly, Arno Mayer argues that victims of "natural" causes cannot be constructed as anything less terrible or less intentional than victims of "intentional" causes. But a timely and important book on the **Historikerstreit, The Unmasterable Past: History, Holocaust, and German National Identity** (Cambridge, Massachusetts, 1988) by Harvard University professor of history Charles S. Maier, rightly assesses uniqueness as the crucial issue. From the introduction we read:

> If Auschwitz is admittedly dreadful, but dreadful as only one specimen of genocide— as the so-called revisionists have implied—then Germany can still as- pire to reclaim a national acceptance that no one denies to perpetrators of other massacares, such as Soviet Russia. But if the Final Solution remains uncomparable— as the opposing historians have in- sisted—the past may never be "worked through," the future never normalized, and German nationhood may forever be tainted like some well forever poisoned...(2)

As the title of Maier's book suggests, Shoah is an essential function of German national identity. Yet we make the mistake of assuming that the German encounter with the horror of National Socialism tells the same story as provided by the victors. Ernst Nolte argues that the Shoah was prompted by German fear of the Soviet Union and the excesses of Bolshevism; and that the Nazi internment of the Jewish population in Europe is justified in the same way as the American detention of U.S. Japanese citizens following the attack at Pearl Harbor. Andreas Hillgruber morally equates the mass murder of Six Million Jews and the expulsion of

Germans from portions of eastern Europe after World War II. Also, he claims, the excesses of Nazism were the fault of Hitler alone, who manipulated currents active in interwar Germany for his own egogentric goals. It is clear in Maier's survey of German approaches to commemorate or contest a traumatic past, the historians are not primarily interested in historiography or social-scientific analysis. Hans Mommsen, Martin Broszat, Karl Dietrich, and others, do not look backward with the aim of discovering facts; rather, they seek to legitimate historical comparison, suggesting that the Shoah is a tragic atrocity among other World War II atrocities, so that Germany can now get on with the normal business of a constructive present. In essence, German efforts to confront the darkest aspects of its immediate past horrors are more about polishing up German patriotism than in pursuing historical truth.

A salient product of the twisted road taken by the West German historians who try to distance the German mind and people from the Nazi aggression and criminiality is a ruptured German historiography. Its advocacy of "truth in scholarship" can be seen as a metaphor for the neutralization of the Jewish catastrophe on the one hand and the denial of the German war guilt and crimes on the other. In reality, the historicizing of Germanism during the Third Reich in categories of causality and accuracy cannot restore the autonomy of the German past; it can only offer an assessment of why the authority of German normalcy was abandoned and can never again be the same.

German revisionism maintains that a) today's Germany cannot be shackled to the past Jewish catastrophe or defined by a priori definitions of guilt; b) categories of historical change affect Germans as they do others; and c) the German historian is wrongly seen as a moral authority condemning Nazism, since he is neither the innovator of the system nor the cause of its perfidy. However, to unburden German guilt by rewriting events of World War II toward the goal of the resurgence and the reunification of Germany is taking a stand. To declare in the words of Franz Josef Strauss, the minister-president of Bavaria, that the Germans "get off their knees and learn to 'walk tall' again," is making a moral - albeit frightening- statment.

What of the future? It is questionable whether models of German significance and commitment can restore German pride if linked only to the controlling political analogies of the Federal Republic. Academic discussion on German identity can report and analyze processes and changes, but it cannot innovate or eliminate components of the German Nazi malady. There is, however, an obligation upon every declared German to justify his/her decision to remain a German. Ultimately German normalcy lies in the activity of Germans of memory who, through a truthful, historical study of Nazism, recognize its unique destructive power and are sworn to uproot it from the German polity in the present and in the future.

An important step in the right direction are the words from the first freely elected Volkskammer (Parliament) of the GDR admitting responsibility as Germans in East Germany for the Shoah (April 12, 1990). [12] Alas, recent racism and violence in the reunified German nation align a survivor's fear: "Nothing has been learned; Auschwitz has not even served as a warning. For more detailed information, consult your daily newspaper."[13]

V. Survivors' Fears and Tears

Survivors have much to say on the Shoah but their testimonies reflect as many Shoahs as there are survivors. If Elie Wiesel is right that "Auschwitz cannot be explained," then we cannot expect a singular authoritative response to cover all. Each response, therefore, is relative to some particular aspect of the Shoah. Survivors are forever having flashbacks. One moment they are here with the living, and the next they are back in a Nazi concentration camp, walking with the dead. A common occurrence can spark traumatic experiences that imprison them. A crowded subway train can recall a crowded railroad cattle car, rumbling toward Auschwitz and exterminating ovens with thousands of Jews. Seeing grandchildren at play can trigger tearful memories over one's stolen childhood. A smokestack can recall the solemn smokestacks that never stopped belching their horrible black soot. Night and day, season in and season out, the survivors breathed the fumes of the "Final Solution," the Nazi annihilation of Six Million Jews. They are forever living the guilt and pain of surviving. Nonetheless, some manage to convert their images of captivity into mental stepping stones to escape their private hells.

There is a caste system in the survivors' community: On top, the concentration camp survivor, who tends to be obsessed with the experience and feels compelled to tell his/her story, and, on the bottom, the hidden child, who lived his/her childhood as a non-Jew, neither deported nor incarcerated, who tends to forget what happened to him/her and keeps the suffering to oneself. Both groups acknowledge that to honor the memory of the brutally murdered, is to never forget, and as such, to reveal what was concealed, denied, minimized, and destroyed by those responsible for these indescribable atrocities.

This may explain why individual survivors and groups believe that "we can't have too many museums and monuments,"[14] and hope that school districts require their students to visit these sites and/or learn about the Shoah in the classroom.

In recent years, survivors have pursued state legislation in behalf of their noble cause, but this has run into controversy. Take the Winnetka denial case, for example. In the Spring of 1989, Sabet and Ingeborg Sarich objected to a state law that requires every Illinois public school to teach "the Nazi atrocities of 1933 to 1945." They withdrew their daughter Sanya from eighth grade history and English classes in Winnetka, IL, which included lessons of history and literature on the Shoah, the Nazi Germany extermination of Six Million Jews and millions of non-Jews in World War II. They argued for their view of the Shoah, based on known revisionist themes: There was no deliberate Nazi program to exterminate the Jews, whose fate correlated with the changing nature of Nazi Germany's changing fortune in its all-or-nothing fiery battle against Bolshevism; and the Jews in the death camps died of so-called "natural causes" rather than by "unnatural ones." They were not successful in convincing the local school board to change its Shoah curriculum.

However, the Sarich crusade in Winnetka and elsewhere—*Newsweek* (12/3/90) reported that the Sarichs mailed lengthy letters to local parents, teachers and clergy in this Waspish suburb (population: 12,500), plus academics and every member of Congress to explain their position—brought forth an unforseen flaw. Illinois state officials conceded that the mandate to teach the lessons of Shoah is vague on three fronts: No suggested instructional material; no added funding from the state for curricular start-up; and no strict monitoring or penalties for failure to comply.

These loopholes cannot be taken lightly if the survivors' campaign to sponsor similar Shoah legislation "with the Illinois law as a model" will have teeth in its guidelines and enforcing mechanism. Our observation is not intended to discourage the political campaign against historical revisionism but to shore up the shaky foundation for mandatory Shoah education.[15]

This task is made more difficult when we consider the fall out from the new enlightenment on campus: The intellectual tradition of Western Europe should not occupy the central place in the history of civilization. If Eurocentric civilization is played down so are its tragic lessons, of which the Shoah is primary. Why the Jewish calamity over other European travesties, including Polish, Ukranian, Senti-Romani, etc? Why European genocide over native American, Asian and African? Worst, the Shoah is seen as the refuse of European culture alone, without input or message to the rest of mankind. A travesty of meaning and catering to the worst fears of the survivors who maintain that the Shoah is an unresolved crime. Thus, the survivors' community is adamant against any attempt to negotiate, renegotiate or abrogate the memory of the sacred martyrs (*kedoshim*): "The wounds of the survivors have not yet healed sufficiently to permit anyone, individual or organization, to arrogate to himself or herself the right to 'close the cycle of pain.' Only the dead can exonerate."[16]

With the above in mind, it becomes clear why the survivors objected to our organized Berlin International Conference: "Addressing the Cycle of Pain," held during the weekend of *Krystallnacht* (November 7-9, 1991), unless we advertised it as exploratory and discussed in existential rather than in idealized terms. The organizers and the Jewish and Christian scholars who participated did just that: The dialogue was conducted in "real life" terms. Given Jews in the New Germany is a reality, we raised pivotal questions that embraced past-future concerns: e.g., the role of German antisemitism in the Judenrein policy of Nazi Germany; the extent of Jewish integration in the new German nationalism, etc. Also, encountering and remembering the Shoah in terms of activism and not quietism is a step forward in assuaging survivors fears in face (Jewish)-to-face (German) colloquy.[17]

VI. Our Task Ahead

The subject of the Shoah, the destruction of the Jews of Europe, and linked to the attempts by the Nazi German state to destroy Europeans during World War II, is one of great moral significance in the history of human civilization.

Consequently, there is a majestic objective in charge of toilers in the cemetery of the Shoah. To relate it, skeletally: Cite evidence from recent reports that tribalism, racism, and revisionist extremism are on the rise; show parallels to the descending importance of the Shoah before the general public; then offer a plethora of suggestions and recommendations to Shoah educators, who are concerned that the thundering voice of the Shoah not be lost in the storms of the future. The matrix around which the data are spun is European Jewry: To instruct the history of European Jewry and how this historic development affected the attitude of others toward the Jews; the plight of European Jewry during the Nazi occupation; extermination, survival, and lessons learned.

In an attempt to stake out a tiny plot in a rocky field, many zealous pilots have steered their nicely loaded Shoah vessel onto some precipitous rocks. Our view is that one cannot superimpose any one philosophy on the Shoah agenda. Suggestions come easily when they deal with inanimate or dead objects. But issues in Shoah education reflect the vitality of live concepts. Thus, interfaith conferences on the Shoah and *Kirchenkampf*[18] mirror causes of existence and conditions of being and respond to the imperative "remember and do not forget" in ways different from exclusively sponsored agency, ecclesiastical or survivors conclaves. Also, Shoah thinking cannot function under ideological imperialism. Its stream of consciousness is like the natural world: Only diversity and adaptation will save it.

The following observations will serve to further explain the agenda which informs this chapter:

The message of the Shoah for the generation after and for future generations is not survival alone. There is something more important than survival, and that is preventing moral bankruptcy. When Auschwitz (survival at any price) contends with Sinai (a moral standard), Sinai must prevail. Nazi Germany is an example of what can happen when Auschwitz prevails. This kind of message must put aside for the time being, those concepts, approaches or perspectives which have become for the moment too familiar or too habitual to stir the imagination. It must seek out new humanistic symbols, expressions of Shoah's unique self-consciousness, which are not only concerned with the past but can look as well to the present/future.

The messengers from planet Auschwitz represent a centrifugal three-tiered system: "Insiders," the murdered victims; "witnesses," the survivors who provide the eye witness accounts and first hand reports that the Shoah happened; and "transmitters," who reassess, reinterpret, rediscover and translate into modern idiom "the raw data" provided by survivors.

In his review of the T.V. mini-series *Holocaust* presented on NBC televison in April 1978, survivor Elie Wiesel had this to say: "The witness feels here duty bound to declare: What you have seen in your screen is not what happened *there*. You may think you know how the victims lived and died, but you do not. Auschwitz cannot be explained nor can it be visualized. Whether culmination or aberration of history, the Holocaust transcends history. Everything about it inspires fear and leads to despair: The dead are in possession of a secret that we, the living, are neither worthy of nor capable of recovering." (*New York Times*, April 16, 1978)

We agree. In the principality of Auschwitz, the only "insiders" are the inhabitants of the Citadel (smokestack). All others are "outsiders."

A final thought, which is construed to be a beginning. Paradoxes inform the road to Shoah and back. On the one hand, those who condone the murder of Jews deny that the murdered are Jews, and on the other, for many, the Shoah is becoming the *raison d'etre* for their Jewishness. Growing numbers of Israeli youth, for example, removed from the Zionist ideal of making the Jews a normal nation like all others, travel to the death camps of Poland and return re-Judaized—via Auschwitz. Sadly, the ashes from cyanide and not the sand from Sinai become the mortar that holds together an Israeli society that fears for the future. We understand: A state made up of people who have suffered the greatest crime in modern history has a special need to be concerned with those who would bring down upon them yet another national catastrophe.

Nonetheless, the tillers of the story must be tellers for the future. We must become "innovators," who understand the mercurial quality of Shoah education (gestation, loss of innocence, atrophy) and choose to revitalize it passionately. Our "rites of remembrance" must be credible for future generations. The guardians of the legacy must not shirk their responsibility.

For whom do we toil? For the dead, for the living, for the unborn.

Endnotes

1. For a discussion of Richard Rubenstein's theology after Auschwitz, see chapter two, pp. 36-37.
2. Hasidic concepts related to the Shoah are presented in Pesach Schindler, **Hasidic Responses to the Holocaust in the Light of Hasidic Thought** (New Jersey: Ktav Publishing House, 1990).
3. Irving Greenberg, "Cloud of Smoke, Pillar of Fire: Judaism, Christianity, and Modernity after the Holocaust," in Eva Fleischner, editor, **Auschwitz: Beginnings of a New Era? Reflections on the Holocaust** (New York: Ktav, 1977, p. 27).
4. Major dicta from the international conference, "Remembering for the Future: The Impact of the Holocaust and Genocide on Jews and Christians," held at Oxford University from July 10-13, 1988. The influence of Franklin H. Littell on these thoughts, representative of the conference theme, is acknowledged.
5. See relevant chapters in Carol Rittner and John K. Roth, editors, **Memory Offended: The Auschwitz Convent Controversy** (New York: Praeger, 1991).
6. Cf. Isa 6:11; 10:3; 47:11; Ezek 38:9; Zeph 1:15; Pss 35:8; 63:10; Job 30:3, 14; 38:27; Prov 1:27; 3:25. Job 13:11a reads, "Shall not His *se'etho* (majesty, excellency, loftiness) terrify you," but the word can be read as *sh'atho* (threat) which parallels "His dread" in Job 13:11b. However, some explain *se'etho* as "His fire" (conceptually related to *sho'atho*/"His Shoah").

7. Branches of right-wing Orthodox Jews remember the destruction of
    European Jewry as *Churban*, and link it with past devastating events.
    See Zev Garber, "Dating the Shoah: In Your Blood Shall You Live,"
    in Alan L. Berger, editor, **Bearing Witness to the Holocaust, 1939-
    1989** (Lewiston, N.Y.: Edwin Mellen Press, 1991), pp. 287-299.
    Also, see further, chapter four.

8. The word Pharisees occurs over a 100 times in the New Testament (29
    times in Matt; 12 times in Mark; 27 times in Luke; 19 times in John;
    9 times in Acts, and one time in Phillipians). There is ample fodder
    in these references to portray Pharisaism as sanctimonius, self-
    righteous, hypocritical petrified formalism, and a degraded religious
    system corroded by casuistry. The bitterest tirade against the Phari-
    sees in any first century Christian literature is Matthew 23 which
    lumps together in an uncritical fashion Pharisees and other groups.
    Also, the world caricature that the Jew worships money has support
    in this chapter.

9. Franklin H. Littell, "Basic Lessons of the Holocaust" from the
    National Institute on the Holocaust (N.I.H.) Notebook: November
    1983, p. 1.

10. John Paul II, **On the Holocaust** (Washington, D.C.: National
    Conference of Catholic Bishops, 1988), p. 1.

11 On Edith Stein, see chapter 5, a reprint of Zev Garber, "Edith Stein:
    Jewish Perspectives on Her Martyrdom," in Harry James Cargas,
    editor, **The Unnecessary Problem of Edith Stein** (Lanham: UPA,
    1994). Also, *ibid.*, "The Problem of Edith Stein: Jewess and Christian
    Martyr," *The Jewish Spectator* (Fall 1991), pp. 13-14.

12. Thirty-nine years to the date when the Knesset decreed the official
    date for observing the Shoah and Ghetto Revolt Rememberance Day
    (*Yom ha-Shoah u-Mered ha-Getaot*). See the chapter, "Dating the
    Shoah: In Your Blood Shall Live," pp. 67-78.

13. Eli Wiesel, **One GenerationAfter** (New York: Avon, 1970 [3]), p.15.

14. Words spoken by LA County Supervisor Ed Edelman at the
    dedication of the Los Angeles Holocaust Monument in Pan Pacific
    Park, April 26, 1992. The city of Los Angeles now boasts three Shoah
    memorials — Simon Wiesenthal Center's Museum of Tolerance, LA
    Jewish Federation Martyrs Memorial, and the Pan Pacific Park—
    more than any other American city.

15. Case in point, California Bill AB 3216 (teaching the Shoah to students
    in California Public Schools), presented to the State Assembly by
    Assemblyman Richard Katz, was signed into law in September
    1992. The goal is commendable: To reach a million California
    students a year and to impart a true and accurate account of this dark

period in history so that all may learn and improve on man's inhumanity to man. It remains to be seen, however, if funding and infrastructure are in place to gurantee the success of this undertaking.

16. From the "Statement on International Conference in Berlin,"by the American Gathering/Federation of Jewish Holocaust Survivors, October 11, 1991.

17. See Zev Garber, "*Reichspogromnacht*: First Berlin International Conference," *Journal of Ecumenical Studies* 28.4, pp. 677-678; and *idem*, "*Gastgeschenk: Panim B'Fanim*," *Shofar* 10.4, pp.76-80.

18. The case for international, interfaith, and inter-disciplinary approach in teaching the Shoah is taken forcibly by Franklin H. Littell, "Normalizing the Holocaust," in G. Jan Colijn and Marcia S. Littell, editors, The **Netherlands and Nazi Genocide** (Lewiston, N.Y.: Edward Mellen Press, 1992), pp.529-533.

References

Broszat, Martin. "Plädoyer fur eine Historisierung des Nationalsozialismus," *Merkur* 39 (1985), pp.373-385.

_____. **The Hitler State**. London and New York : Longman, 1981; German original [**Der Staat Hitlers**] published in 1969.

Hildebrand, Klaus. "Wer dem Abgrund entrinnen will, muss ihn aufs genaueste ausloten Ist die neue ;Deutsche Geschichtsschreibung revisionististisch?" *Die Welt*, November 22, 1986.

Hillgruber, Andreas. **Zweierlei Untergang. Die Zerschlangung des Deutschen Reiches und das End des europaisshen Judentums**. Berlin: Corso dei Seidler, 1986.

Mommsen, Hans."Stehen wir von einer neuen Polarisierung des Geschichtsbildes in der Bundesrepublik?" in **Geschichte in der demokratischen Gesellschfat. Eine Dokumentation**, ed. Susanna Miller. Düsseldorf: Schwann-Begel, 1975, pp. 71-82.

Nolte, Ernest. "Vergangenheit, die nicht vergehen will," *Frankfurter Allgemeine Zeitung*, June 6, 1986.
____. Der euröpaische Bürgerkrieg. **Nationalsozialismus und Bolschewismus**. Frankfurt am Main.: Propyläen, 1987.

CHAPTER TWO

Teaching the Shoah: The Introductory Course

The experience of the Shoah is truly unique. Nothing can compare to the enactment of absolute evil that attacked the Jewish people and other minorities during the 1930s and 1940s. Some say that all speaking about Shoah and its consequences is thoroughly inadequate and sacrilegious to the memory of the millions murdered, maimed and orphaned. Others say that silence is ultimately a posthumous victory to Hitlerism. However, all agree that education is the key to understanding the Great Catastrophe. But how to teach a subject that most educators believe is like no other course taught in the basic college curriculum of today?

The main thrust of this essay, an attempt at an objective presentation, is to provide some direction for possible standards in an introductory (i.e., lower division) class in Shoah Studies. This article discusses background, objective, methodology, theological responses, and limitations. It concludes with comments on the Written Assignment. Not the final word but a beginning, which perceives the material it teaches from a student's point of view, and attempts to make the Shoah learning experience meaningful and academically responsible.

*Much of the essay that follows first appeared in Z. Garber, A. Berger, and R. Libowitz (eds.), **Methodology in the Academic Teaching of the Holocaust** (Lanham: UPA, 1988). The superimposed bibliography is extracted from my "Response to the Holocaust," in G. Shimoni (ed.), **The Holocaust in University Teaching** (Oxford: Program Press, 1991).*

The subject of the Shoah, the destruction of the Jews of Europe, and others, at the hands of the Nazis and their collaborators, is one of great moral significance in the history of human civilization. Genocide, the obliteration of all members of a national group, is the most horrible of crimes and one of the most difficult to deal with in the field of social studies, revealing the human race in its worst perspective. After presenting a Course Outline (Part I), suggesting some direction for possible standards in an introductory (i.e., lower division) class in Shoah Studies, this chapter will probe a number of Jewish theological responses to Judaism's perpetual dilemma and tragedy (Part II). The chapter concludes with comments on the Written Assignment, emphasizing a view of the Shoah from a student's perspective (Part III).

I. Course Outline[1]

Purpose
A. To study the background, meaning, and practice of antisemitism.
B. To learn about, and analyze, the assault against the Jewish people waged by Nazi Germany between 1933 and 1945.
C. To consider, in their various implications, the results of the Shoah in Europe and the rest of the world.
D. To examine how the Shoah differs from other examples of Genocide.
E. To evaluate responses to the Shoah from the following perspectives: Biblical, rabbinic, existentialist, literary, secular, Christian, etc.
F. Using the materials presented and discussed in this course, to consider whether a Shoah can happen again.

Objectives
A. To develop an awareness and understanding of racial and religious prejudice in the minds of our student body.
B. To clarify the unique nature of the Shoah and its significance for Jews and non-Jews alike.
C. To highlight the problems of Jewish-Christian relations and seek a better understanding of these problems.
D. To attempt to develop some insight into the motives and purposes of those responsible for the Shoah.
E. To analyze the attitudes of the leaders of the democratic nations before, during, and after the event.
F. To consider the results of the Shoah upon the Jewish communities in Europe and the rest of the world.
G. To study the relationship between the Shoah and the attitude of world Jewry to Zionism and the concept of a Jewish state.
H. To study the Shoah as background for the UN decision to support the reestablishment of a Jewish state.
I. To study the Shoah as a factor in the national awakening of Soviet, Arab, and Ethiopian Jewry and as a force in the support of Israel by

the Jewish people of the world.

J. To understand that the Shoah and its aftermath represent a vast reservoir of feelings, thoughts, values, concerns, and actions preserved by victims and survivors in artifacts, signs, symbols, calendars, legal traditions, nature, history, persons, documents, and ideas.

K. To feel the personal and the group, the parochial and the universal, the legal and the mystic, the spiritual and secular dimensions of the Shoah.

L. To discover the change and development of Jewish religious experiences and theology due to the Shoah.

M. To develop a self-awareness in the relevancy and legitimacy of Shoah Studies.

N. To acquire the basic vocabulary for study of, and oral and written presentations in, a basic introduction to Shoah Studies.

O. To be made aware of the laborious work involved in a critical, disciplined study of origins, sources, and materials, and to obtain skills in oral and written presentations on a given problem in Shoah Studies.

P. To enhance for the identifying Jewish student a self-concept and self-pride in the relevancy of Reb Dodye Feig's last charge in Spring, 1944, to his grandson, Elie Wiesel: "You are Jewish, your task is to remain Jewish"; to develop by all a sensitivity to the way of life, thought and faith of Shoah victims and survivors.

Method
Analysis of historical experience; literature, newspapers, TV programs, movies, plays; linguistic and rhetorical evidence; reports from local survivors, liberators of the camps and their experiences; group discussions of this material and dilemmas involving choice; and written evaluation of quality and extent of thinking and reasoning demonstrated.

Topics
"Responses to the Holocaust" is a course designed to introduce students to Shoah Studies. It is selective of but influenced by much that is written above. Suggested topics include:

Topic 1 -*Defining the subject*
Is the Shoah different only in degree, not in kind, from previous and contempoorary acts of man's inhumanity to man?

Zev Garber and Bruce Zuckerman, "Why Do we Call the Holocaust 'the

Holocaust'? An Inquiry into the Psychology of Labels, **"Remembering for the Future: The Impact of the Holocaust on the Contemporary World**, Oxford, 1988, pp.1879-1892.

John Fox, "The Holocaust, A Non-Unique Event for All Humanity," **Remembering for the Future: The Impact of the Holocaust on the Contemporary World**, Oxford, 1988, pp. 1863-1878.

Irwin L. Horowitz "Many Genocides, One Holocaust?" *Modern Judaism*, vol. 1, 1, 1981, pp. 74-89.

Steven Katz, "The Unique intentionality of the Holocaust," *Modern Judaism*, vol. 1, 2, 1981, pp. 161-183.

Yehuda Bauer, "Whose Holocaust?" *Midstream*, Nov. 1980, pp. 42-46.

Emil Fackenheim, Foreword to Yehuda Bauer, **The Jewish Emergence from Powerlessness,** Toronto, 1979.

Yehuda Bauer, **The Holocaust in Historical Perspective,** Seattle, Wash., 1978, pp. 30-49

Topic 2 -*Understanding Antisemitism and the Nature of Prejudice.*
The unifying link of antisemitism, yesterday, today, and forever, is the "dislike of the unlike."

Saul Friedlander, From Antisemitism to Extermination," **Yad Vashem Studies XVI**, Jerusalem, 1984, pp. 1-50.

Jacob Katz, **From Prejudice to Destruction: Anti-Semitism 1700-1993**, Cambridge, 1983, pp. 1-10, 74-91, 303-327.

Michael R. Marrus, "The Theory and Practice of Antisemitism," *Commentray*, vol. 74, 2, August 1982, pp. 38-42.

Ben Halpern, "What Is Anti-Semitism?"*Modern Judaism*, vol. 1.3, 1981, pp.251-262.

Shmuel Ettinger, "The Origins of Modern Anti-Semitism," Y. Gutman and L. Rothkirchen,eds., **The Catastrophe of European Jewry,** 1976, pp. 3-39.

Jacob L. Talmon, "European History as the Seedbed of the Holocaust," *Midstream*, May 1973,pp. 3-25.

Topic 3 -*Nihilism of Murder*
How to explain the role of the Jews in Nazi Ideology and policy?

Emil Fackenheim, "Holocaust and Weltanschauung: Philosophical Reflections on Why They Did It,"*Holocaust and Genocide Studies*, vol. 3, 2, 1988, pp. 191-208.

Raul Hilberg, **The Destruction of the European Jews** (student edition), New York, 1985. Selections.

Gerhard Fleming, **Hitler and the Final Solution**, Berkeley, 1984.

Randolph L. Braham,"What Did They Know and When?," Y. Bauer and N. Rotenstreich, eds., **The Holocaust as Historical Experience**, New York, 1981, pp. 109-132.

Jacob Katz, "Was the Holocaust Predictable?," Y.Bauer and N. Rotenstreich, eds., **The Holocaust as Historical Experience**, pp. 23-41.

Lucy Dawidowicz, **The War Against the Jews, 1933-1945**, New York, 1975. Selections.

Eberhard Jaeckel, **Hitler's Weltanschauung, A Blueprint for Power,** Middletown, Conn.,1972, chs. 1-3.

Topic 4 -*The Biblical Response*
The Structure and dimensions of the Bible have much to say about human suffering. What can Creation, Akedah ("Binding of Issac"), "the Hidden Face," Test of Job, Valley of the Bones, Sinai, and other biblical selections tell us about the silence of Auschwitz?

Selections from the TaNak (Bible).

Topic 5-*The Rabbinic Response*
The Rabbis endured the destruction of the Temple and Jerusalem in the year 70 C.E. and the tragedy of the abortive revolt in 135 C.E. How does the classical rabbinic mind respond to the Holocaust?

Selections from Mishnah, Gemara, and Midrash.

Topic 6-*The Mystical Response*

In every generation there have been those who contemplated the problem of evil in a context which, while not obliterating its reality, diminished its power by virtue of cosmic or mythic perspective. What is a Kabbalistic response to the Shoah?

David R. Blumenthal, **Understanding Jewish Mysticism:The Merkabah Tradition and the Zoharic Tradition**, New York, 1978, pp. 141-180.

Maimonides, **Guide of the Perplexed, Part III**, Chapter 51 (translation of S. Pines), Chicago, 1963.

Topic 7-*The Hasidic Response*

Chutzpah and *Ahavat Yisrael* - courage bordering on the reckless and love of the Jewish people - are characteristics of the tales about R. Levi Yitzhak of Berditchev. How does Hasidic optimism prevail against impossible odds?

Yaffa Eliach, **Hasidic Tales of the Holocaust**, New York, 1982.
Pesach Schindler, **Hasidic Responses to the Holocaust in the Light of Hasidic Thought**, New Jersey, 1990.
Anonymous, "The Last Song of the Jewish Community of Lublin."

Topic 8-*The Literary Response*

The Literary imagination does not merely deal with the Shoah as *Historie*: Controlled, objective facts of historiography. Rather, it sees the Shoah as *Geschichte*: A paradigm, above the historical; attached to history but by no means limited by it. What are some of the responses of the creative artist"to show what cannot be shown, to explain what is not explained, to recapture an experience that cannot be relived" (Elie Wiesel).

Alan L. Berger, **Crisis and Covenant: The Holocaust in American Jewish Fiction**, New York, 1985.

Sidra DeKoven Ezrahi, **By Words Alone: The Holocaust in Literature**, Chicago, 1980.

Elie Wiesel, **Night**, New York, 1982.

Jerzy Kosiniski, **The Painted Bird**, New York, 1981.

Andre Schwarz-Bart, **The Last of the Just**, New York, 1973.

Topic 9-*Film Response*
In recent years, significant films on the destruction of European Jewry have been produced for television and theatre release, including *Sophie's Choice*, *Genocide*, *Night and Fog*, *Who Shall Live and Who Shall Die?*, *The Wall*, *Inside the Third Reich*, *Skokie*, *The Wannsee Conference*, S*hoah*, *Weapons of the Spirit*, *Schindler's List*, etc. How does filmography contribute to our understanding of the Shoah?

Judith E. Doneson, **The Holocaust in American Film**, Philadelphia, 1987.

Annette Insdiorf, **Indelible Shadows; Film and the Holocaust**, New York, 1983.

Topic 10- *The Traditionalist Response*
Many notable rabbis endured the Nazi era and later wrote about it. Leo Baeck commenced his study of **This People Israel in Theresienstadt**. Ignaz Maybaum contemplated the **Face of God After Auschwitz**. Ephraim Oshry wrote voluminous responsa in the ghetto of Kovno, in midst of Lithuanian fascistic cruelty. Emil Fackenheim reaffirmed **God's Presence in History**. Eliezer Berkovits responded with **Faith After the Holocaust**. What is the quality of faith and Halachah in response to the Holocaust?

Eliezer Berkovitz, **With God in Hell**, New York, 1979.

Irving Greenberg, "Cloud of Smoke, Pillar of Fire: Judaism, Christianity and Modernity After the Holocaust," in E. Fleischner, ed., **Auschwitz: Begining of a New Era? Reflections on the Holocaust**, New York, 1977, pp. 7-55.

Irving J. Rosenbaum, **The Holocaust and Halachah**, New York, 1976, pp. 17-46.

Eliezer Berkovitz, **Faith After the Holocaust**, New York, 1973, pp. 37-85.

Emil Fackenheim, **God's Presence in History**, New York, 1970, pp. 67-104.

Topic 11-*The Humanist Response*

For the religious theist, responding to the Shoah is intolerable. How could the Guardian of Israel have failed to intervene? For the religious humanist, responding is no less agonizing. How could Man have done it? What are the responses of Jewish humanists, e.g., Martin Buber, Mordecai Kaplan, Richard Rubenstein, and others, to the Shoah?

Richard Rubenstein, **After Auschwitz**, Indianapolis, 1966.

Topic 12-*The Christian Response*

Whether or not we take the extreme view that there is a direct causal link between two thousand years of the "teaching of contempt" and the Shoah, Christian culpability for the Holocaust cannot be denied. What is the Christian response to the Shoah?

Paul M. van Buren, "Ecclesia Semper Reformanda: The Challenge of Israel," R. Libowitz, ed., **Faith and Freedom: A Tribute to Franklin H. Littell**, Oxford, 1987, pp. 119-125

Eugene Fisher, "Theological Education and Christian-Jewish Relations," Z. Garber, ed., **Methodology in the Academic Teaching of Judaism**, Lanham, MD, 1986/87, pp. 189-200

Alice Eckardt, "Post-Holocaust Theology: A Journey Out of the Kingdom of Night," *Holocaust and Genocide Studies*, vol. 1, 2, 1986, pp. 229-240

Norman Ravitch,"The Problem of Christian Anti-Semitism," *Commentary*, vol. 73, 4, 1982, pp. 41-52

Rosemary Radford Reuther,"Anti-Semitism and Christian Theology," E. Fleischner, ed., **Auschwitz: Beginning of a New Era? Reflections on the Holocaust**, New York, 1977, pp. 79-92

Franklin H. Littell, **The Crucifixion of the Jews: The Failure of the Christians to Undestand the Jewish Experience**, New York, 1975, pp.24-99.

Topic 13-*The American Jewish Response*

How effective was the American Jewish Response to the Holocaust? Why did a prestigious Shoah fact-finding group, made up of prominent Jews and headed by former Supreme Justice Arthur J. Goldberg "split up in anger and dissension" (*New York Times*, week of January 2, 1983) while investigating the American Jewish community's response to the Nazi extermination program?

Henry L. Feingold, "Did American Jewry Do Enough During the Holocaust?," **B.G. Randolph Lecture in Judaic Studies,** Sryacuse University, April 1985, 33 pp.

David Wyman, **The Abandonment of the Jews,** New York, 1984. Selections.

Yehuda Bauer, **American Jewry and the Holocaust,** Detroit, 1981.

Walter Laqueur, **The Terrible Secret,** London, 1980.

Topic 14- *A Dialogue Response*
For centuries the Jewish community in Poland prospered, but memories of the Shoah have tainted the relationship. Can looking honestly at the past begin the healing? Or must one conclude that anti-Jewish prejudice is very strong among Poles in and outside Poland, the land of Auschwitz?

Wladyslaw T. Bartoszewski, **The Convent at Auschwitz,** London, 1990.

J. Kermisz and S. Krakowski, **Polish-Jewish Relations During the Second World War,** Jerusalem, 1974. Selections.

John Grondelski, "Theological Literature in Poland on Catholic-Jewish Relations Since Auschwitz Convent Controversy: A Survey," *The Polish Review,* Vol. 37.3 (1992), pp. 285-296.

Claude Lanzmann, **Shoah,** New Yorker Films; Pantheon Books, 1985.

Ronald Modras, "Jews and Poles: A Relationship Reconsidered," *America,* January 1982.

Carol Rittner and John Roth, editors, **Memory Offended: The Auschwitz Convent Controversy,** New York, 1991. Selections.

Topic 15-*An Israeli Response*
Never since 1948 has one camppaign and one massacre- the summer of 1982 Peace for Galilee Operation and the Phalangist murder of Palestinian refugees at Sabra and Shatila - caused so many in and outside Israel

to raise questions concering Israeliness and Jewishness, Israeli state and Jewish state, and to suggest that "Judaism does not need a political entity in the Land of Israel to survive worldwide. A State of Israel that can conspire with Phalangist thugs is not a proper response to the Shoah. And we are not one people if that means condoning blatantly immoral Israeli acts" (Eugene B. Borowitz writing in *Sh'ma*, November 5, 1982). Similarly, the *Intifada* ("Uprising") of 1987-1993 tests Jewish morality. Can Jewish morality and Jewish power coexist in the land of Zion, in the second generation after Auschwitz?

Zev Garber, "Triumph on the Gallows," *Israel Today* (Perspective column) August 1987; "Blood and Thunder: Israel Under Siege," March 1988.

Kahan Commision Report, *Jerusalem Post*, November 9, 1983.

Jacobo Timmerman, **The Longest War: Israel in Lebanon**, New York, 1982.

Elie Wiesel, **Dawn**, New York, 1982.

Yehuda Bauer, **The Jewish Emergence from Powerlessness,** Toronto, 1979, pp. 41-78.

Emil Fackenheim, **The Jewish Return into History,** New York, 1978, pp. 129-286.

Topic 16-*Can it Happen Again?*
The question of whether or not the Shoah could happen again depends for an answer upon our model of an "I and Thou" society. The major traits of Hitlerism - isolation, vilification, expulsion, slavery, and extermination - are not the will of heaven but the act of Everyman, the bitter fruits of the freedom he has abused. Consequently, man can stamp out these evils if he so chooses by demonstrating intelligence, wisdom, and moral will. This then, is the commandment after the Great Tragedy: All are made in the image of God, and the interdependence of humankind is the only rational road to survival.
Zev Garber,"Auschwitz: The Real Problem," *Israel Today*, April 15, 1988.

Zev Garber, "Sinai and not Cyanide: Witness and not Survivor," remarks given at the Utah State Capitol Rotunda on April 19, 1985, in conjunction with the Governor's proclamation of Holocaust Memorial Week 1985 (5745).

"Teshuvah," a Hasidic sermon by Yehuda Leib Alter (1847-1905), Barry W. Holtz, ed., **Back to the Sources, Reading the Classic Jewish Texts**, New York, 1984, pp. 393-399.

Irving Greenberg,"Religious Values After the Holocaust," A.J. Peck,ed., **Jews and Christians After the Holocaust,** Philadelphia, 1982, pp. 63-86.

Simon Wiesenthal, **The Sunflower**, New York, 1977.

"The Indestructible Dignity of Man," (The Last Musar Lecture in Slabodka), *Judaism*, vol. 19, 2, 1970, pp. 262-263.

Observations

A.   The subject of the Shoah with its universal qualities of human nature is unusually broad. Can it encompass all within a course unit or even within one course alone?

B.   The effort would be not to cover *all* the history, sociology, psychology, philosophy, theology, etc., relating to the Shoah. Rather, the introductory course provides a context for asking questions and providing a frame of reference through which insights would be provided and further applications would be suggested.

C.   The emphasis should be on tolerance, diversity, and understanding. It is important that an initial class in Shoah (1) represents a universal, humanistic approach; (2) focus on the student rather than the event, utilizing an interdisciplinary approach; and (3) endeavor to heighten the student's awareness of ethical themes and human tendencies toward prejudice.

D.   There are, of course, many examples of history's excesses being repeated and exceeded. However, there is also progress. We have changed. The United States of 1994 is significantly improved in many ways from the United States of 1954. The same can be said of Germany of January 1933 and United Germany today. Mankind is "improvable"; we must all be reminded of this and educators, above all, must believe it.

E.   The essence of Shoah thinking is "dislike of the unlike." It is the recognition of this force in our lives that must be at the core of any Shoah presentation. Also at the core must be the students' feelings and recognition of how this distrust of the unfamiliar often dominates our lives.

F. The message of Shoah for the generation after and for future generations is not survival alone. There is something more important than survival, and that is preventing moral bankruptcy. When Auschwitz (survival at any price) contends with Sinai (a moral standard), Sinai must prevail. Nazi Germany is an example of what can happen when Auschwitz prevails.

G. A number of college, university, and seminary programs may lack the mechanism (staff, funding, sources, etc.) to offer a class in Shoah Studies, or the subject matter may be limited in appeal. If so, themes from the Shoah may be generalized within a topic such as "Studies in Human Values," "Civil Liberties," etc., or a one-day seminar can be given on "Moral Choices," etc. This should not be seen as *the* Shoah course or symposium but should utilize the Shoah experience and other comparable experiences as part of its context. The approach should be universal and interdisciplinary, and other examples of human "holocausts" should be included (American Indians, Armenians, etc.).

H. Los Angeles Valley College, to my knowledge, is the only public community college which offers a class on the Shoah on a regular/continuing basis. The method used is a "response" approach, which the writer feels is more effective than the "traditional" lecture presentation. There should be readings but not "difficult" ones, so that the students' feelings and, thus, interest should be engaged. The aim should be the transformation of values. A caring, understanding delivery is essential.

A final observation. A course such as "Teaching the Shoah" is lacking in the social science curriculum of many State and University Schools of Education and many local teachers feel the lack of preparation to deal with the Shoah issue knowledgeably and capably. This is especially true, given the publicity and success of Claude Lanzmann's film, "Shoah", and a segment on the Shoah as part of the very popular film series "Heritage: Civilization and the Jews." Our attempt to discuss several approaches to Shoah curricula represents an invitation to "learn Shoah" for junior high or high school teachers in the social sciences and literature. Becoming capable in directing students through this historical, theological, and ethical problem will help one give a sharpened focus to the courses one teaches in the area.

II. Thoughts on Theological Responses [2]

The theology from Jewish Tradition is that God is good, merciful, compassionate, omniscient, just, loving, etc. He is, above all, a redeemer God.

This theology has its origins in the Hebrew world view, conditioned by the wanderings of the Jewish people from place to place and environment to environment which, in contrast to the other cultures (stationary, static) of the Ancient Near East, sees God as incorporeal, ineffable and transcendent; neither restricted by nor embedded in nature; and whose fuller presence is immanent not in space but in time. Not cosmic phenomena but history is pregnant with meaning; history becomes a revelation of the divine will and the arena in which man acts out his responsibility in this encounter. In the Hebrew myth of origins, the interrelationship between history (Sinai) and nature (nomadic freedom) produces a religion (Judaism) which upholds man's power to reason and freedom of will. Without this power, man cannot be responsible for his actions and the fabric of society will dissolve into chaos and anarchy.

Yet traditional theology clashes with the Shoah and all that the Jewish genocide of World War II represent: The silence of God and His non-intervention in the Nazi treatment of Europe's Jews and millions of non-Jews. How then to resolve the problem from a Jewish theological perspective?

Option One

If theology is tied to history then historical events can create and dislodge theological imperatives, doctrines and values. The historical events of the Exodus and Sinai created Jewish convenantal theology and its important corollary, the Jews are God's Chosen People.

From the earliest biblical record to the eve of Emancipation, Jews took seriously the belief that Israel is the firstborn of God (Exod 4:22), a unique people, chosen from all the nations as God's treasured people (Deut 7:6; 14:2; 26:18, 19; 28:9, etc.), and singled out for the mission of bringing all life closer to the kinship of God on earth. The mission of Israel was cemented in a mutual covenant of love between God and Israel (Deut 6:5; 7:12, 13; 10:15, etc.). This belief helped compensate Jews for the hurts and humiliations of life in the exile.

Traditionally defined within and outside of the group as "a people that dwells alone, not reckoned among the nations" (Num 23:9), Jews sustained this role, for they believed they were part of "a kingdom of priests, and a holy nation" (Exod 19:6), divinely commissioned to advance the day that the "Lord shall be king over all the earth; on that day shall the Lord be one and His name be one" (Zech 14:9).

Enlightenment and Emancipation brought a radical departure from traditional thought patterns and aspirations. Emancipation destroyed the authority of the Jewish community and Enlightenment offered an ideological justification of surrendering the authority of Jewish tradition. The organic relationship of God-Torah-Israel (religion, culture, peoplehood) was now challenged by reason and equalitarianism. Count Clermont Tonnerre's declaration to the French National Assembly in 1791: "To the Jew as an individual — everything; to the Jew as a nation — nothing," and the positions adopted by the French Great Sanhedrin in February 1807, though bestowing equal civic rights upon Jews, began the process of redefining Jewish doctrines and values.

Unlike the national-religious identifying Jews in the Arab world and in Eastern Europe, Jews of the West now saw themselves as nationals of their countries of citizenship and worshippers in the "Mosaic faith." However, what Jews as individuals may have gained by Emancipation, Jews as a group lost. By leaving the ghetto and attaining the status of citizens, the Western European Jews loosened the bounds of Jewish group identity which in many cases led to total assimilation or worse, expulsion, conversion, and extermination.

Quantitatively and qualitatively, the Nazi near-complete destruction of European Jewry represents the worst threat to Judaism's self-definition: A people made in the image of Torah, commanded by God to bring mankind ever closer to the prophetic ideal of the Fatherhood of God and the brotherhood of man. In the radical theology of Richard Rubenstein, the Nazi Third Reich (history) successfully overthrows a mature Jewish acceptance of convenant belief (theology). The evil that the Nazis unleashed against the Jewish people requires as a basic minimum that the Jews give up the notion that they are the Chosen People of a personal deity. Simply put, how can God permit the senseless slaughter of millions of Jewish victims, including 1.5 million children? Likewise shocking and tragic is the biblical-rabbinic belief that Nazi bestiality is a just compensation for collective Jewish sins. Equally absurd are Deutero-Isaiah's "Servant of the Lord" and Judah HaLevi's "Israel is the heart of mankind" themes which proclaim vicarious suffering by Israel for the sins of mankind. That is to say, the Jewish people's continuous suffering and misery at the hands of the nations in different climes of geography and shifting sands of history are not because of its sins, but because of its role in history as teacher and witness to God's law of justice, freedom, love, and peace. Rubenstein rejects these positions because a) they suggest that God is a powerless God and b) if not omnipotent, He enters into a pact with Hitlerism which sanctions the destruction of the Six Million.

Other harmony theodicies are presented and rejected. 1) The view that universal harmony exists now but we cannot recognize it due to our finite knowledge. Basic to this position is that everything that happened and is happening was/is part of a harmonious, cosmic order of things. Since we cannot fathom the total harmony of the universe, we therefore believe that certain events of history are inherently evil. In the total view of things, however, evil together with good are necessary components to the total harmony. Thus the miracle of the rise of the State of Israel is seen as a proper adjustment to the tragic loss incurred by the Shoah. 2) Universal harmony does not presently exist but continual tragedies in the present will ensure its futuristic appearance. Variations of this theodicy theme are that evil exists to test our faith and challenge our freedom; and the victims of Hitler's war against the Jews are rewarded on earth by the posthumous citizenship granted to them in the State of Israel (act of Knesset, 1953) and in heaven by the bliss of the world to come. 3) The classic Jewish eschatological teaching that in the end of days, the messianic future, all known evils of mankind will be abolished.

Objections to the harmony theories are two-fold: a) Do the extremities of present distress ethically command a future harmony?; and b) can we morally believe and rationally accept that the Shoah kingdom of enslavement, torture, pain, murder and death is necessary for eternal harmony? Also, pietists reject harmony theodicy because it questions the power and goodness of God. Could God plan His perfect kingdom on earth without exacting such a heavy price for the sake of His name? If God could not, then why call Him omnipotent? If God could but chose not — the Shoah, for example — then why call Him good? Thus we have come full circle with the initial statement of Rubenstein's death of God theology, i.e., letting go of traditional Judaism's doctrine of God for a new symbol of God's reality conducive to the lessons learned from Auschwitz. Rubenstein's Godless Judaism is aptly put this way:

> The religious symbol and the God to whom the religious symbol points were never more meaningful than they are today. It is no accident that the twentieth century is characterized by theological excitement and renewal. Our myths and rituals have been stripped of their historic covering. No man can seriously pretend that the literal meanings given to our traditions before our time retain much authority today. Happily, in losing some of the old meanings we have also lost some of the old fears. God stands before us no longer as the final censor but as the final reality before which and in terms of which all partial realities are to be measured. The last paradox is that in time of the death of God we have begun a voyage of discovery wherein we may, hopefully, find the true God. [R. Rubenstein, **After Auschwitz** (Indianapolis: the Bobbs-Merrill Co., 1966), p. 241]

Option Two

Recognizes that the Holocaust differs not in kind from the other destructive events of Jewish history; meaning, Jewish faith in the convenantal God of history persists before, during and after the Shoah.

For Elie Wiesel, recipient of the 1986 Nobel Peace Prize, the experience of the Shoah is truly *sui generis*. Nothing can compare to the enactment of absolute human and historical evil that attacked the Jewish people and other minorities during the 1930s and 1940s. Wiesel suggests that all speaking about the Holocaust is throughly inadequate and sacrilegious to its millions of victims. Perhaps silence is the only proper posture.

In **The Oath**, (New York: Random House, 1973), Wiesel talks about Moshe, mad survivor of a pogrom, who has sworn never to tell of his ordeal. He is bound to silence as a testimony on behalf of all humanity to life against death. To scream about radical dehumanization raises the possibility that the world is not listening or does not care, which would be a victory for absolute evil. Within the Jewish tradition humanity is made in the image of God, and must imitate God. God's silence during centuries of Jewish pogroms and destruction may be interpreted as God's presence in suffering.

Yet one person's loyalty to the memory of the dead becomes another person's reason to go on living. This is the position taken by the famed Nazi hunter Simon Wiesenthal in the **Sunflower** (New York: Schocken Books, 1977). In a sensitive and provocative story, Wiesenthal tells of a Nazi soldier, a participant in the slaughter of innocents, terrified of dying with the burden of his guilt. He asks forgiveness from a concentration camp Jew, one who knows well the meaning of the Jewish moral millenia, when victim-survivor shakes hands and makes peace with the enslaver-destroyer. The Jew, for his part, listens with horror and feeling to the German's deathbed wish, and walks quietly out of his presence without giving absolution.

The author's moral dilemma now becomes the reader's as the latter is asked to confront the question, "What would I (you) have done?" A collection of 32 responses, from Jew and non-Jew alike, then follows, providing the reader with a situation which s/he cannot help but enter, analyze, and internalize. The result is a significant post-Auschwitz reality, echoing in part Elie Wiesel's mystical insistence that the Shoah

> can still be experienced ... even now. Any Jew born before, during or after the Holocaust must enter it again in order to take it upon himself. We all stood at Sinai ... we all heard the *Anochi* — "I am the Lord ..." If this is true then we are also linked to Auschwitz. Those who were not there can discover

it now. How? I do not know. But I know that it is possible ...
One does not speak about the beginning of creation and the
end-time ... Today we know that all roads and all words lead
to the Holocaust. What it was we may never know; but we
must proclaim, at least, that it was, that it is.
[**Hunter and Hunted: Human History of the
Holocaust**, selected and edited by Gerd Korman.
New York: Viking Press, 1973, p. 19]

The neo-mystical Hasidic strain of Elie Wiesel emphasizes that the
Shoah must be understood first and foremost as a unique Jewish experience; and the universal ramifications of the Shoah flow from its Jewish
specificity. On the other hand, Simon Wiesenthal suggests that the
parochial aspects of the Jewish Destruction be externalized in the objective
world in such a manner to enable the Gentiles to join Jews in questioning,
reflecting, and answering to the phenomenon of the Shoah.

This brings us to the theocentric religious philosophy of Emil
Fackenheim, who combines metaphysics and epistemology to satisfy two
responses to the Shoah, one practical, the other, theoretical. Starting with
Quest for Past and Future (Boston: Beacon Press, 1970), continued in
**God's Presence in History: Jewish Affirmations and Philosophical
Reflections** (New York: Harper Torchbooks, 1970), and elaborated in
**The Jewish Return into History: Reflections in the Age of Auschwitz
and a New Jerusalem** (New York: Schocken Books, 1978), Fackenheim
continually maintains that Jewish existence and world consciousness must
be reconsidered after the destruction of the Shoah and the rebirth of the
State of Israel. He insists that every survivor of the Shoah is gradually
becoming a paradigm for the entire Jewish people. The State of Israel is
collectively what the survivor is individually — testimony in behalf of all
mankind to life against death, to sanity against madness, to Jewish self-
affirmation against every form of flight from it, and loyalty to the God of
the Sinaitic Covenant against all lapses into paganism. These paradigms
confront the contemporary Jewish crisis wherein some Jews seek a
universalism in which to lose their "Jewishness." Regarding the uniqueness of Jewish existence as a scandal amounts to a victory of Auschwitz
over Israel.

"Auschwitz" is defined by Fackenheim as the extreme technological
dehumanization which, to varying degrees, may in the end become the fate
of us all. Nazism was simply the machine radically dehumanized, and its
millions of victims, its waste products. Nazism was a murder camp: A
nihilistic, demonic celebration of death; destruction was its animating
principle. This was revealed during the last stages of the war when Nazis
continued to transport Jews to death camps, choosing not to utilize the

trains for immediate and necessary military operations. Hatred of Jews was a Nazi obsession and transcended the drive for self-preservation. Similarly, at the end, in the Berlin bunker, Hitler and Goebbels expressed demonic satisfaction that their downfall might doom not only the enemies but the "master race." The point is illustrated by Hitler's bunker-order to flood the subways of Berlin in an attempt to stop the Russian advance, though it was clear that thousands of Germans seeking shelter from air attacks would perish in the action. As Hitler had said in 1944 to his associate Walter Schellenberg:

> In this war there can be no compromise. There is only victory to extinction. In case the German nation should fall it will perish... Yes, in that case let it perish, let it croak; for the best will have fallen, and the rest should give way to those who are biologically stronger. In case the German nation falls, the end of Germany will be cruel. However, it will have deserved nothing better. [W. Jochmann and B. Nellesson, **Adolf Hitler: Personlichkeit-Ideologie-Taktik** (Paderborn, 1960), pp. 34-35; cited by E. Fackenheim, "Concerning Authentic and Unauthentic Responses to the Holocaust," in *Holocaust and Genocide Studies, An International Journal*, p. 118 (Vol. 1, Number 1, 1986].

The mind shrinks from systematic murder which serves no purpose beyond itself, for it is ultimately unintelligible. Yet in Nazism this unintelligibility was real

In addition to the murder machine, the Nazis played with the living, who were enslaved, prostituted, beaten, dismembered, experimented on, and subjected to all conceivable forms of dehumanization. An example cited by Fackenheim to illustrate the diabolical scenario of Nazism is the "two work permits." By this scheme able-bodied Jews were permitted to "live" and permit one member of the family to live-work; the others the Jew consigned to death. Certainly this was not an efficient plan for laborers ("able-bodied only" was not the rule) but reflected the satirical humor of the Nazis: To rob the Jew of his/her soul and make him/her forever guilty of the murder of all his/her family (mother, father, brother, sisters, children) save one.

Despite even this, the Jew rejected suicide, rejected the relief of insanity, preserved the tie with his/her God and remained a witness against darkness in an age of darkness, a witness whose like the world has not seen. How else to explain the last and lasting testimony of many Jewish victims in the Nazi murder machine as they were led to the gas chambers and crematoria. They sang the 12th article of the Maimonidean Creed, belief in the messianic age to come, and by this, in contrast to a depraved world that failed them, proclaimed hope in an improved humanity as the divine goal of history.

Notwithstanding this heroism and humanism of the Jew, there is in the world today an identity crisis for many Jews who elect freedom from and not of Judaism. To surrender one's Judaism is a victory for Hitler. For a post-Shoah Jew to act as though his Jewishness required justification is to allow for the possibility that none might be found. This is an act of betrayal, betrayal of the world as well as the Jewish people. Thus Fackenheim has suggested that though God was utterly silent, the Jews had heard a "commanding voice" come from Auschwitz, "The 614th Commandment": Jews must survive as Jews and under no circumstances must there be posthumous victories granted Hitler. If there is a Jewish hero today, it is s/he who confronts the demons of Auschwitz and defies them; the Jew who has defied equally antisemitism and self-hatred. It is the Jew at home in his/her own skin and at peace with his/her Jewish identity and destiny. It is the Jew who is whole, complete, *shalem*.

How is the Jew to aspire to and to acquire authenticity? Fackenheim's definitive statement is found in **To Mend the World: Foundations of Future Jewish Thought** (New York: Schocken Books 1982). The first part of the work explores the options in Jewish thought caused by modernity and reflected in the writings of Spinoza and Rosenzweig. According to Fackenheim, the holocaustal experience in history makes folly Spinoza's absolute of reason and Rosenzweig's Jewish antihistoricisms. Here, as found in earlier writings, he insistently argues that the Auschwitz experience cannot be compared to anything. One who minimalizes, universalizes, parochializes, assimilates, hyphenates, etc., Shoah to any human experience is committing the unpardonable *pesha'*, ultimate rebellion against God and man. The uniqueness of Shoah, the only example of absolute *novum*/evil in history, renders absurd all words, ideas, apologies, and actions derived therefrom. If rational thinking is rendered bankrupt in the post-Shoah age, we give life and acts priority in the now Jewish existence. He posits that Jewish survival after Auschwitz cannot be regarded in mere physical terms. The individual and collective survival of Jews have become a religious commandment, which is seen and learned from the everyday acts nurtured in the way of Torah (*tikkun*) in the death camps. The standard for millions of Jews trapped in Hitler's inferno — religious and secular alike — was not nihilism nor despair nor suicide but the sanctification of the deeds of everyday. The constant in the shifting sands of the Holocaust kingdom was the belief (for many) and the practice of Judaism to the extent possible under the most horrendous circumstances. It now challenges all Jews to act Jewishly, morally, ethically, and ritually.

In conclusion, it may be said that Fackenheim's lessons from the Shoah are summarized in the divine imperative from the ashes, his often quoted 614th Commandment: No posthumous victories to Hitlerism; Jews must never forget the sacrifices and acts done by and to their holy martyrs; they must not despair of God, Torah, and Israel lest Judaism perish; and Judaism must be understood in its *own* self-hood, i.e., Jews are a kingdom of priests, and a holy nation (Exod 19:6), witnesses of God in the world (cf. Isaiah 43:10). Genuine Jewishness is living Jewishly, i.e., testifying against idolizing nature and paganism; it is to proclaim the transnatural God whose operative commandment is to mend the world (*tikkun 'olam*). [The phrase is associated with the 16th century kabbalist, Isaac Luria, but its original thought is biblical, cf., *na'aseh venishma'*, Exod 24:7.]

Option Three

This option finds fault with Options One and Two, and charts its own course between the Death of God agnosticism of Richard Rubenstein and the existentialist thought of Elie Wiesel and Emil Fackenheim on the meaning of a post-Shoah Jewish future. It asks of Rubenstein, if Holy Nothingness and Death are lord of us all and if man, responsible only to himself and his progeny, exists by his own resources (wit and animalistic instinct to survive as a group, people, race) then what constraints are there to distinguish between good and bad, murdered and murderer, victim and victimizer? To paraphrase Hannah Arendt's *Banality of Evil* thesis, if everyone, under particular historical conditions, is potentially guilty of murder then no one is actually guilty of this heinous crime or its facsimile. But there is something more important than survival, and that is preventing moral bankruptcy. When Auschwitz (survival at any cost) contends with Sinai (the Jewish moral standard) then Sinai must prevail. Cyanide succeeded because Sinai was removed from the thoughts and actions of man. In his **Morality and Eros** (New York: McGraw-Hill, 1970) and **The Cunning of History: The Holocaust and the American Future** (New York: Harper and Row, 1975), Rubenstein uses secular, moral imperatives to explain the symbolism of evil in the Western tradition, but this is not an effective response to the Shoah, which saw Jews exterminated as Jews. Elie Wiesel's words are instructive:

> ...Listen to such *hutzpah*: First they make us suffer, and now
> they resent it when we acknowledge the suffering as ours ...
> And why take away from the dead the only thing left to them
> — their Jewishness and their uniqueness? Don't they deserve

at least that?

(cited in K. Gorman, *loc. cit.*)

Recognition of this anger coupled with the lessons that we must not trivialize, minimize, compromise nor wrongly universalize the Shoah are at the core of a theistic response (Option Two) to the Great Destruction. The Shoah was unique. Its dead and maimed were not the victims of war and famine or politics in the normal sense. The Nazi bureaucratic murder machine claimed victims of all European nationalities, but Jews were the people for whom it was designed, the only people whose right to live was denied in principle. Thus Wiesel's above cited admonition and Fackenheim's suggested truism, the Shoah claims another victim whenever a Jew doubts his Jewishness. Conversely, when a Jew lives up to Judaism's creeds and deeds, s/he defeats Hitlerism and carries out the legacy of the dead: "You are Jewish, your task is to remain Jewish" (Elie Wiesel's grandfather, Reb Dodye Feig's last charge to his grandson in Spring, 1944).

But the issue is more complicated than some theists are willing to admit. We want to make two observations. First, must we understand that the mandate for the present and future was forged in the crucible of the crematorium? No intelligent person can deny the heroism and the heroic acts of Jewish martyrs done in the shadow of Auschwitz; they serve as the exemplar of Kiddush Hashem. But is this a healthy model for "sanctify Thy name in the presence of all men" (from the morning service)? Second, the holocaustal experience has shown and today's headlines verify that adherence to God's moral law can bring destruction and evil in its path. In September, 1986, two masked gunmen stormed into one of Istanbul's oldest synagogues (Neve Shalom Synagogue) during a Sabbath service and sprayed automatic weapon fire on the worshippers, killing 21 Jews and burning the bodies with gasoline before blowing themselves up. True, the evil deed of the murderers caused their own deaths, but how to explain the fright, suffering and death brought upon the victims?

Traditionally, an answer to this question may be cultivated from the biblical book of Job. The prologue to Job suggests a question: Will the righteous Job, once deprived of the good things of life, abandon and curse his God? In 44 chapters of narrative and discussion, Job does not because he is righteous and his cry for justice is vindicated at the end. The author(s) of Job ask, if God is just and in control of life, if righteousness is rewarded and wrongdoing punished, then why does the righteous Job suffer horrendous misfortune? The traditional answers of Job's friends [Eliphaz: no man could achieve perfection and the punishment was a chastening for Job's own good; Bildad: suffering is rooted in human fallibility; Zophar:

Job's challenging the justice of his suffering was akin to blasphemy; Elihu: God leads man to the brink of death only to rescue him so that man might forever be grateful in blessing God the redeemer] are inadequate and ultimately God declares them to be inaccurate (Job 42:7-8). Job's challenge is not to God but to popular theology. He stubbornly insists on his innocence, and so represents the refusal of Judaism to account for evil entirely as punishment for sins. Similarly, the trial and tribulations of millions and the spilled blood of innocent victims suggest that evil is unleashed by man, that it is not of God and, in the end, justice and righteousness will prevail.

The Jobian message that righteous man and righteous nation must in moments of dark despair live in unconditional trust with God is a central motif in the writings of contemporary Jewish theists. But the neo-Orthodox Jewish thinker, Irving Greenberg, insists that the biblical-rabbinic categories of redeeming faith are no longer valid due to the long history of Jewish pain, especially the quintessential expression of that pain, the Shoah. After Auschwitz, he declares, we live not in ever-present faith but in "moments of faith, moments when Redeemer and vision of redemption are present, interspersed with times when the flames and smoke of the burning children blot out faith — though it flickers again ["Cloud of Smoke, Pillar of Fire: Judaism, Christianity and Modernity after the Holocaust," in Eva Fleischner, editor, **Auschwitz: Beginning of a New Era? Reflections on the Holocaust** (New York: Ktav, 1977, p. 27)]. Greenberg's limited God theodicy argues that God is perhaps not all powerful as traditional theistic belief maintains, but He is limited in power.

How so? In the classical Jewish myth of origins, God is portrayed as an absolute, pure existence, unqualified and ineffable, by whose will the world was created. History, not cosmic phenomena, becomes the vehicle of the revelation of God's word to man. Man's dialogue with God began at creation, was ratified at Sinai, challenged at Auschwitz, and redeemed in the survival of Israel. The record of coming to grips with the dialogue in every age since Sinai and the emphasis on action rather than creed as the primary religious expression is Halachah, a pan-Judaic movement that subscribes to set systems of methodology and interpretation, whose insights, written and oral, are authoritative but never final in Jewish teaching and law. Greenberg's writings on religious problems are illustrative of the Halachic commitment to tradition through change in accordance with concessions of history. However, his chapters dealing with theodicean issues of faith precipitated by the Holocaust are more indebted to rabbinic midrash than rabbinic Halachah. Midrash means biblical inquiry; it is an attempt to explain the biblical text in as many ways as seemed possible to the inquiring mind of the Jewish sage. Thus midrash has a variety of interpretations and includes exegesis of Scriptures, sermons, and nonlegal discussions. The genius of midrash lies in its ethical and hermeneutical pronouncements peppered with philosophical wisdom and a vast amount of folk tradition. In summation, when Greenberg writes on holocaustal issues, he utilizes the traditional midrashic line of communication between God and Israel. This working principle is neither absolute nor relative but in a continuous, dynamic state of flux. His theology, therefore, is process theology, which by its very nature reveals a certain self-limitation, so chosen, on the part of an originally omnipotent God (*ṣimṣum*).

Central to Greenberg's thinking on the Holocaust are his thoughts on the role of Israel's covenant and the nature of Israel's chosenness. In midrashic language, God and Israel enter into a partnership at Sinai; God promises protection for the Jews proportional to the Jews' promise of doing commandments (*na'aseh venishma*, Exod 24:7). In the course of history both covenant partners reneged on their word: Israel collectively does not live up to its obligatory covenant, and God, in every generation, withdraws further and further from Jewish destiny. The cutting edge is the Shoah, the murderous death of millions coupled with the horrific absence of God, which proclaims that a new age has begun: Religionless Judaism. Greenberg holds that in the perspective of what the Shoah presents, the self-definition of the Jew and his covenant with God must be totally revised, reevaluated and renegotiated. Greenberg is saying that the imposed covenant of Sinai is no longer valid after Auschwitz. How can it be otherwise? It has failed. Centuries of persecution have chipped away at its words and the flames of the Shoah have obliterated its authoritative voice. Yet, in its place, a new covenant has arisen by virtue of the actions of survivors and other Jews who choose not to assimilate but to survive as a people. Jewish survival is the central tenet of the new voluntary covenant; all the rest, including performance of Jewish law, though important, is commentary.

The peculiar character of Greenberg's theology is his belief that God's original will for the Jews has been and remains operative. He is not willing to sacrifice the unity of Judaism any more than the unity of God Himself. But he acknowledges that the unity of Judaism is different from what one may have thought it to be. His maverick covenant theology emphasizes the transcendence of God so that the Jews, in some type of dialogical process with God/covenant, come into independence and maturity. This represents a beginning to reconstruct Jewish thought from the ashes of Auschwitz and to redirect meaningful Jewish living in a post-Auschwitz age. This plays havoc with the orthodoxy of many religious people who insist that their religious forms are equal to the ultimate reality and that the sacred tenets of Judaism, e.g., God gave an obligatory Torah to follow at Sinai, were, are, and will always be. Greenberg's orthodoxy is otherwise. He takes seriously the rabbinic suggestion that the Torah speaks in the language of man (TB Berachot 32B), and that Torah after Sinai is not in heaven (TB Bava Metzia 59A-B), and he reasons that an authentic religious person does not place his/her hope in religious language and symbols which represent the ultimate but in the ultimate itself. God is what He is; His plan for Israel is what it is. What is being altered by Greenberg is our understanding of God and His design as expressed in age-old sancta, dogma, doctrine, etc. Judaism's ultimate challenge is to survive, but the language of survival must reflect contemporary Jewish reality. Thus Voluntary Covenant and not Imposed Covenant since today's religionless Jew, according to Greenberg, lives Judaism either by being or in the process of becoming, and not by doing traditional beliefs.

Peoplehood and a contracting deity, parochialism and sheer existence as a Jew are consistent leitmotifs in the covenant theology of Irving Greenberg. But others say that today's Jewish survivalist is not concerned with creating methodologies in thinking about Judaism but rather in doing Judaism; in producing philosophies cut off from belief; is concerned disproportionately with emphasizing Jewish ethnicity over Jewish morality and ritual. One generation after the rebirth of the State of Israel and the Shoah, s/he is asking searching questions of who God is, and what God wants, perhaps even needs of him/her as a Jew. S/he is finding meaningful answers in Jewish tradition, ethnicity, and in the performance of (obligatory) Halachah and mitzvah. S/he chooses to live Jewishly and not merely survive as a Jew. By returning home to Sinai, s/he exposes the secularism of today's religionless Jew as a deceptive disguise for a displaced commitment to Israel's covenant. Clearly, a new conservatism in modern Judaism prevails in rite and rights, *Zeitgeist* and timelessness, but it is forged in modern thought patterns of rationalism, democracy, pluralism, and humanism. Furthermore, Greenberg's process midrash relates directly to the Bible and offers existential observations *juxtaposed* to the text which at times are inconsistent with the accepted classical Jewish interpretations found in Midrash (collections of accepted rabbinical pronouncements intimately related to Scriptures), Talmud, or Codes. Classical Jewish faith affirms unhesitatingly the belief that God fulfills His promises (of redemption, for example) even though the overt evidence seems to indicate the opposite. Shoah, therefore, is not the culmination of the eclipse of God but the supreme test of Israel's faith, thereby strengthening the faith by the heroic exercise of it. It is the celebration of the covenant at Sinai and not its demise.

III. The Written Assignment

Of the many aspects of the learning process, perhaps the most frustrating is the cross purpose of students and professors. The professor's lectures are for the most part not understood, and his/her intelligence is further insulted by the students' seeming anti-intellectualism. The professor blames his/her failure on his/her young charges. S/he vents dissatisfaction by "popping" quizzes, assigning busy work, asking trick questions on exams, and springing a host of other tricks which only his/her mind can issue. Students become apathetic, turn off, and consider class attendance a punishing jail sentence.

In reality, the problem grows out of the diversified roles played by the professor and the student. The professor sees him/herself as a knowledge dispenser, developing a new generation of scholars who share his/her philosophy and concerns, and are willing to spend infinite hours reading, researching, writing, and discussing the problems at hand. The average student does not embrace the scholarly way defined by the professor. S/he is a tradesman interested only in the bare essentials of the job: How, when, where, what is required of him/her to obtain his/her grade. S/he could care less about schools of thought, philosophy, sociology, history, literary analysis, and theoretical abstractions; s/he is interested only in the here and now.

The nature of a college program, introductory classes in particular, is such that a professor does not trust his/her student and a student does not trust his/her professor. Students are regimented through a structured program which allots them little time to reflect, think, and mature. No wonder passivity and inertia set in. To rectify this problem the professor could help his student understand the beauty of being a professional and not a mere worker. One of the ways in which this can be done is to change the nature of the Written Assignment. In place of hourly examinations, mid-terms, and finals, which often represent the scribbled jottings derived from a lecture hour, there can be the book review, article review, journal, and synthesizing project. The major pedagogical principle gained is that the students will learn better and appreciate more their understanding of the subject matter if they are actively involved in learning rather than being passively taught.

Book Review

There are two types of book review, "scholarly" and "popular."

A. Scholarly Text

The review is brief and direct. About four double-spaced typewritten sheets in proper length. An essay style and not a question-and-answer format is suggested. The structure of the paper is constructed from the viewpoint of writing college quality work, using Kate L. Turabian's **A Manual for Writers of Term Papers** or the **MLA Style Sheet**

The goals of the student's report are to demonstrate to the professor that s/he has read the book, has understood why it was written, and has related it consciously to the material presented in the lectures. In addition to writing on the main thesis of the book, the student discusses language and terminology used, the background presupposed in the reader, whether the material is presented in a predominantly explanatory or a predominantly argumentative form, etc. S/he is asked, finally, to discuss how the book affected his/her previous notions of the particular aspect or aspects of Shoah with which it deals.

B.   Novel and Biography

An interesting way for a student to learn about Shoah ideas, values, and history is through fiction and/or biography which shift the course curriculum from subject matter to activity, from subjects of study to experience. The reading of Shoah novels and biographies is a Shoah happening and is more popular than historical reading in fashioning meaningful, lasting ties to an awareness of Shoah in Jewish and world history and culture. A good story provides a more vivid and intimate insight into life than does a textbook. A textbook must generalize but a story makes the subject matter more particular and personal. In addition, the novelist and/or biographer give a different dimension to what Shoah and Final Solution mean than is found in the "heavy" findings of a theologian, historian, social scientist, etc.

An impressionistic essay is suitable for a novel or biography review. By "impressionistic" is meant: Students' reactions, feelings about the book, how s/he experienced the book, any questions it may have raised in his/her mind to the central themes of the course, etc. The student may also approach the review by extracting those significant facts or observations related to aspects of Shoah which the book purports to cover. Points to look for include: What can we learn from the author's life?; is his/her style distinctive?; age and type of Jew portrayed; historical background and implications of the story; changes in the religious life of the Jew caused by knowledge of the Final Solution; growing knowledge about the Shoah and Jewish destiny in Europe, Israel, America, etc.; the Jewish minority in an overwhelming gentile environment; what message is there for the continuation of Jewish life, etc.

Article Review

An Article Review is short; approximate length is 2-3 pages. The review should contain (1) author, title of article, reference; (2) summary of main points of article; (3) statement of whether the article is empirical, analytical, or both.

  A. If the article is empirical, what hypothesis does the article support? Can the empirical article be related to a more general statement?
  B. If the article is analytical, describe the analysis. Does the analysis suggest hypotheses which could be tested?;

(4) the student's evaluation of the article. Articles are selected from assigned articles or readings in the course outline or from relevant periodical literature on the subject matter.

Journal

The journal is intended to combine aspects of the formal essay with that of a diary. The entries are short exercises, 5 typewritten double-spaced pages are recommended, though there is no limitation on length. Thoughts associated with the lecture topics are written-up as a journal entry and turned in during the class session at which the related topic is discussed. Thoughts and activities are many and varied, and provide an opportunity for the student to develop critical methodology and preserve or alter deep-seated commitments in his/her view of self, society, and history in light of the Shoah.

Synthesizing Project

A synthesizing project permits a direct encounter of student with material and can serve as an option or alternative to a writing-only presentation. The depth, variety, nature, and breadth of the Shoah are forcibly brought home if the student pursues his/her own special academic preference (e.g., art, music, religion, psychology, literature, sociology, etc.) in whatever media s/he deems most productive (short story, collage, audio-visual, etc.) in showing the relationship between these disciplines and some aspect of Shoah Studies. If done properly, a synthesizing project can weave a thread of continuity into complex and diversified material, and make the course content more particular and personal. The project is clearly intended not only to synthesize the different motifs within the course but to provide a goal for the students from the very day it is appropriately introduced.

Role-Playing, Problem Solving

A writing exercise, old in years but recently discovered, designed to enhance a learning process is role-playing or problem solving. This method takes seriously the four sequential steps of learning: Confrontation, analysis, interaction, and internalization.

Role-playing or problem solving offers a number of positive claims seldom found by other teaching strategies. It deals with real life situations and not theoretical abstractions; it enables the student to confront deep philosophical ideas in remarkable simplicity and convincing application; more cognitive avenues of knowledge are relied upon by this method than any other; students develop sensitivity and learn empathy when they interpret the different roles, often in conflict one with another, of a problem solving exercise; finally, values, commitments, aspirations, etc., can be discovered or developed or changed when a student is engaged in ethical decision making and moral development, the twin pillars of a role-playing sequence.

Problem solving activities can be enacted in almost every phase of Shoah Studies, from the Nazi-Jew-Church confrontation in the rise of the Third Reich to the different post-Auschwitz theologies and histories, from learning about the outlook and mentality of European Jewry in the inter-war years to understanding Israelis, 1948-present, and with all responses ever since Sinai to choose life and not death or stagnation.

Endnotes

1. My views on what can and cannot be obtainable in teaching an initial class in Shoah Studies are drawn from teaching experiences in a variety of educational settings: A one-day seminar, University of California at Riverside; adult education, University of Judaism; community college, Los Angeles Valley Colege; and a state university, University of Utah. In Spring 1988, I began offering Shoah and Zionism within a singular class setting at UCR.

2. This section is a presentation of mind sets associated with Response topics 10 and 11 (above). A part of its content is stimulated by Eugene B. Borowitz' fine chapter on "Confronting the Holocaust," in his **Choices in Modern Jewish Thought** (New York: Behrman House, 1983), pp. 185-217.

CHAPTER THREE

WHY DO WE CALL THE HOLOCAUST "THE HOLOCAUST?" AN INQUIRY INTO THE PSYCHOLOGY OF LABELS

*At the 1988 Oxford Conference, **Remembering for the Future: The Impact of the Holocaust and Genocide on Jews and Christians**, I served as chairperson of the section on "Philosophical and Moral Implications." Here Bruce Zuckerman (USC) and I presented our word study on the term "Holocaust," giving historic background and implications of the term, as well as a critical assessment of the role Elie Wiesel played in perpetuating this term of record for the Judeocide of World War II (see above p. 4). Our original text was published in Y. Bauer et al (eds.), **Remembering for the Future**, vol. 2 (Oxford: Pergamon Press, 1989), but a revised, tighter version appeared in Modern Judaism, vol. 7, no. 2 (1989). The shorter version appears below.*

Language is really a reciprocal tool: it reveals and, at the same time, it is revealing. That is, not only do we use language to explain the things that define our world, but, by the same token, the way we use language also necessarily discloses how we explain and define ourselves within that world. In general, everyone can instinctively grasp how a given word or phrase is used to demarcate, even create that small bit of the universe which it encompasses in linguistic terms. But the more subtle aspects of how this same word or phrase might disclose a part of our own identities is less obvious and is usually less consciously considered.

A case in point: the phrase, "The Holocaust" in contemporary American language. There can be little question exactly what this terminology means in common parlance. Indeed, "The Holocaust" has very narrow and specific connotations well recognized and well understood by anyone who has a reasonable working knowledge of the American idiom. Actually, one can delineate two connotations in this rubric-one general, the other specific. In general, a "holocaust" now is commonly used to connote a genocide, i.e., the systematic murder of any ethnic group. When used in this manner, the term is usually qualified so it is clear what "holocaust" is meant; for example, "the Armenian holocaust" or "the Biafran holocaust." When the systematic elimination of the entire human race is meant, one simply shifts the qualifier from the object to the agent of destruction: i.e., "nuclear holocaust."

But the most common and most prominent use of this phrasing does not seem to require any qualification; after all, it is taken to be the archetype, the prime case, against which all secondary applications of "holocaust" are measured and from which they each draw their sense of meaning. It is for this reason that one rarely sees this preeminent genocide designated as "the Jewish holocaust"-the qualification seems redundant. Instead, one simply acknowledges the primacy of what has come to be identified as the most horrific event of the Twentieth Century—the destruction of European Jewry by the Nazis—by capitalizing the "T" of "The" and the "H" of "Holocaust." Beyond the resulting, unadorned "The Holocaust" nothing more needs to be said.

And yet, on second thought, perhaps there is more to be said about "The Holocaust" than simply this. The sense one has today of what "The Holocaust" means did not evolve in a vacuum but, like all semantic developments, has a context. Moreover, in examining that context, one is necessarily drawn into a consideration of that other side of language, the self-revelatory aspect involved in the choice of a given word or phrase. For, as it turns out, "holocaust" is a rather strange term; and its use as the label to designate the Jewish genocide is neither obvious nor inevitable- in fact, it is surprising.

One might be tempted to say, "so what?"-why should we worry about the shades of meanings in "holocaust"? The semantics of "holocaust" might reasonably be said to be of minor importance when measured against the magnitude of the events that the term has come to designate. But it is precisely because "The Holocaust" has become the rubric of record under whose umbrella all discussions of the genocide of the Jews has come to be grouped that it bears close semantic consideration. The power latent in words and phrases must be taken seriously, especially when they come to bear as much cultural weight as "The Holocaust" has been made to bear in the modern world. If only for this reason, one may well wish to probe more closely exactly what "The Holocaust" means, or perhaps better: What the term "holocaust" has always meant before it came to have its current application.

We can begin with etymology. As the *Oxford English Dictionary*[1] attests, the term comes via the Latin *holocaustum*[2] from the Greek *holokaustos*.[3] This, in turn, is a compound composed of *holos*,[4] an adjective (or adjectival substantive) meaning "whole, entire, complete in all its parts" and *kaustos*, another adjectival form meaning "burnt, red-hot."[5] Thus, the basic, etymological meaning of *holokaustos* — and indeed, of its English equivalent "holocaust" — appears to be "something wholly burnt up." From this basic meaning, a broader, more generalized sense for the term can be naturally desiderated: "total destruction." We can trace this development from the particular to the general, for example, in the way the OED gives one of its definitions of the term: "Complete consumption by fire, or that which is so consumed; complete destruction, esp. of a large number of persons; a great slaughter or massacre." Seen in this light, "holocaust" appears a most apt term to characterize what the Nazis did to the Jews. The connotation of not merely massacre, but destruction by fire seems to give the term appropriately tangible overtones: The horror of the event may be said to be properly emphasized by a term that evokes the smell of burning corpses in the Nazi furnaces.

However, this is not the entire story. The picture presented above of a term that developed from a basic meaning of "something wholly burnt up" to an applied meaning of "total destruction" is largely misleading. For such a view of "holocaust" totally ignores what is originally the most common nuance of the term. "Holocaust," in its pre-World War II usage, has a connotation of which few who now use the term are aware; for most often the term was actually employed to characterize a particular sort of consumption by fire: The religious sacrifice. Thus, the first definition in the OED is not the one we have cited above but rather: "a sacrifice wholly consumed by fire; a whole burnt offering"; while the second definition applies this sense of sacrifice in a more general fashion: "a complete sacrifice or offering; a sacrifice on a large scale." Only thereafter does the nuance "general destruction, massacre" find its listing. A check of modern dictionaries will show that virtually all have retained "sacrifice" as the first definition of the term. For example, *Webster's Ninth New, Collegiate Dictionary* is typical in making its first definition of "holocaust" "a sacrifice consumed by fire."[6]

That the term should have the primary meaning of "sacrifice, whole burnt offering" in pre-Nazi era English is not at all surprising, considering that this falls completely in line with the sense of the term in both Latin and Greek. Not only do the Greek and Latin dictionaries list "sacrifice, burnt-offering" as the first definition of the term in these ancient languages, but this sense is employed virtually to the exclusion of any other sense.

Note, in particular, that the Septuagint, i.e., the Greek translation of the Hebrew Bible, employs various forms of our term, (*holokaustos, holokaustuma, holokaustosis*) well over 200 times, and without exception the term is used to designate a sacrifice— in the vast majority of instances an *'olah*, sacrifice to God–the exact Hebrew term employed in Biblical contexts to designate something offered to God which is to be wholly consumed by fire.[7]

Undoubtedly this fact duly impressed the editors of the King James Version of the Bible, who therefore also translated the Hebrew term for whole-burnt offering, the *'olah*, with what they thought was certainly the most appropriate English equivalent: "holocaust." Indeed, the adoption by the King James editors of this use of the term probably played the decisive role in fixing "religious sacrifice" as the primary sense of the term in English up until the mid-Twentieth Century. The lexicographers of the OED and other English/American dictionaries have simply reflected this fact.

Only in the post-war period has "holocaust" become largely divorced from its heretofore most common sense, "religious sacrifice." Yet we must consider: Why was this term the one that was chosen to characterize what the Nazis did to the Jews in the first place? One might argue that it was chosen primarily, if not exclusively, because of its nuance of "total destruction." Yet there were certainly other terms that would have appropriately described the sense of utter devastation that "holocaust" conveys without adding a religious, sacrificial connotation to the event: e.g.,"genocide," "extermination," "annihilation,'"destruction,'" massacre," or "slaughter." Note, in this respect, that the modern Hebrew term for the Jewish genocide, "Shoah," has no religious or sacrificial overtones. This term, which comes into modern Hebrew from biblical Hebrew, simply means "destruction, ruin."

In fact, the evidence——on linguistic grounds alone–points to just the opposite being the case. It seems most unlikely that anyone could have employed "holocaust" without taking cognizance of its most common definition. Rather. it was precisely because "holocaust" not only conveyed a sense of general and complete destruction, but also because it conveyed connotations of the religious sacrifice that it was the term of choice. But if this is so, we must consider the motivation: *The* psychology that led to the choice of this particular label to connote what the Jews suffered under the Nazis.

This is especially so since the implications of this choice, upon close consideration, are disturbing. For—whether intended or not—when one adopts the "holocaust" label, one also implies a particular religious correspondence between the Jews and the Nazis: If the former are the holocaust sacrifice, then it implicitly follows that the latter are the sacrificers, the officiants who offer up the sacrifice. In effect, one casts the Nazis into a quasi-"priestly" role. Even more seriously, the sacrificial connotation of "holocaust" also implies a third party to this "ceremony," — He to whom the sacrifice is offered: God, Himself. There are also other distressing elements that are injected into the interpretation of what the Jews suffered under the Nazis when one calls this "The Holocaust." The act of sacrifice involves a tacit religious agreement between sacrificer and deity; if the sacrificer offers the sacrifice, then the deity will benefit him. Indeed, often times it is the deity who demands the sacrifice; it is then the demanding god who must be propitiated by the slaughter and burning of flesh.

In consideration of these implications that can be so easily tied to the term *"holocaust,"* one would think that this would be the *last* term that Jews would accept as the proper characterization of their genocide. Yet this is clearly not so. Today, it is the term of choice — and, clearly, at some point this choice was made, and made (or, at minimum, accepted) by Jews. Still, it has to be equally obvious that when this term was adopted as the title of record, it was not meant to carry the connotations that — nonetheless — it definitely does carry. Why then, this choice? Why focus on a term that could be said to suggest that God and the Nazis were co-conspirators in the sacrifice of the Jews? Why do we call the Holocaust "The Holocaust"?

One possible explanation is simple: The label was chosen out of ignorance. Some time ago, James Kugel noted that "l'holocauste" was used by the French to describe the carnage of World War I and that this label was used by French writers once again at the conclusion of World War II in much the same manner.[8] In this respect, the connotation, "great destruction" for "holocauste" in post-war France apparently carried no obvious religious overtones. If the dead were viewed as sacrifices, it was on the altar of war, not of God, that they were slain. Even more to the point, presumably the battle dead were not called a "holocauste" in the sense that they were devoted offerings, but rather more as though they were ignorant "lambs for the slaughter" or, to use a slightly different, synonymous idiom, "cannon-fodder."

Along similar lines, it is interesting to note that the usage "atomic holocaust" (later, "nuclear holocaust") also had widespread currency within a few years after the conclusion of World War II–well before "holocaust" started to be used to designate the Jewish genocide.[9] Once again, when "holocaust" was used in this sense, no apparent religious connotations were implied. Instead, it was the sense of "holocaust" in terms of world conflagration, i.e., the earth being burnt to a cinder, that was clearly intended. Perhaps, therefore, we should not be surprised that the first American book (to our knowledge) in the Twentieth Century to be entitled **Holocaust!** was not about the destruction of European Jewry–but rather about the great "Coconut Grove" disaster in Boston, where an entire theater full of people lost their lives in the most devastatingly fatal fire of the early 1940s.[10]

In consideration of this history of usage, it might be possible to argue that "holocaust" was adopted as the label for the Nazis' extermination of the Jews independent of the term's religious/sacrificial nuance. Instead, it might be suggested that this word came into American usage primarily because it had a sense of destructive meaning associated with fire and war. Note, in this respect, David Roskies' comment:

> For the British and Americans who experienced the Nazi genocide at a distance, the word "Holocaust," capitalized and bracketed in time, did not reverberate with echoes of past destructions. Such terms as Deluge, Armageddon, Great War and Great Patriotic War carried specific historical and theological imperatives, but Holocaust to the English ear, was an apocalyptic term for a vicarious destruction. Like so many other weighty words in the English language, "Holocaust" had its roots in Latin, and though it did establish a vague connection back to the Bible for both Jews and Gentiles, ("holocaust" as burnt offering), it had none of the ready connotations of the alternative names just mentioned. So much the better, for it was precisely the nonreferential quality of "Holocaust" that made it so appealing.[11]

Roskies is certainly correct when he concludes that "Holocaust" has largely endured as the term of record for the Jewish genocide because those who use it are almost always ignorant of its meaning. Indeed, it is the very "strangeness" of the term, coupled with its vaguely "biblical" flavor, that has allowed this label to cast its spell over those who employ it. Still, once someone is told what "holocaust" actually means (or at least can mean) this spell of strangeness can be broken suddenly and dramatically. The usual reaction is shock and incredulity–followed by an affirmation to the effect- "Regardless of what the term means (or used to mean), that's not what I mean when I use "The Holocaust."

But in the final analysis, this argument from ignorance simply cannot hold up. While it is certainly true that the vast majority of people (Jew and Gentile) continue to use "The Holocaust" without understanding its religious/sacrificial connotations, it strains credulity to argue that those Jewish thinkers and writers who first adopted the term and, even more importantly, then allowed it to flourish, totally ignored information that could easily be found simply by opening a dictionary. The choice of a term to describe so horrific, so decisive, so all-encompassing an event in the shaping of modern Jewish identity as "The Holocaust" cannot be assumed to be a decision taken lightly or ignorantly. It must have been done with care and with due consideration. Besides, there is little doubt that the one man who has done most to establish "The Holocaust" in the modern consciousness was well aware of what he was doing and well aware of what the term "holocaust" meant in all its nuances. That man is Elie Wiesel.

Wiesel is a key-figure, whose work and thought are decisive in the development of the Jewish response to what European Jewry suffered under the Nazis. When he received the Nobel Peace Prize, a number of newspapers, for example, the *New York Times* (October 15, 1986), listed among his accomplishments the coining of the term "The Holocaust" to characterize the Jewish genocide. Whether Wiesel actually was the very first to employ "holocaust" in this manner or not, for all intents and purposes his adoption of the term was the single most important factor involved in legitimizing it in its current usage. We might say that Wiesel is to "The Holocaust" what Columbus is to the discovery of America. Whether he was strictly the first or not is really beside the point—he was the one who put "The Holocaust," as it were, "on the map." As he mentioned to us in private communication, he began to use the term in the late 1950s—and first recalls employing it in print in a review of Josef Bor's *The Terezin Requiem* in the *New York Times Book Review* of October 27, 1963.[12] From that point on, the term and its popularization developed throughout the 1960s (especially stimulated by the Eichmann trial in 1961)[13] until by the 1970s and 80s it came to its current broad application.[14]

And the motivation for Wiesel's use of "The Holocaust" has unmistakable religious/sacrificial overtones, as his own writings reveal. Indeed, in invoking the "holocaust" terminology, it was a particular scene of sacrifice that Wiesel had in mind–the *Akedah*, i.e., the story in Genesis 22 where God orders Abraham to offer his son as an *'olah* sacrifice. Wiesel has commented in a number of places regarding what he meant when he joined the concept of holocaust/sacrifice to the *Akedat Yitzhak*. For example in a statement he made in Skokie, Illinois in 1980, he declared:

> The *Akedah* is the most mysterious, one of the most heartbreaking, and, at the same time, one of the most beautiful chapters in our history. All of Jewish history can actually be comprehended in that chapter. I call Isaac the first survivor of the Holocaust because he survived the first tragedy. Isaac was going to be a burnt offering, a *korban olah*, which is really the Holocaust. The word "holocaust" has a religious connotation. Isaac was meant to be given to God as a sacrifice.[15]

It is not all that surprising that Wiesel would turn to the Akedah as a means by which to come to terms with horrific disaster. Since the time when mother Miriam or Hannah cried out in the face of Hadrian's persecutions, "Abraham! Be not proud!" Jews have turned to this strange and difficult story and seen it as emblematic of their plight. Especially, in the modern context, this story can be seen as being fraught with meaningfulness and relevance. Particularly, the figure of Isaac offers potent archetypes through which Jews can seek comprehension of what might otherwise seem too horrible to be comprehended. We believe that it is these "Isaac-arche-types" to which Wiesel turned when he endeavored to see the Holocaust as "The Holocaust." It is therefore important to explore the implications of these archetypes if one is to understand how the Akedah can stand in the background of "The Holocaust."

One such archetype is that of Isaac, the silent sacrificial offering. He goes to the slaughter without complaint, without protest and with only the mildest of questions. There is a palpable sense of nobility and bravery in Isaac's obedience to the commands of his father and, through the patriarch, the commands of God. There is the sense, too, of someone who seems, deep down, to comprehend what is about to happen to him but who is nonetheless not quite told of the fate awaiting until the very last possible moment. These strongly etched, biblically sanctioned standards of what is deemed to be ultimate piety clearly can hold a message for a survivor of "The Holocaust" like Wiesel. For in the *Akedah* one may find a kind of answer to the sharpest of questions that victims of the Nazi genocide have had to try to answer: Why did you not resist? Why did you not throw yourselves on the Nazi enemies—killing even as you were killed?

Such questions. of course, are both cruel and unfair, but they are asked (or thought) nonetheless. Perhaps the only *meaningful* response a survivor feels he can give to those who were not there and who could not possibly understood what it was like in the Nazi camps is a response of silence— a silence that the Akedah helps to explain. If what happened to the Jews in the camps was not exactly like what happened to Isaac, still on some profound level of meaningfulness, they share a sense o[identity.

Another potent archetype invoked by the *Akedah* is that to Isaac, the chosen victim. One might well imagine that Isaac would just as soon not have been chosen to be the object-lesson through which his father's righteousness and obedience were to be tested. But this was not Isaac's choice. He is the sacrificial pawn in the gambit, the peculiar object of focus in this game of wills between He who tests and he who is tested. Wiesel calls it "the game played only between God and Abraham."[16]

Still, Isaac is nonetheless a special victim, *yaḥid*. This is usually translated as "only son," but a more precise translation would be "only one." That is, Isaac is the one singled out for special treatment–specifically, he is the one promised to Abraham, the miraculously born malechild of the special wife Sarah, he who is to carry the covenantal blessing and whose progeny will be like the sands of the sea and the stars of the heavens. Isaac is Israel, or at least, the crucial, single antecedent of Israel.

Moreover. Isaac's death would mean the destruction of a complete people before they could ever be born—a genocide in microcosm. Even more to the point, he is an innocent victim. It is simply the special attention that God gives to Israel that seems to motivate the *Akedah*, as if to say, if you are going to be God's *yahid*, you are also going to be probed, tested and always at risk.

One can well understand how Wiesel could gravitate towards the archetype of Isaac as chosen victim and see in this figure the embodiment of Jewish history from biblical times until its modern culmination in "The Holocaust." For Jews have always perceived themselves as *yehidim*, the "only ones" chosen by God and this very chosenness has often had deadly consequences. To be sure, the Bible typically goes to great lengths to point out that the disasters in ancient times were a consequence of the people's inability to keep the covenant promises made at Sinai or to their incapacity to hold to the idealistic standards of justice demanded by the prophets. These demands are also seen as Israel's special burden —a standard required of no other nation and to which no other nation could even hope to aspire. If Israel cannot always hold to this standard, it is not so much because they are an especially degenerate people, but instead because, like the others, they are human, and their humanity defeats them. Hence, there is a sense of unfairness involved in Israel's chosenness. To some extent when God chose Israel, He victimized them, leading them into danger "like lambs to the slaughter" just as certainly as He led Isaac in the *Akedah* to the sacrificial altar.

Thus the archetype of the chosen victim is very likely the key to Wiesel's connecting "The Holocaust" to the *Akedah*. Certainly, Wiesel had no desire to suggest that "The Holocaust" was visited upon the Jews by God as a direct consequence of their disobedience to the covenant. At a minimum, the "punishment" did not suit the "crime" or, at least, if Israel was "guilty," all the other nations–the *goyim*, to use the appropriate biblical term–were equally, if not more guilty. After all, the other nations either were the agents of destruction or stood silently by and allowed destruction to occur.

Rather, it is Israel's special status that has caused the Jews to be separated out for special treatment–it is their burden, and their burden alone. Indeed, though in some respects this may seem perverse if not masochistic, Jews have found throughout their tragic history a certain confirmation of their peculiar status in the disasters that have befallen them–as if to say, God still acts in history with intentionality towards His Chosen People.

Finally and most crucially, Wiesel sees in the *Akedah* one further archetype of vital importance to him: Isaac as first survivor. Wiesel explains this sense of the story as follows:

> Almost to the last minute, the tragedy [*of the Akedah*] was going to occur. Yet Isaac remained a believer. Furthermore, Isaac, Yitzhak in Hebrew, means "he will laugh." So I asked myself, "How will he laugh?" And that is where I make the leap: Isaac, the first survivor of a tragedy, of a holocaust, will teach us how to laugh, how to survive, and how to go on believing.[17]

Wiesel would find it intolerable to view "The Holocaust" in terms of the *Akedah* if doing so would lead to utter despair—if he saw the victimization of the Jews by the Nazis solely in terms of the victimization of Isaac in the *Akedah*. There is life after the *Akedah*, although the relationship between God and man can never be quite the same in a post-Akedah world. So, likewise, Wiesel finally comes to believe that there is life after "The Holocaust": There is survival although things can never really be the same in a post-Holocaust world.

Ultimately, Wiesel sees beneath the silence and the singular victimization in the *Akedah* the promise that God gave to Abraham that not only is his the chosen line, but that his descendants *will* survive. If a disaster of the proportions of the Jewish genocide exterminates hope as much as it exterminates existence, something, Wiesel believes, always remains. One must make some kind of leap—like Isaac one has to learn to laugh if one is to continue to exist at all. He declares:

> We look at one another with pride and gratitude and we think that whatever happened to Abraham and Isaac happened to us too. The *Akedah*, after all, was not consummated. The testimony of our life and death will not vanish. Our memories will not die with us.[18]

In the final analysis, we suspect that Wiesel felt compelled to connect the Jewish genocide to the *Akedah* and hence to conceive of it as a holocaust for one overarching reason: That it was essential that God be encompassed within the universe of this ultimate Jewish catastrophe. Certainly, to see God as having a role in the destruction of the Jews is difficult, nearly intolerable–but to divorce God from this most horrific of events would be far worse. For without the God of the Bible, who established the special relationship with the Chosen People, the genocide ceases to be a *Jewish* event. The Jews who suffered so much would be robbed of their chosenness, their unique victimization—and for Wiesel this is unthinkable. Wiesel well understood all of the factors that could come into play when he called the Holocaust "The Holocaust"; he chose this term nonetheless because it seemed to him the only way to preserve the specialness of the tragedy as a Jewish tragedy. To all of this, one must respond with sympathy and empathy. Still, as the trauma of events in the first half of the Twentieth Century lessens as the Twenty-First approaches, one may begin to reconsider: Do we *still* wish to characterize the Holocaust as "The Holocaust"? Is the "Isaac-archetype" appropriate?

To begin with, should one see the Jews who were exterminated by the Nazis as the embodiment of the first Isaac-archetype, the silent sacrificial offering? We have already considered how such an assumption turns the Nazis into agents of sacrifice and God into Him for whom the sacrifice is made. Is there any way to mitigate these potentialities? A possible mitigation appears in certain Christian interpretations of "The Holocaust," in which the Jews are seen as Christ-like sacrificial "lambs of God," and, like Christ, turning the other cheek and loving their enemies who know not what they do. The sacrifice can then be seen as serving a greater purpose, as with Jesus: The redemption and salvation of mankind. In some versions of this Christian interpretation, the "reward" of the reclamation of Israel by the Jews is seen as the preliminary step to the Second Coming of Christ. Thus, "The Holocaust" will lead to the coming of a mutual Messiah.

Most Jews would discount this Christological view of "The Holocaust." They prefer to think of themselves as Wiesel thinks of Isaac, as one put upon by a circumstance he did not make or choose. They have never willingly sought out the martyr's role. Besides this, the idea of the Nazis as the agents of evil who, nonetheless, serve a greater good, is distasteful to Jews–especially because the parallel agents of destruction from the Christian story, the priests and Pharisees, are none other than the Jews themselves. Finally, most Jews find it unconscionable to see the state of Israel as their tangible "reward" for sacrifice—least of all if this reward is to be viewed as a preliminary step to the return of the Christian Messiah.

Still, there is one element that the Jewish and Christian views of "The Holocaust" share. It follows from seeing the Jewish genocide as a sacrifice to God, whether after the model of Isaac or of Jesus. In either case the silent object of deadly intent has been elevated to "heroic"[19] status. If an Isaac did not cry out, if a Jesus turned the other cheek, cannot the Jews who went silently to their deaths also be seen as "heroes" who had to endure a special testing that no ordinary men and women have ever had to endure? And did they not pass this test, as did Isaac and Jesus, with "flying colors"? Further, if the Jews who died in the camps did not begin as paragons of virtue, could it not be argued that their ultimate sacrifice made them so—just as the testing of Isaac confirmed his role as patriarch and the crucifixion of Jesus confirmed his role as Messiah?

Although such arguments might seem attractive, they distort the reality. There were no Isaacs or Jesuses in the camps but rather simply human beings in desperate straits—ordinary people who did the ordinary, desperate things that people do in order to prolong their existence, however, pitiful, however short-lived. In fact, the lack of resistance in the camps is precisely what one would expect from ordinary people who were always left with an element of doubt (however small) about their final fate.

It is a fundamental disservice to those who died to transform them all into images of Isaac or Jesus. Their deaths should not be elevated to grand, even cosmic tragedy, but kept grounded on earth. The meanness of their ends should not be aggrandized because to do so would make this grim course of events more palatable. Like the *Akedah* or the crucifixion of Christ, the story would become "beautiful."

It is not beauty, nobility, "heroism" or even silence that should be celebrated when one speaks of this Jewish calamity. Instead, the elemental human struggle manifest in this event can be properly grasped only if the Jewish genocide is kept ugly, ignoble, unheroic, punctuated by the screams of those who found themselves in mortal peril. To turn the Jewish genocide into a sacrifice makes it a "biblical" event rather than an event of our own time–a myth rather than a reality.

A closer look at the second Isaac-archetype reveals not only specially chosen victims, but also specially chosen destroyers to be the rods of divine anger. The prophets have told us that God created these victimizers solely for that purpose. Similarly, the Nazis can be seen as the ultimate foreign nation destined to make Israel suffer. They are unique devils, perpetrating cruelty on their unique victims, the Jews. This conception sometimes leads to making no distinction between Nazis and Germans, including those who acquiesced, those who did not, and new generations of Germans who are wrestling with collective guilt. This fails into the racial stereotyping that Jews have resisted for centuries, a license for Jews to see others as sub-human, just as the Nazis categorized them in that way.

A more humane model would see the Germans, even the Nazis, as ordinary human beings, who showed in the Jewish genocide that ordinary people in certain circumstances are capable of extraordinary cruelty. To say this does not exonerate or mitigate in any way the enormity of the Nazi cruelty. In fact, the dreadfulness of the Jewish genocide comes into focus only when the Nazis are deemed to be ordinary. Then the event cannot be so easily dismissed as an isolated instance. It becomes a warning of what can all too easily happen at any time, at any place, with anyone in the role of victim or victimizer. This is the way "The Holocaust" should be characterized and especially how it should be taught.

We should not be swayed by arguments that Six Million, efficiently killed Jews represent a more horrific slaughter than one or two million inefficiently murdered Armenians. In fact, even the "Six Million" figure, often invoked in characterizations of "The Holocaust," points up the problem of stressing uniqueness and chosenness over commonality. The truth is that eleven million people were killed by the Nazis in the concentration camps. Nearly half of these are excluded in most characterizations of "The Holocaust," and this seems to imply that Gentile deaths are not as significant as Jewish deaths.

"The Holocaust" should not be isolated, labeled as *sui generis*, the cataclysmic event, the discontinuity in history—all those things that necessarily follow when the Holocaust is seen as "The Holocaust." Rather, it must be taken to be emblematic. If it is to remain "The Primary Case" then it must be a case that shows the true horror, i.e., what all people are capable of doing and what all people are capable of suffering.

The third, and last, archetype to consider is that of Isaac as survivor. Here we must note that Isaac miraculously escaped, whereas the victims of the Final Solution had no such miracle. Further, Abraham's pious acceptance of God's testing does not sit well as a "parallel" to the cruelty of the Nazis, although both could say that they were just following orders.

Despite these interpretive drawbacks, it must be recognized that Wiesel feels compelled to use an *Akedah*-model of survival, as opposed to other potential models (e.g., Job) because its theme of Jewish survival includes God who grants an eternal promise to his people that some remnant will always survive.

Needless to say, no Jew in his right mind would oppose the concept of Jewish survival in a post-Holocaust world. However, when Jews urge each other, "Never again" the sub-text is really more "Never again for us!" This stress can have a subtle effect of desensitizing the Jewish community to the suffering of others as the community takes whatever steps it feels are necessary to insure its own survival. Moreover, because the authority of this survival, according to the patriarchal covenant, is God and His promise to Abraham, those who zealously press for whatever measures are necessary to guarantee that the Jews endure or even triumph can claim that any action is justified as a furthering of God's will.

We emphasize, however, that most Jews have resisted this tendency to a remarkable degree. In the current crisis in Israel, there is extensive moral self-examination. At the same time, however, there has been a disturbing increase in aggressive demands for Jewish-survival-at-all-costs. Although certainly Wiesel and most survivors of the Jewish genocide find the latter development a perversion of the Isaac-archetype of survival, still it is an idea set in motion by the term "The Holocaust." It does not fit with the fact that overall, Jews still pay heed to prophets' warning that a Jewish society cannot endure without justice–even as they wrestle with the exigencies of survival in an increasingly dangerous world.

This detailed critique of the implications of the term "The Holocaust" is not intended to discredit Wiesel's interpretations, but to explore what the acceptance of this rubric reveals about how the Jewish community thinks about itself in a post-Auschwitz world. The concepts evoked by the "Isaac-archetypes" remain active and concerns about them therefore need to be raised publicly. Wiesel himself has expressed doubts about this terminology, yet he has not explicitly opposed it.

The term may endure because of a second silence added to that of the victims — a silence that anyone must feel in the presence of a "Holocaust" survivor. When such a survivor demands that we understand "The Holocaust" as the most profound, cataclysmic calamity in history, this second silence tends to encourage acquiescence. For how can anyone bring him or herself to enter into open dispute with those who have suffered and witnessed so much? If they wish to see and define their experience as a kind of religious sacrifice, if they see themselves in the image of Isaac, who are we who have not so suffered and have not so witnessed to raise objection? Like Job we wish instead to lay our hands upon our mouths and speak no more.

The thoughts conveyed here are therefore painful thoughts. We are concerned that they may give offense, that they may cause further pain to those who have suffered enough. But we also believe that the time has come when what happened to the Jews in the first half of the Twentieth Century be placed in a more dispassionate perspective. The Jewish genocide needs to be humanized; its saints and devils need to be demythologized back into the mere people that they always were, its message of survival must be shared with all who have suffered and will suffer.

If language is a reciprocal tool, as was suggested at the outset of this study, then the tool must be used in both its facilities — as a window through which to discover and define our world and as a mirror through which to discover and define ourselves.

Endnotes

1. Cf. vol. 5 p. 344.
2. Cf. C.T. Lewis, C. Short, **A Latin Dictionary** (Oxford, 1879; rpt. 1969), p. 859.
3. Cf. H.G. Liddell, R. Scott, **A Greek-English Lexicon**, revised, H.S. Jones (Oxford, 1968), p. 1217.
4. *Ibid.*, p. 1218.
5. *Ibid.*, p. 932.
6. Cf. p. 576.
7. Cf. E. Hatch, H. Redpath, **Concordance to the Septuagint** (Oxford, 1897), pp. 987-989.
8. In an unpublished lecture delivered at Harvard University Hillel, Cambridge, MA; February 10, 1973; cited and summarized by D. Roskies, *Against the Apocalypse; Responses to Catastrophe in Modern Jewish Culture* (Cambridge, 1984), p. 261 with n. 7 p. 346.
9. The first use of "holocaust" in this sense of which we are aware is from the *Yale Review*, Spring, 1949. Therein, C.O. Dunbar declares (p.538):
   ...the people of the world should know the menace of atomic warfare so that they may match natural laws with civil laws while there is yet time to avoid such a holocaust.
   We are grateful to Frederick C. Mish, Editorial Director for Merriam-Webster Inc., who drew our attention to this and a number of other early references to "atomic/nuclear holocaust" in a private communication of August 19, 1986.
10. Cf. P. Benzaquin, *Holocaust!* (New York, 1959). Another early volume which includes "holocaust" in its title is G. Sherrard, *The Holocaust; Poems to the Children of England That They Might be Spared* (London, 1944).
11. Roskies, *op. cit.*
12. Cf. also, "A Sacred Realm," interview of Elie Wiesel by Ellen S. Fine, in *Centerpoint*, Fall, 1980; reprinted in **Against Silence; The Voice and Vision of Elie Wiesel**, I. Abrahamson (ed.) (New York, 1985), Vol. 1, pp. 185-190; cf. p. 185. For the review, cf. E. Wiesel, "In the Face of Barbarians, A Victory of Spirit," reprinted in *ibid.*, Vol. 2, pp. 269-270.
13. As Wiesel himself has noted. He declares, for example, in his interview with Fine (*ibid., p. 185*), "since the Eichmann trial there has been a breakthrough."
14. An indication of how "The Holocaust" came to be used and popularized may be found by making reference to Ph.D. dissertations utilizing

"Holocaust" as part of their title as found in a computer readout of dissertation abstracts from 1861-1985. There are no such titles listed before 1970. Between 1970-1975 there are 21, between 1976-1980 there are 97, between 1981-1985 there are 274.

15. E. Wiesel, "The First Survivor," Statement for the Niles Township Jewish Congregation, Skokie, Illinois, December 7, 1980; reprinted in Abrahamson, *op. cit.*, Vol. 1. p. 385. For similar statements, cf., for example, "Jewish Atheist: A Quarrel with God," *Baltimore Jewish Times*, April 9, 1965; reprinted in *ibid.*, Vol. 1. pp. 243-244; "What is a Jew?" interview of Wiesel by H. J. Cargas, *U.S. Catholic/Jubilee*, September, 1971; reprinted in *ibid.*, Vol. 1 pp. 271-275; cf. esp. p. 274; "The Three Times I Saw Jerusalem ," Address to the World Federation of Bergen-Belsen Associations, Jerusalem, July 9, 1970; reprinted in *ibid.*, Vol. 2 pp. 3-8; cf. esp. p. 8. Abrahamson is therefore quite correct when he observes: "The *Akedah* preceded the Holocaust, but for Wiesel the Holocaust is already in the *Akedah*, foreshadowed there." Cf. I. Abrahamson, "Introductory Essay," *ibid*, Vol. I; cf. p. 40.

16. "First Survivor," *op. cit.*; cf. also, for example, "The Question of God," Lecture for the Olin-sang Institute, Oconomowoc, Wisconsin, Sum mer, 1966; reprinted in Abrahamson, *op. cit.*, Vol. 2 pp. 139-144; cf. esp. p. 140.

17. Wiesel, "Survivor," *op. cit.*

18. E. Wiesel, "To Our Children," Keynote Address, Plenary Session of the First international Conference of Children of Holocaust Survivors, New York, May 28, 1984; reprinted in Abrahamson, *op. cit.*, Vol. 3; cf. p. 324.

19. The word hero/heroic has been intentionally placed in quotation marks in order to signal a particular nuance ol the term-i.e., a "hero" in the sense of an individual who does exceptional, courageous feats, usually at the risk of life–and–limb, over and above the sorts of acts that "ordinary" individuals ever do. In particular, a "hero" ol this sort willingly embraces great danger and even welcomes martyrdom. However, in using the terms "hero/heroic" in this manner, it is not being implied that the Jews and others who endured sufferings at the hands of the Nazis were not heroic on a much more basic *human* level; for certainly it is correct to view their endurance as being of heroic proportions.

CHAPTER FOUR

Dating the Shoah:
In Your Blood Shall You Live

In July 1988, I participated in a workshop entitled, "University Teaching About the Holocaust: Concepts and Resources," under the aegis of the International Center for University Teaching of Jewish Civilization established by Professor Moshe Davis in 1980. My participation in the workshop, where I and others introduced our book, **Methodology in the Academic Teaching of the Holocaust** *(Lanham: UPA, 1988), led to an invitation to participate in a panel discussion on the importance of the Shoah for Jew and non-Jew alike before the 1988 Yad Vashem Summer Institute. My attempt to answer a question from the audience on the date of the Shoah commemoration became the catalyst for the paper I delivered at the 19th Annual Scholars' Conference on the Holocaust and the Church Struggle held in Philadelphia, March, 5-7, 1989. My midrashic essay on the meaning of the choice of 27 Nisan as the date commemorating the Shoah is an exercise in linkage between providential design and history in the choice. In an appendix to the paper, I provide the first English translation of the Knesset decree formalizing 27 Nisan as Yom HaShoah. The essay initially appeared in A. Berger (ed.),* **Bearing Witness to the Holocaust 1939-1989** *(Symposium Series 31; Lewiston/Queenston/ Lampeter: The Edward Mellen Press, 1991).*

On April 12, 1951, the Knesset of Israel decreed *Nisan* 27 to be the official date for observing the Shoah and Ghetto Revolt Remembrance Day (*Yom ha-Shoah u-Mered ha-Getaot*). The date is commemorated worldwide by all who wish to recall the Great Catastrophe, honor its victims and heroes, and pledge that the devastation caused by the Nazis will never again be repeated.

The emminent Jewish philosopher and prisoner of Sachsenhausen concentration camp, Emil Fackenheim, has observed, "We cannot give meaning to Auschwitz with Jerusalem. Still less is it possible, however, to give meaning to the catastrophe without Jerusalem: Indeed, we cannot give meaning to Auschwitz at all."[1] Yet the decision of the Knesset has insured the meaning of Auschwitz for eternity.

However, the choice of *Nisan* 27 as the date of record to recall the most significant event of the 20th century disappointed religionists and secularists alike. To understand the "Day of Remembrance" decision is to disclose contemporary Jewish thinking on the Shoah: Is it an act of providential design, history, or a combination of both?

Asarah b'Tevet is one of four fast days in the Jewish calendar which recalls the end of the First Jewish Commonwealth, signified by the destruction of the First Temple (*Churban*) and the Babylonian Exile of the Jewish people from Eretz Israel (586-539 B.C.E.).

To label the destruction of European Jewry as a *Churban* is to link it with a past devastating event, but, in the words of Neo-Orthodox thinker, Rabbi Irving Greenberg, this does not come to grips with the awesome emotional, historical, and theological weight of the Holocaust; the Shoah as a category-shattering event.[2] In addition, it can be said, classical *Churban* catastrophe takes place within the Land of Israel; Shoah outside the Land.

Tishah b'Av. This major fast day in midsummer is *the* day of reflection on catastrophies of Jewish history in *and* outside the Land of Israel: Destruction of the First and Second Temples, the expulsion of Jews from Spain in 1492, the Chmielnicki murder of Polish Jewry in 1648-49 (in addition, Sivan 20 is specifically set aside to remember these massacres), and all other major atrocities committed against the Jews.

To remember Shoah on *Tisha b'Av* is to teach that the causes, reasons, and politics of genocide past have repeated themselves in the Nazi destruction of Six Million Jews, and to suggest that learning the proper responses to *Churban*, depicted in Jewish literature and Halachah (Jewish law), could have averted or diminished the evil decree unleashed on millions of innocents during World War II.

However, to observe Shoah on *Tisha b'Av* (day of *Jewish* tragedies) could make the event parochial and not universal — lest we forget, millions of others were murdered in Hitler's inferno. Also, if Shoah were recalled with other Jewish calamities, then the uniqueness of Hitler's war against the Jews would be dramatically diminished.

Never in history was a people so radically abandoned, dehumanized, and murdered. Emil Fackenheim puts it well:

...to lump the Holocaust with all the others would be to act as if nothing new had happened in the history of horror when the attempt was made to "exterminate" the Jewish people, that is to murder saints as well as sinners, new born babies as well as adults, and no exception was made even for those already near the grave; and the attempt was successful beyond the wildest nightmares of anyone.[3]

Furthermore, *Tisha b'Av* in the minds of many is of biblical origin and its observance is dictated by Halachah. Would the non-religious feel comfortable observing Shoah on a day guided by minutiae of rabbinic guidelines?

April 19. On this day in 1943, the liquidation of the Warsaw Ghetto began, and Mordechai Anielewicz led the Warsaw Getto revolt; the liquidation was completed on May 16. Secularists, Yiddishists, Bundists, among others, feel that this freedom fighter image — the revolt of the few against the many — is the proper way to record the Shoah

Opposition to "April 19," however, was mounted on three major ideological points.

(1) The Warsaw Ghetto uprising was by no means the only revolt against the Germans; why then should this act of heroism be singled out?

(2) Not all moments of heroism took place with gun in hand. Many simple Jews who participated not in "uprisings" did exceptional, courageous feats, usually at the risk of life and limb, over and above the sorts of acts that "ordinary" individuals ever do. These Jews and others who endured sufferings at the hands of Nazis were heroes on a much more basic human level; for certainly it is correct to view their endurance itself as something of heroic proportion.

(3) "April 19" is a solar date; issues of Jewish destiny demonstrate permanence only when they are commemorated in the Jewish lunar year (providential calendar).

Nisan 15 is the Hebrew date on which the Warsaw Ghetto uprising began. Setting aside the objections mentioned above, *Nisan 15* is the first day of Passover. Many would agree that the birthday of the Jewish people (Hebrew tribes became a nation on the first Passover) is a time for joy and celebration, not a time for pain and remembering destruction.

Others say if there is no Jewish people there can be no celebration as Jews; hence, Shoah should take precedence over Passover. Curiously, this argument may be supported by a reading from the Book of Esther, and a midrash (rabbinic hermeneutical pronouncement) thereupon:

> In the first month, that is, the month of *Nisan*, in the twelfth
> year of King Ahasuerus, *pur* - - which means "the lot" — was
> cast before Haman concerning every day and every month,
> (until it fell on) the twelfth month, that is, the month of
> *Adar*.

> On the thirteenth day of the first month, the king's
> scribes were summoned and a decree was issued, as
> Haman directed ... to destroy, massacre, and extermi-
> nate all the Jews, young and old, children and women,
> on a single day, in the thirteenth day of the twelfth
> month — that is, the month of *Adar* — and to plunder
> their possessions. (Esther 3:7, 12-13)

When told of this evil decree by her wise and informed cousin,
Mordechai, Esther bids the Jews of Shushan and her court maidens to fast
for three days and three nights (Esther 4:15). The rabbinic view is that the
fast followed immediately after Esther heard Mordechai's report on the
13th of *Nisan*. According to the midrash, the fast embraced *Nisan* 13, 14,
and 15.

The fast days, proclaimed to avert the decree of extermination,
coincided with and took precedence over Passover (*Nisan* 15). The text
records, *va-Ya'avor Mordechai/* "And Mordechai went his way (in the
city)" (Esther 4:17), but the talmudic sage Rav takes *va-Ya'avor* (= he
violated) to mean, "transgressed the Passover law by fasting on a festival
day."[4] The Sages' embellishment of this account presents Mordechai as
protesting to Esther, "But these three fast days include the first day of
Passover," and Esther as replying, "If there is no Israel, how can there be
a Passover?"

Rabbinic legislation permits the cancellation or minimization of joy
due to pain or shame. The Talmud speaks about God's anger at angels for
singing a song of victory after the pursuing Egyptians drowned in the sea:
"The work of My hands are drowning in the sea, and you sing my praises?"
(BT Megillah 10B). Consequently, Jews intentionally curtail their Passover joy by not reciting the complete Hallel (Psalms 113-118) during
Passover week, by diminishing the second cup of wine at the Seder, and
by the Fast of the First Born on the eve of Passover, out of empathy for the
dying Egyptians.

In the midrashic account, Esther's decision to cancel Passover may be
seen as an act of *Pikkuah Nefesh* ("saving life"), and Jewish law permits
the suspension of Jewish practice if life is at stake. Esther's cancellation

of Passover was an act *before* destruction in order to avoid it; Shoah observance, however, is an act of obedience *after* destruction in order to lament and learn from it.

Today on 'erev Passover many read Holocaust selections during the recitation of the "Pour Out Thy Wrath" paragraph accompanying the Cup of Elijah. But reference to Shoah here does not dominate the Passover tiding of freedom and birth. Rather they are part of a liturgical message invoking the Judge-of-all-the-Earth to deal justly with the murderers, and on another level, the nations of the world, who did nothing to condemn Nazism and do nothing to abolish the cry that Zionism is racism,[5] as He continuously judges Israel. Only then, can the complete messianic fulfillment of the future, a siblinghood of man under the parenthood of God and inspired by the Torah way, be realized swiftly in our days.

On this point, we should note that the anthem of many Jews as they were led to extermination was the 12th article of the Maimonidean Creed ("I firmly believe in the coming of the messiah, and although he may tarry, I daily wait his coming"). These helpless victims of Nazism sang of a better day for humanity — a humanity that chose to be silent at the hour of their destruction. This is an authentic Jewish understanding of hope and *Heilsgeschichte*, conducted without politics, politeness, and paternalism. The message: The major traits of Hitlerism — isolation, vilification, expulsion, slavery, and extermination — are not the will of heaven but the act of Everyman, the bitter fruits of the freedom he has abused.

Shoah cannot cancel Passover because the latter is transformed by Sinai (providence), and the former is the leaven waste of cyanide (history).

On the 12th of April 1951, the Knesset arrested Heaven and Earth and declared *Nisan* 27 as the national holiday commemorating the Shoah. The declaration (see Appendix) recalls antecedents to the Nazi brutality done to Ashkenazi Jewry in European lands; chooses biblical prooftexts that narrate exile, plight, mercy, justice, return, redemption, and responsibility; maintains that in the month of *Nisan*, many communities were destroyed by the forbears of the Nazis, the Crusaders; and offers a fable emphasizing some useful truth:

> A man and his son were walking along the path. The son tired and asked the father: "Father, where is the state?" The father replied: "Son, this should be your sign, if you see a cemetery close by, the state is near."

In our day, the catastrophic destruction of the Jewish people is the Shoah ("cemetery"), which is forever linked to the rise of Israel ("state"). Indeed, Israel Independence Day is celebrated on *Iyar* 5, showing a connection between *Yom ha-Shoah* and *Yom ha-Atzmaut*.

Thus on April 12, 1951, the Knesset read first the declaration on *Yom ha-Atzmaut* followed by the declaration on *Yom ha-Shoah*. The order of the readings is important; it suggests that only an unrelentless commitment to life and hope (Zionist dream and hope) can withstand the pain and grief of remembering the Shoah. The reverse is unthinkable.

So we count the days from *Yom ha-Shoah* to *Yom ha-Atzmaut* and we compute nine. Who knows nine? Nine, in the words of the Passover Haggadah, "are the months of pregnancy." Pregnancy means life and life is ushered in by covenant. And in the Covenant of Abraham, Jews recite this prophetic utterance:

> And I pass by thee (Jerusalem) and
> I (God) saw thee wallowing in thy blood,
> And I said unto thee
> In thy blood live. Yea, I said unto thee,
> In thy blood live.
> (Ezekiel 16:6)

The cited verse is found in the Knesset statement on the Shoah.

At the Wannsee Conference in January 1942, the blueprint for the "Final Solution" was unveiled in 58 minutes. In less than 20 minutes on April 12, 1951, people, history, God, Shoah, and Zion were sealed in an eternal manifesto committing a post-Holocaust age to life, hope, and action.

On 6 *Nisan* 5711 (April 12, 1951), clouds gathered over Auschwitz, Poland, and in Jerusalem the Golden, the sun rose over Zion.

"In your blood, Israel, in your blood shall you live."

Endnotes

1. Fackenheim, Emil L. **What is Judaism?** New York: Summit Books, 1987, p. 37.
2. An insightful summary of Rabbi Irving Greenberg's thinking on Shoah is his "The Shattered Paradigm: Yom Hashoah," in **The Jewish Way.** New York: Summit Books, 1988, pp. 314-372.
3. Fackenheim, *loc. cit.*, p. 37.
4. See S. Goldman's comment on Esther 4:17 in **The Five Megilloth.** London: Soncino Press, 1961, p. 218.
5. The resolution declaring Zionism to be racism, introduced by the UN sponsored Women's Conference in Mexico, was subsequently accepted by 72 member nations of the General Assembly (contra 35 against with 32 abstentions and three delegations absent) in 1975. US

Ambassador Daniel Moynehan, now US Senator from New York, called the resolution "an obscene act," and Israel's Ambassador Hayyim Herzog, later elected Israel's sixth president by the Knesset, declared: "This day will live in infamy. Hitler would have felt at home in this hall."

Sixteen years later, in the aftermath of the failed Soviet coup against M. Gorbachov and the dismantlement of the USSR, President George Bush called for the repeal of the 72 infamous nays. In an address before the UN General Assembly on September 23, 1991, he stated: "To equate Zionism with the intolerable sin of racism is to twist history and forget the terrible plight of the Jews in World War II, indeed, throughout history." On the day that the President spoke, which contributed successfully to the abogation of the infamous declaration, Jews were celebrating the Succot festival. And on the first day of "Our Season of Joy," they intoned the biblical lesson from Num 29, which narrates the offering of the 70 bullocks, corresponding to the Nations of the World, intended as an atonement for all mankind.

Appendix

The Decision Regarding the Establishment of a National Holiday Commemorating the Holocaust and Ghetto Revolt Remembrance Day.

Chairperson Yosef Sprinzak:

I request the subcommittee chairperson of the House Committee, Knesset member Nourok, to present us with the decision regarding *Yom ha-Shoah*. Mordechai Norouk (in the name of the House Committee):

The Heaven weeps, the Land weeps, and Israel weeps.

High Court, sisters and brothers in suffering. On behalf of the House Committee, I am honored to present to you an important and significant proposal. Six years have passed since the removel of the iron bars enclosing the European countries occupied by Nazi Germany during World War II, when we finally realized the awful truth, that our expectation was in vain and our hope was nought, and our worst fears came to be: Six Million of our people were murdered, a third of our nation, most of our sons, in cold blood were killed, with frightening brutality, using a system horrifying in its completeness, fathers and sons, women and children, a million two hundred thousand Jewish children, the Jewish youth, the hope and future of a nation, who could have become the pride of our people and a beacon to the nation.

The significant thousand- year period of European Jewry came to a tragic end. Carved in our minds is the intricate and complete social and political life of the various Jewish communities in the European diaspora. A wide network of schools teaching in other languages, from pre-school through higher education, supported by the state and local authorities, encouraged by the cultural, national autonomy; the large yeshivas, their reputation preceeding them throughout the Jewish world; splendid institutions cultural, financial, philanthropic; various organizations, rich daily newspapers, libraries, publishing; parliament representatives elected by Jewish parties, who continuously protected equal rights for all, with integrity and respect of Jewish values; tens of thousands, study halls and prayer quorums, hundreds of thousands Jewish books and millions upon millions of worshippers — "a wind passes by and it is no more"[1] — this is, the Third Destruction (*Churban*) of the House of Israel.

We hear the voice of the blood of our brethren screaming from the earth:"Earth, do not cover my blood,"[2] so that all future generations will know the horrendous acts done by the vicious animals disguised as human beings.

We hear the cry of our beloved sons: Raise the flag which is drowning in blood and tears, that fell from our hands, and carry it with pride and reverance. If we mourn on *Tisha b'Av* for the communities of Magneza (Mainz), Vermiza (Wurms), and Smyrna (Speyer), that were destroyed by the ancestors of the Nazis, then we must know how many Jews these communities numbered — five thousand at the most. And yet now we have witnessed communities such as Warsaw, which numbered during the war as much as half a million residents, Lodz, Lemberg, Cracow, Lublin, Tzintuchov, Pinsk, Luzak, Rona, Vilna (the Jerusalem of Lithuania), Kovna, Grodna, Brisk, Bialistock, Riga, Mitaov, Lvov, Berlin, Frankfurt, Hamburg, Breslau, Vienna, Strasburg, Budapest, Bucharest, Kishinev, Tzernovitz, Belgrade, Zagreb, Thessalonica, Prague, Odessa, Charson (Kherson), Kiev, Vitvask, Mohil (Mogilez), and many, many more, who is able to count them? In all these communities there were no less than 50,000 Jews.

"When I think of this, I pour out my soul."[3]

"Oh, that my head were water
My eyes a fount of tears!
Then would I weep day and night
for the slain of my poor people."[4]

"For how can I bear to see the disaster
which will befall my people! And how can I
bear to see the destruction of my kindred!"[5]

I am a prayer to the God of our ancestors: "Before our eyes let it be known among the nations that You avenge the spilled blood of Your servants!"[6] When the Romans found Rabbi Hananya ben Teradyon, one of the Ten Martyrs, who gathered unto him crowds and Torah in public, they sentenced him to burn at the stake. And as he took his last breath, he declared: "The parchments are burning, but the letters of the Torah soar upward." Our enemies can destroy us in body, the parchments are burning, but the spirit of Israel, the infinite treasure, lives on forever, the letters soar from country to country, from one part of the earth to another.

Those that remain, the survivors, who were subjugated to incomprehensible suffering, do not know where the ashes of the holy and pure have spread: "And no man knows their sepulchre unto this day."[7]
Every Jew has a proper memorial day, a day he commemorates the memory of his dear beloved ones. They died a natural death, we know when they left us; we ourselves buried them and we have always opportunity to shed tears on their graves. On days that we rejoice and on days of sadness, when we stand at their graves, we can almost see our dearly beloved, we can practically hear their voices, and our hearts warm to the sound.

However, dear Knesset members, brothers and sisters in suffering, different is the other kind, the uncommon; we have no knowledge of neither the day or the year of death of the innocent souls of all the martyrs, nor any idea to where their ashes were spread.

Even this small consolation, the vicious animals, posing as humans, take from us.

Even in our history, submerged in blood and tears, which knows Pharaoh, Nebuchadnezzar, Vespasian, Titus, Hadrian, the Crusades, the Poisoning of the Wells, Blood Libels, the Inquisition, the Pogroms — there is no equivalent to the annihilation of a third of our people in such a form.

And we feel compelled to commemorate the memory of our loved ones, but we must designate a day that will be commemorated by all, to remember all the martyrs. On this day the unity of the nation in its entirety will be reflected for "there was no house where there was not someone dead."[8]

It is our national duty to designate for the generations to come a memorial day for our martyrs. We are proud of the ghetto uprisings, and of our brothers and sisters who saved the honor of Israel with miraculous feats accomplished in great courage, and they showed the vicious animals that the people of Israel will not be led like sheep to slaughter, and that it will die heroically, the death of righteous and courageous people. So that all future generations will know how to honor and respect the memory of these sacrificial victims of our nation. This is our consolation.

Our forebears have dedicated days of fast and mourning to certain events, such as the 20th of *Sivan*,[9] etc., which cannot be compared in any shape to this modern tragedy.

We must choose a significant day which will reflect the days of slaughter and the days of uprising that took place in the month of *Nisan*. Therefore, the House Committee has chosen the end of the month of *Nisan*, in the days of *Sefirah*, [10] during which many sacred communities were destroyed by the ancestors of the Nazis, the Crusaders.

The commemoration of the victims of the Holocaust is an issue in and of itself. I hope we will do so when the people of Israel will dwell secure in our country, and by the grace of God, we will achieve a normalized state. In evidence is an elaborate plan conceived by Yad Vashem and sponsored by the World Jewish Congress with the participation of the Jewish Agency and the National Committee.

The people of Israel have always excelled in the commemoration of their departed. Our forebears carried Joseph's coffin 40 years in the desert in order that he be buried in the Land of Israel.

Let us commemorate the memory of our martyrs and the future generations will pass down from generation to generation the glory and honor of our martyrs, and from them they will draw the strength and courage to continue the chain of generations. Our martyrs have a significant part in the building of our people and the land. And we ask with pain gripping our hearts: Why didn't our dear and beloved ones live to see their hopes and dreams, from which they dedicated their lives, come to be?

I take the liberty to find the answer in a fable. A man and his son were walking along the path. The son tired and asked his father: "Father, where is the state?" The father replied: "Son, this shall be your sign, if you see a cemetery close by, the state is near."

Honored Knesset: We too have seen a cemetery before us, a graveyard of Six Million of our sisters and brothers, and perhaps by the merit of their blood spilled like water, we achieved a state and the beginning of redemption, as in the words of the prophet spoken from the hills of Zion: " And when I passed by you, and saw you wallowing in your blood, I said unto you: In your blood live; yea, I said unto you: In your blood live!"[11] In other words, my oppressed and persecuted people — do not despair! You will rise to a new life, to an independent life, to a glorious life.

I have the great pleasure to present to the Knesset the following legislation formulated by the House Committee:

The First Knesset declares and states that the 27th day of the month of *Nisan* of every year will be the Day of the Shoah and Ghetto Revolt Remembrance — an eternal day of memory for Israel.

Honored Knesset, the elected of the Land, with the permission of the chairperson, we will stand for a moment of silence in the memory of our martyrs. (The Knesset stood at attention.)

I hope,[12] that at this moment, when the images of the martyrs and their communities appear before us, we will think of them with respect, with sympathy and admiration, and we will decide unanimously to commemorate their memory on this established day, this year and forever. And we call to the sacred communities destroyed, as Jonathan called to David: "You will be missed when your seat remains vacant."[13]

We will not forget you, you who have left an empty space in the Jewish world.

Chairperson Sprinzak:

I declare the decision.

The First Knesset declares and establishes the 27th day of the month of *Nisan* of every year as the Shoah and Ghetto Remembrance Day — an eternal day of memory for the House of Israel.

The meeting adjourned at 9:20 A.M.

The meeting resumed at 10:35 A.M.

Translation by Zev Garber

Endnotes

1. Psalm 103:16.
2. Job 16:18.
3. Psalm 42:5.
4. Jeremiah 8:23.
5. Esther 8:6.
6. Psalm 79:10b.
7. Deuteronomy 34:6b. Text speaks of "his sepulchre," i.e., Moses; likewise, an unknown burial place is the fate of millions of Shoah victims.
8. Exodus 12:30b.
9. The Council of the Four Lands, the central institution of Jewish self-government in Poland and Lithuania from the middle of the 16th century until 1764, decreed the Fast of *Sivan* 20, the day upon which Chmielnicki massacres began in Nemirov (*Gezeirot Tah ve-Tat*).
10. *Sefirah* = count; the counting of the Omer (a measure of grain) for seven full weeks starting from the second day of Passover to the beginning of Shavuot (Pentecost); see Lev 23:9-15. In addition, rabbinic memory has changed this biblical season of joy to one of pain

as it remembers the slaughter of Rabbi Akiva and his students for the "crime" of teaching Torah in Eretz Israel against the wishes of Rome.

11. Ezekiel 16:6.
12. Error in text; word should read *mekaveh* and not *tikvah*.
13. I Samuel 20:18b. The prooftext has the verbs in the singular, understandably changed to the plural in the Knesset quotation.

CHAPTER FIVE

Edith Stein: Jewish Perspectives on Her Martyrdom

Murdered in Auschwitz in 1942, Edith Stein has become a figure of controversy in the Jewish-Catholic dialogue. Some Jews and Christians say that Stein was sent to her death because of her proud affinity with the people of her birth, and others find in her canonization a symbol of retributive repentance for the atrocities committed against the Jews in the heart of European Christendom during World War II. I consider and reject both alternatives and then offer other possibilities in an effort to unravel the enigma of Edith Stein, Jewess and Christian martyr. My views were first presented at the 21st Annual Scholars' Conference, hosted by Stockton State College in New Jersey. They are found in Harry James Cargas (ed.), The Unnecessary Problem of Edith Stein (Studies in the Shoah 4: Lanham: UPA, 1994).

Edith Stein, a Jewish intellectual convert to Catholicism, became a Carmelite nun, Sister Teresa, and ultimately was murdered at Auschwitz in 1942. Our primary purpose here is to set up the basic premises which may allow us to answer the neccessary question on Edith Stein: Was she a Jewish martyr or Christian martyr or both? We begin by reviewing the dialectics of who is a Jew?; move on to the tensions of Catholic-Jewish dialogue; proceed to the factuality of her martyrdom; and conclude with the actuality of her canonization.

I. The Dialectics of Who is a Jew?

The prominent antrhopologist, folklorist, and historian, Raphael Patai, has done more than most in tackling the perpetual problem, "Who is a Jew?" In articles and books spanning over a half-century, he offers salient observations.

Jews as a Race

Are the Jews a race? In **The Myth of the Jewish Race**,[1] written jointly with his daughter, Jennifer Patai Wing, the authors cite the Oxford English Dictionary (OED) definition of "Jew" as a "person of the Hebrew race." Patai and Wing then proceed to destroy the validity of this definition as they discuss all available physical, historical, psychological, genetic, morphological, and behavioral data that bear on this topic.

They conclude that there is much genetic diversity among Jews today, reflecting the populations and environments in which they live, and that there are very few genetic differences between Jews and non-Jews. Thus Jewish "racial" types are a product of non-Jewish environment, and not the result of unique Jewish genes.

Jews as a Religion

In America, and throughout most of the world, a Jew is perceived as an adherent to Judaism, a system of commandments and concepts enshrined in a philosophy of ethical monotheism. Thus for many, a Jew is defined in religious categories. But Patai in **The Jewish Mind**[2] points out how fragile is this association.

Unquestionably, Jewish religion is the most important component of the Jewish civilization, but significant number of Jews identify not by a spiritual Being but by ethnic and secular belonging. God may choose the People Israel yet certain of the People choose not God.

Even if Jews are qualified by religion, one may ask, whose model of Judaism? In cultural terms, Ashkenazic, Sephardic, Oriental? In geographic terms, Israeli rabbinic, American pluralistic, European Hasidic or Mitnagdic, etc.?

Also, past and present definitions differ in the same branch of Judaism. In November 1885, leading Reform rabbis convened in Pittsburgh and declared:

> We hold that all such Mosaic and Rabbinic laws as regulate diet, priestly purity, and dress, originated in ages and under the influence of ideas altogether *foreign* to our present and spatial state...
> We recognize in the modern era of universal culture of heart and intellect the approach of the realization of Israel's great messianic hope for the establishment of the kingdom, truth, justice, and peace among all men.
> We consider ourselves no longer a nation, but a reli-

gious community, and therefore, expect neither a return
to Palestine nor a sacrifical worship under the adminis-
tration of the sons of Aaron, more the restoration of any
of the laws concerning the Jewish state.[3]

However, in today's Liberal Judaism (contra Classical Reform of
19th and early 20th centuries), it is common place for congregants to wear
skull caps and prayer shawls, and for some, to pray with phylacteries and
observe dietary laws in order to be *distinguishable* from Christians at pray
and play.

Further, the full disclosure of the Shoah radicalized the Reform
movement to endorse the goals of Jewish statehood. The Association of
Reform Zionists of America's (ARZA) success in World Zionist Con-
gresses, coupled with Reform institutions in Israel, including Kibbutzim
Yahel, Lotan, and Har Halutz, may be seen as a true barometer of today's
Reform involvement in a Jewish state, committed to prophetic Judaism
and social justice.

Jews as a Nation

The notion that a Jew belongs to a Jewish nation is common among
many Israeli and diaspora Jews.

Hear the words of Amos Oz (born in Jerusalem in 1939), one of
Israel's most gifted writers, in an article published a few weeks after the
Six-Day War of 1967 and republished in the January, 1988 issue of *New
Outlook:*

> I am a Jew and a Zionist. In defining the nature
> of my identity I do not rely on religion, for I stand
> outside it. I have not learned to have recourse to verbal
> compromises like 'the spirit of our Jewish past' or 'the
> values of Jewish tradition', for values and tradition alike
> derive directly from tenets of faith in which I cannot
> believe. I am incapable of separating Jewish values and
> Jewish tradition from their source, which is command-
> ment, revelation and faith ... A Jew, in my vocabulary,
> is someone who regards himself as a Jew, and also
> someone who is forced to be a Jew. A Jew is someone
> who admits to being a Jew... If he does not admit to any
> connection with the Jewish people, then, in my view, at
> least, he is not a Jew, though religious law defines him

as such. A Jew, in my opinion, is one who chooses to share the fate of other Jews, or who is condemned to do so. To be a Jew means to relate to the Jewish present ... to take pride and participate in the achievement of Jews as Jews, and to share responsibility for injustice done by Jews as Jews (responsibility, not guilt). Finally, to be a Jew means to feel that when a Jew is persecuted because he is a Jew - that means you.

> (cited by Alan Montifiore, grandson of the founder of Liberal Judaism in Great Britain, in a paper on Jewish identity delivered at the Oxford Conference, "Remembering for the Future," 10-13 July, 1988).

Oz (Hebrew for "strength") speaks for many Jews who identify ethnically and culturally sans religion, or who are defined Jewish by antisemitism. The latter echoes Jean-Paul Sartre's "existentialist" inter-pretation of *the* Jew as someone who is regarded and defined as such by others irrespective of *Jewish* input.

Yet the term Jewish people is the expression '*Am Yisrael* ("people of Israel"), an age-old identification rooted in biblical *religious* tradition. Note the start of the Ten Commandments: "God spoke all these words saying: I am the Lord your God who brought you (*the people*) out of the land of Egypt, the house of bondage: You shall have no other gods beside Me." (Exod 20: 1,2,; Deut 5: 6,7).

If the *religion* of biblical Israel had not developed and infused the *history* of the ancient Israelites, would there be a Jew today? In fact, the peoplehood of Israel embraces Judaism (ethical monotheism in the image of the dual Torah, Mosaic and Rabbinic) and Jewishness (status of a Jew, delineated by humanistic, social, and ethical values, and community involvement).

Jews as a Lineage

In Jewish law (Halachah), biological descent plays a significant role in defining who is a Jew. Classical Halachah designates a child to be a Jew if a) both parents are Jews; b) the natural mother is a Jew; and c) Halachic ritual conversion (spiritual descent from "our father Abraham") is per-formed. But does biological parentage guarantee transmission of Jewishness?

This is hard to comprehend if the child is raised in a non-Jewish faith or in no Jewish faith. What to do with "Jews for Jesus," and similar groups, who claim Jewishness ("born a Jew, always a Jew"), while distorting Judaism? .

Reform Judaism's ascent of patrilineal descent (child of a Jewish father and non-Jewish mother, who is supposedly raised Jewishly, e.g., Jewish rites of passage, observance of Jewish holy time and space, etc.) is one step forward and two steps backward. It is correct in emphasizing the importance of the father's Jewish line, but fails a) to appreciate the *closer* relationship between (Gentile) mother and child; b) to comprehend the harsh realities of Jewish history, namely, children of Jewish women fathered willingly or unwillingly by Gentile fathers who abandoned them, which contributed to rabbinic recognition of matrilineal exclusivity; and c) to deal with the possible impediment of Jewish religious instruction of the child brought about by later non-interest or non-involvement by intermarried parents, Gentile and/or Jew alike.

Halachic definitions of a Jew are the modus operandi today. Ironically, questions prevail within the *tolerance* exhibited by Halachah as interpreted on the one hand by the Orthodox/Conservative, and on the other, by Reform/ Reconstructionist.

For the Traditionalist: Can a Jew by birth who chooses not to obey and observe Halachah contribute meaningfully to Jewishness? For the Modernist: If Halachah is voluntary and not mandatory, when does a person cease to be a Jew? Also, what to do with non-halachic (traditional) converts and patrilineal descent if faith committments are reneged?

Patai in his seminal work, **The Jewish Mind** (cited above), concludes that "a Jew is a person who considers himself a Jew and is so considered by others."[4] Thus to be Jewish is a matter of feeling, emotional commitment. In Patai's assessment, to feel Jewish is the result of one or more factors: Heritage, peoplehood, nationality, religion, and moral behavior; and, we may add, reinforced by a battery of -isms: Antisemitism, Hitlerism, Zionism, heroism, humanism, etc.

For Patai, the bottom line in all these categories is knowing something about the Jews, and from feelings produced by that knowledge. Thus, in the ultimate analysis, to be Jewish is a state of *mind*.

However, in a post-Auschwitz age, where the entire enterprise of being Jewish has been called into serious question, to be Jewish in head and heart is not sufficient. What if one suffers from amnesia?

It is a great mistake, based on an entire misconception and misunderstanding of Judaism, to assume that Jews are capable to living in a world of ideas only, and can dispense with *action* that should embody these ideas and give them tangibility and visible form.

Admittedly, knowledge and feelings about Judaism are important, but they must be challenged and channeled by *doing* Judaism. It is not a question of "Who is a Jew?" but how and why be a Jew?

The voluntary Sinaitic oath, *na'aseh venishma'* ("we do therefore we hear, understand, obey") is today's post-Auschwitz obligation: You're Jewish, your task is to remain Jewish.

Memory of the past is a central component of the Jewish experience (who a Jew is) and determination to live the memories actively preserves a Jewish present (why be a Jew) and transmits a Jewish future.

It is clear that Edith Stein as Sister Teresa Benedicta of the Cross — as the one blessed by the Cross — does not fulfill the categorical definitions nor obligations of one who is a Jew. Yet the Church insists that she died as a daughter of Israel," for the glorification of the most holy name (of God)."

II. Dialogue: Understanding Self and Other

The case for or against Edith Stein's classification as a Jew presents an opportune time to review the progress made, not withstanding the setbacks caused by the Kurt Waldheim affair [5] and the "Carmelite convent at Auschwitz" controversy,[6] in Catholic-Jewish relations since the Shoah.

Fifty-six years ago, in September, 1938, Pious XI addressed a group of Catholic pilgrims: "Through Christ and in Christ we are of the spiritual lineage of Abraham. Spiritually, we are Semites." These words were spoken two months before the burning of synagogues, destruction of Jewish property, and the arrest of countless Jewish men at the infamous *Kristallnacht*.

In addition, Pious XI warned co-religionists not to be taken in by Nazi racial theories. He spoke out aginst antisemitism, and taught that contempt for Jews was not only a violation of justice and charity, but a sin against faith.

Twenty-five years later, Pope John XXIII agreed and instructed Vatican Council II to make a statement on the Jews, which will repudiate the notion of collective Jewish guilt in the crucificion of Jesus and will instruct Catholics to eliminate false views that in the past have caused Jews to undergo suffering and discrimination. The primary statement was uttered by Cardinal Bea on November 19, 1963, and approved by Pope John XXIII several months before he died. Revised, it is article IV of the Declaration on the Relationship of the Church to Non-Christian Religions (*Nostra Aetate*, Vatican Council II, 1965).

The message and meaning of *Nostra Aetate* came forth in action too. Pope John XXIII's deletion of the phrase "perfidious Jews" from the Good Friday prayer for Jews and his successor, Pope Paul VI's revision "For the Jews" instead of "For the Conversion of the Jews," etc., were steps in the direction of mutual understanding and respect.

Also, on the day *Nostra Aetate* was promulgated, the Congregation of Rites issued a decree banning further veneration of Simon of Trent, a small boy allegedly murdered by Jews in 1475 in order that his Christian blood might be used by Jews in the celebration of Passover. Actually, Simon was killed by non-Jews who blamed Trent's Jewish community for the crime.

Vatican Council II's document on the Jews inspired numerous dioceses and archdioceses in Europe, Latin America, and the United States to issue their own local guidelines to implement article IV and to rid the anti-Jewish bias of *contra Judaeos* found at the crossroads of Christian preaching and teaching.

Among the important authoritative directives endorsed by the Vatican are **Guidelines for Catholic-Jewish Relations**, and **Notes on the Current Way to Present Jews and Judaism**, both published in 1985. They are distributed in the U.S.A. by the United States Catholic Conference, which includes the national Conference of Catholic Bishops. **Notes** and **Guidelines** are an important step toward correcting the "injustices directed against the Jews at any time from any source," and a significant contribution to ongoing Jewish-Christian dialogue.

By encouraging lessons learned from the Shoah and the reality of the State of Israel, the documents correct an ambivalent teaching about the Jews in *Nostra Aetate*, IV: "The Jews remain most dear to God because of their fathers" (suggesting past but not present validity), but "He does not repent of the gifts He makes nor of the calls He issues" (suggesting continual validity).

However, many Jews read these pamphlets with mixed emotions: Respect for the sincere efforts of the **Notes** and **Guidelines** to eliminate misrepresentation of the Jews and "to strive to learn by what essential traits the Jews define themselves," but disappointment with denominationally oriented language, which reveals a flawed or condescending view of contemporary Judaism.

To say, for example, that the establishment of the State of Israel is not "in itself religious" is irritating. To apologize in the **Notes** for the continual use of the term "Old Testament" ("'old' does not mean 'out-of-date' or 'outworn'") and to report the "sad fact" that most Jews did/do not accept for themselves the salvific role of Jesus in history (but proclaim so for Christians, respecting the teaching of classical Christianity, which joins belief and salvation) is disturbing. Also controversial and seen as dangerous by many Jews is the **Guidelines** recognition and tacit support for inter-religious (Jewish-Catholic) marriages.

The Church must not overlook the tensions of Christian-Jewish relations in the past, nor allow misguided judgments of the present to pass by. The Jews, on their part, must understand that the Roman Catholic Church of John Paul II is not the Roman Catholic Church of Pious XII, whose silence and compromise in the early 1940s contributed to Hitler's long night of terror against the Jews.

Yet the move to beatify Edith Stein poses an important challenge to the spirit of ecumenical dialogue: Can the Church and the Jewish people overcome familiar roadblocks of mistrust, indifference and intrageance on the road from Auschwitz to Zion?

III. The Martyrdom of Edith Stein

Edith Stein was born in 1891 to a wealthy Jewish family in Breslau (now a part of Poland and known as Wroclaw). She studied philosphy at the University of Gottingen and earned a doctorate in 1916. She became an atheist, but in 1922, inspired by a biography of St. Teresa of Avila, she was baptized as a Catholic and, eleven years later, entered a Carmelite convent at Cologne. In the same year, she started her autobiography entitled **Life in a Jewish Family**.

In 1938, she wrote to the Pope and urged him to condemn the Nazis for the attacks on Jewish synagogues and Jewish business places in an event known as *Kristallnacht*, "Night of the Broken Glass." Not long afterward, her order sent her to Echt, in the Netherlands, where it was thought she would be safer than in Germany.

In the early morning of May 10, 1940, the Germans marched into Holland, and ushered in the period of occupation. Two years later, the Dutch Catholic bishops protested the Nazi authorites' transporting of Jews to concentration camps in Eastern Europe. In reprisal, the Germans ruled that Jewish converts to Catholicism were to be seized and sent to the camps.

On August 2, 1942, Sister Teresa was arrested at the Carmelite convent at Echt, along with her sister Rosa. A week later, they were both dead, gassed at Auschwitz.

Catholic authorities say that Edith Stein "died as a daughter of Israel, 'for the glorification of the most holy name of God,' and at the same time as Sister Teresa Benedicta of the Cross."[7] There is no doubt that she died as a Christian; but can a "baptized Jew" qualify as a Jew? Eugene J. Fisher, Executive Secretary of the Secretariate for Catholic-Jewish Relations of the National Conference of Catholic Bishops (NCCB), believes so and he points out" that there does exist Orthodox halachic opinion that one who is born Jewish does not cease to be a Jew, albeit an apostate Jew, simply by conversion to another faith, even Christianity."[8]

However, a careful reading of the Halachah in the name of R. Avda bar Zavda (Sanh. 44a) says otherwise. For it is said (Josh 7:11): "Israel has sinned," meaning that even though *he has sinned* (italics added) he is still an Israelite. This applies in the case of all these forced converts who at heart are still loyal to God and Torah acceptance. Forced converts to Christianity during the days of the First Crusade (1096-1105) and during the period of persecutions in Spain qualify. Their historic experience, sooner or later, permitted them, some secretly and some openly, to renounce the vows imposed upon them by persecutions and by the Inquisition. When they returned to Judaism, they are seen as Jews *who have sinned*, past experience and not present reality.

The decision of Edith Stein to leave Judaism cannot be considered as an act of forced abandonment from her ancestral faith. She voluntarily chose "a change of name and street where she lives."[9] Her apostasy is one of essence and not accidental. And the Church does not deny this:

> The entire course of Edith's life is formed by an unremitting search for truth, elucidated by the benediction of the cross. The message was first revealed to her in the person of a fellow-student's widow, who, deeply religious, didn't despair confronted with the loss of her husband, but obtained strength and confidence out of the cross. Later Edith will write conferring to this experience: "that was my first meeting with the cross, with the strengh of God, which is communicated to the ones who carry it ... In this moment, my disbelief was destroyed and Jesus Christ appeared in his glory, Jesus Christ in the secret of the cross".[10]

The responsibility of resolving the age-old question, "Who is a Jew?," lies with Jewish decision and not Christian opinion. The fundamental assertion of Jewish self-definition may be seen in Exod 24:7, where Moses read before the people from the book of the covenant (*berith*) and they responded, "all that the Lord has spoken we shall do and obey (*na'aseh venishma'*)." Moses transmitted 'creeds' reflecting 'revelation' for this is the biblical intent of *berith* (partnership between God and people). The masses experienced revelation as a people, not individually but communally (see also Exod 19,20 and Deut 5). As such, they lived their religious memories as a nation. Further, "We shall do and obey" suggests voluntaryism, signals of nationalism, and not "thou shall do and obey," which implies obligation, characteristic of religion.

The mixture of religion and nationality is particularly noteworthy in Judaism's basic creed of monotheism: "Hear O' Israel (nation), the Lord our God, the Lord is one (religion)" (Deut 6:4). Also, the revelation of the Decalogue is introduced by an historical note: "I am the Lord your God, who brought you out of the Land of Egypt, out of the house of bondage" (Exod 20:2; Deut 5:6). Thus, the Torah's designation of Israel as an *'am/* people suggests *'im/*together, and *'am yisrael* is the people Israel held together by religion *and* nationality.

Irrespective of intra-Jewish interpretation, the Halachah understanding of Jewishness is hereditary or halachic conversion (individuality), historic experience (group memory), and Torah acceptance (divine legislation). If one lives by the latter alone (e.g., an ethical monotheist who follows the covenant of Noah), he/she is not a Jew; but if one is of the former, he/she is considered a Jew, albeit not an ideal halachicly defined Jew.

To identify with the Jewish people (*guf*=body) and not practice the Jewish religion (*neshama*=soul) is not grounds for group or self excommunication. However, to proclaim Jewish ethnicity and to practice voluntarily another religious sancta (e.g., Christianity) is grounds for self and group removal from Jewish identity. Paradoxically, according to Halachah, Edith Stein in her state of disbelief (from the tenets of Judaism)[11] is considered a Jew, but in her decision to convert to Catholicism and later join the Carmelite order at Cologne, she has removed herself from the Jewish fold. She has substituted one bridal garland for another: "Marriage to the Lord under the symbol of the Cross" in place of the thrice-fold marriage espousal said daily in Jewish worship, a symbol of the devotion and affection between God and Israel.[12]

In addition to Halachah, secular sensitivity may question the Jewish status of Edith Stein. Her biographers and defenders claim that she remained loyal to her Jewish roots and publicly proclaimed her Jewish identity, as a form of protest against virulent German antisemitism.[13] In this regard, her case is similiar to Oswald Rufeisin (b. 1920), who became a Christian in 1942 and entered the Carmelite order as Brother Daniel in 1945. His appeal to become a citizen of Israel under the Law of Return, and based on Jewish birth, Zionist activity, and active resistence against the Nazis, was denied on the ordinary secular usage of the term "Jew" as understood in the national-historical consciousness of the Jewish people. The comments of Judge Silberg, speaking for the Court, are instructive:

> I have reached the conclusion that what Brother Daniel
> is asking us (the High Court of Israel) to do is to erase the
> historical and sanctified significance of the term "Jew" and to
> deny all spiritual values for which our people were killed
> during various periods in our long dispersion. For us to
> comply with his request would mean to dim the luster and
> darken the glory of the martyrs who sanctified the Holy Name

(*Kiddush Hashem*) in the Middle Ages to the extent of making them quite unrecognizable; it would make our history lose its unbroken continuity and our people counting its days from emancipation which followed the French Revolution. A sacrifice such as this no one is entitled to ask us, even one so meritorious as the petitioner before this court.[14]

The signal from the highest judicial body in the Jewish State is strikingly decisive: there is no compromising of the Jewish *guf* and *neshama*. This decision affects Brother Daniel, Sister Teresa and any Jew by birth who has become a Christian.

An additional consideration. Quantitatively and qualitatively, the Nazi near-complete destruction of European Jewry represents the worst threat to Judaism's self-definition: A people made in the image of Torah, commanded by God to bring humankind closer to the prophetic ideal of the parenthood of God and the peoplehood of humanity. Many talmudic and modern authorities maintain that a Jew who is murdered because of being a Jew is forgiven by divine compassion of all sins, public and private. The millions of murdered Jewish victims of Hitler's war against the Jews are rewarded on earth by the posthumous citizenship granted to them in the State of Israel (act of Knesset, 1953) and in heaven by the bliss of the world to come. The Six Million, including thousands who are outside the pale of halachic recognition, are revered as the exemplar of the meaning and glory of Kiddush Hashem. It is suggested by Eugene Fisher that Edith Stein was "simply one more Jew to be murdered with bureaucratic efficiency"[15]; her Catholic tradition was not able to save her. Thus, may her sin of apostasy be considered as null and void in light of her victimization and martyrdom?

Perhaps, but unfortunately this does not nullify her act of apostasy, an affront to the *locus classicus* of Kiddush Hashem: "You shall keep my commandments and do them: I am the Lord. You shall not profane my holy name; but I will be hallowed among the children of Israel; I am the Lord who hallow you" (Lev 22: 31,32). Judaism's regard for human life (*Pikkuah Nefesh*) permits under circumstances of pain or death violations of most commandments. Under no circumstances, however, may the three cardinal sins be willingly entertained: Idolatry (apostasy), unchastity (incest, adultery) and murder (Sanh. 74a). The dispensation of sins brought about by acts of Jewish martyrdom embrace "normal" transgressions (Sabbath ordinances, dietary laws, rites of passage, etc.) and do not contain the serious offenses against man and God.

A final point. Some authorities permit forced apostasy in private, i.e., less than ten Jews (male and/or female), in order to save one's life.[16] But Edith Stein's choice of Christianity was not coerced nor did she celebrate her conversion privately. In a prayer, she confesses to her savior, "that it is his cross, which now be imposed on the Jewish people."[17] By the most lenient stretch of Jewish compassion, Edith Stein, an individual, is a martyred Jewish victim; ironically, however, the Church's beatification makes her a blessed symbol of the Cross thereby declaring she *was* (and not is) a Jew. Unlike living "baptized" Jews, who are potential returnees to Judaism, Sister Teresa's faith as a Christian and fate as a martyr are sealed by Auschwitz and the Vatican.

IV. Edith Stein: Christian Martyr

"When the Germans marched into Holland in the early morning of May 10, 1940, they ushered in a new phase in Dutch history in general and in the life of Dutch Jewry in particular." So reads the opening line of Dr. J. Presser's 15-year study on the destruction of Dutch Jewry by the Nazis,[18] from Aryan attestation and isolation to disenfranchisement to deportation, and finally, to extermination. The extent to which the process of Hitlerism succeeded in the Netherlands depended upon Dutch capitulation. Of the 140,000 Dutch Jews, including German Jews who escaped to Holland, 107,000 were deported. Only 5,500 survived and returned, a mere 5%. According to German racial laws, Edith Stein was murdered as a Jew, but it cannot be denied that her arrest and deportation were part of a selection of "Catholic Jews" in the Netherlands in order to punish the Danish bishops for speaking out against the deportation of Jews. The direct cause for the death of Edith Stein, then, was due to an act of Nazi reprisal against the Church; her road to Auschwitz was by way of the cross.

Catholic authorities say that sainthood for Sister Teresa is recommended because of her pious life, her religious writings, her good works and her execution. Her act of Christian martyrdom gives the Church every right to claim her ultimate sacrifice as an act of testimony to the Passion of Jesus, preparing the world for the Kingdom of God. Jewish fears that the veneration of Sister Teresa would promote conversion among Jews or appropriate the Shoah event as a Church tragedy are properly laid to rest in a statement of the Bishops' Committee for Ecumenical and Interreligious Affairs of the National Council of Catholic Bishops:

> Catholic resepct for the integrity of Judaism and for
> the ongoing validity of God's irrevocable covenant with the

Jewish people is solidly founded on our faith in the unshakable faithfulness of God's own word. Therefore, in no way can the beatification of Edith Stein be understood by Catholics as giving impetus to unwarranted proslytizing among the Jewish community. On the contrary, it urges us to ponder the continuing religous significance of Jewish traditions, with which we have so much in common, and to approach Jews not as potential "objects" of conversion but rather as bearers of a unique witness to the Name of the One God of Israel.[19]

"To venerate Edith Stein," says Eugene Fisher, "should help Christians begin to deal more seriously with their own history of erroneous teaching about the Jewish people,"[20] viz., supercessionism and "teaching of contempt," including the charges of deicide and misanthropy.[21] Continuing the Bishops' statement cited above, "in honoring Edith Stein, the Church wishes to honor all the six million Jewish victims of the Shoah ... Catholic veneration will necessarily contribute to a continuing and deepened examination of conscience regarding sins of commission and omission perpetrated by Christians against Jews during the dark years of World War II."

The Church's condemnation of antisemitism from any place, time, source, and person is welcomed; the Church's commitment to correct centuries-old misteaching about the Jews is appreciated. But it is in the reflection on Catholic-Jewish reconciliation vis-a-vis the words of Edith Stein and the Church's understanding of her martyrdom that major obstacles continue to exist:

• She has devoted her life to the honor and glorification of Christ, especially for the preservation and fulfillment of her order, namely the Cologne and Echt Carmelites, and for the sins of the "unbelieving Jewish people."

• In a number of personal prayers, she likened herself to Queen Esther: "I am only a helpless poor little Esther, but the king, I was chosen by, he is infinitely great and merciful."[22] Relief and deliverance for Edith's biblical namesake comes from an unnamed "another place" (Esth 4:14). But Edith has "confidence in the fact that the Lord has taken my life in exchange for all (the Jews)."[23]

• Edith died with the people of her birth and she is reported to have said to her sister, also a convert to Catholicism, "Let us go, we will go for our people."[24]

• In her last will, written some years before her death, she wrote: "With joy I will accept now the death which God already intended for me, being entirely subject to his most holy will."[25]

The words of Edith Stein bear testimony to her Christian advocation: Expiatory sacrificial offering, imitating his "Heilig Blut," for the atonement of the Jewish people. No wonder the Church has seen fit to beatify her as the quintessential Shoah martyr: She is of Jewish birth and loyal to the Jewish people; a confessor of human sins, which, theologically, crucified Jesus; and a participant in the "theology of suffering," who is redeemed by self-sacrifice inherent in Christ-like creeds and deeds.

Consequently, knowingly or unknowingly, Pope John Paul II inserted the controversial dynamics of *Veritas Israel* in his homily during the beatification ceremony on May 1, 1987, when he made reference to the words of Jesus to the Samaritan woman at a place tradition calls Jacob's well:

> Believe me, woman, a time is coming when you will worship the Father neither on this mountain nor in Jerusalem. You Samaritans worship what you do not know; we worship what we understand, because salvation is from the Jews. But the hour is coming, and is now here, when true worshippers will worship the father in spirit and truth; and indeed the father seeks such people to worship him. God is spirit, and those who worship him must worship in spirit and truth.[26]

By representing Edith Stein as a great daughter of the Jewish people who was among the tortured millions, and by insisting upon the word Shoah and not Holocaust as the term of record for the Judeocide, the Church is confirming the inestricable connection between Israel and the Great Catastrophe. However, by beatifying Sister Teresa Benedicta of the Cross, a true worshipper of God — in spirit and in truth (contra Judaism's spiritual *Lebensphilosophie* — this wordly realism and spirtuality), the Church is signaling supercessionist Christology: A Christ-like sacrifice of the salvation of Edith's people, her church, and the entire world.

We would suggest, with all deference, that the Church and the Jewish people can agree that the courage and passion of Edith Stein should help Christians learn the lessons of Shoah but they necessarily differ in their theology of redemption. For the Church, it is the Easter faith, spirit over matter, that enables victory to be proclaimed over Golgotha and Auschwitz. For the Synagogue, it is the covenantal oath at Sinai, uniting spirit and matter and resulting in everyday acts of holiness, that permits Zion to triumph over Auschwitz. Recognition of this difference may lessen the Jewish objection to Pope John Paul II's homily in his advocacy for the canonization of a "Jewish" nun.

The present pope is a confessing pope. In a June 14, 1987 address to the Jewish community in Warsaw, he spoke of the Jewish people as a force of conscience in the world today and of Jewish memory of the Shoah as a "warning, a witness and a silent cry to all humanity."[27]

The Church is a confessing Church: "We Christians approach with immense respect the terrifying experience of the extermination, the Shoah, suffered by Jews during the Second World War, and we seek to grasp its most authentic, specific and universal meaning."[28]

Acknowledgment of antisemitism and the Shoah by the Church is of paramount importance. But equally just and right is the full acceptance by the Church of Jewish peoplehood and statehood. Recognition of Jewish self-definition challenges the Church to be a professing Church.

Confessing and professing are appropriate directives for the Pope and the Church in the aftermath of the beatification of Edith Stein. May the Holy Father and the Holy Church not forget the voice of the Holy People: "Without sensitivity to Judaism, as fully understood and practiced by Jews, Sister Teresa Benedicta of the Cross is only a parochial event."

We maintain that the Church and Synagogue are paths to the reign of God, but not identical to it — a sound position recommended to all who take seriously the doctrine of religious diversity in speaking of Shoah today.

Respect [29] (Jews) and veneration (Church) for the life of Edith Stein is a start; we must now move beyond the icon.

Endnotes

1. Raphael Patai and Jennifer Patai Wing, **The Myth of the Jewish Race** (New York: Charles Scribner's Sons, 1975).
2. Raphael Patai, **The Jewish Mind** (New York: Charles Scribner's Sons, 1977).
3. A summary of the Pittsburgh Platform is found in David Rudavsky, **Modern Jewish Religious Movements** (New York: Behrman House, 1979), pp. 298-301.
4. R. Patai, *op cit.*, p. 24. 5.
5. A dissenting and decisive Catholic view on the Waldheim affairs is suggested by Harry James Cargas, **Reflections of a Post-Auschwitz Christian** (Detroit: Wayne State University Press, 1989), pp. 121-138.
6. The controversy began in 1983, when a group of Carmelite nuns contracted from the city of Oswiecim a 99-year lease of a former Nazi building which was used to store the Zyklon B gas for the gas chambers at Auschwitz-Birkenau. The intent of the nuns was to convert the building into a Catholic Church in order to offer prayers in behalf of Polish people (Catholics and presumably also Jews) who were killed here and for atonement between peoples. But for Jews, Auschwitz is Hell on Earth and no consecration or Catholic good will can change this. "Let this hell speak of the horrors done here where millions of Jews were killed. Let this be a memorial to such Jews and anyone else killed here. Whatever else this place is, Catholic Poland, it is not yours to preempt" (Martin E. Marty, "The Convent at Auschwitz Recalls a Polish Past Most Want to Forget," *LA Times*, September 17, 1989).
   After years of conflict and strife, the nuns vacated the Auschwitz convent on June 30, 1993. But the ten-year controversy over this site has not ended as it was revealed that The Society for the Victims of War (a little-known Polish nationalist group) has begun efforts to turn it into a museum to Polish victims of World War II (not Jewish victims of Nazism). Mother Therese of the Carmelite Convent, without consulting church or local government officials, has given support to this venture (news item, June 29, 1993). As of this writing, the Vatican has not spoken on this matter.
7. **John Paul II, On the Holocaust**, selected and introduced by Eugene J. Fisher (NCCB, Washington, D.C., 1988), p. 8.
8. *Ecumenical Trends*, February 1988, p. 25.
9. Title description of "forced ones" (Marranos) in the Responsa of R. Isaac b. Moses Arama (1420-1494).

10. *NC News Service*, May 4, 1987, p. 23. This is the 3,100 word homily (in German) given by Pope Paul John II at the mass for the beatification of Edith Stein in Cologne, May 1, 1987.
11. Edith Stein was an atheist from age 14 to age 31.
12. And I (God) will betroth thee (Israel) for ever; Yea, I will betroth thee unto me in righteousness, and in judgment, and in loving kindness, and in mercy; I will even betroth thee unto me in faithfulness: And thou shall know the Lord. (Hos 2: 21,22)
13. A selection of works is cited in Rachel Feldhay Brenner, "Edith Stein: The Phenomenological Ethics in Her Religion," a paper presented before the 20th Annual Scholars' Conference on the Holocaust and the Churches, Vanderbilt University, March 5, 1990.
14. **Encyclopaedia Judaica**, vol. 3, p. 209.
15. *Ecumenical Trends*, February 1988, p. 25.
16. See a list of authors of Responsa on the Shoah in Philip Friedman, **Bibliography of Books in Hebrew on the Jewish Catastrophe and Heroism in Europe** (Jerusalem: Yad Vashem=YIVO, 1960), pp. 139ff. Important books available in English include Robert Kirschner, translator and editor, **Rabbinic Responsa of the Holocaust Era** (New York: Schocken Books, 1985); Ephraim Oshry, **Responsa from the Holocaust** (New York: Judaica Press, 1983; an abridged English version of the original five-volume **Sh'eilos U'Teshuvos M'Ma'amakim**); Irving J. Rosenbaum, **The Holocaust and the Halakhah** (New York: Ktav, 1976); and especially, H.J. Zimmels, **The Echo of the Nazi Holocaust in Rabbinic Literature** (printed in the Republic of Ireland, 1975). Major *poskim* (rabbinic decisors) differ as to when martyrdom (Kiddush Hashem) is more praiseworthy (Tos. Av. Zar. 27b) than preserving life (*Pikkuah Nefesh*; "he shall live by them (commandments)," Lev 18: 5). Maimonides ruled that in times of religious persecution of the entire community, one must choose to die for the Sanctification of God's Name and one must not violate any commandment (Maim. Yad, Yesodei ha-Torah, 5:3). The talmudic principle of logic, *Kal-va-Homer* ("Inference from minor to major, or from major to minor") clearly rules against voluntary apostasy in times of persecution and (how much more so) in "normal" times.
17. *NC News Service*, May 4, 1987, p. 23.
18. J. Presser, **Ashes in the Wind : The Destruction of Dutch Jewry** (Detroit: Wayne State University Press, 1968), translated by A. Pomerans.
19. April 24, 1987, Secretariat for Catholic- Jewish Relations, NCBB

on the occasion of the beatification of Edith Stein.

20. *Our Sunday Visitor* (Los Angeles), May 22, 1988, p. 8.

21. See Matt 27:11-26; Mark 14:1,11,43ff.,55,64; 15:11-15; Luke 23:1-25; John 8:42-47; 19:1-16; Acts 2:22-24; 7:51-53; I Thess 2:14-16.

22. *NC News Service*, May 4, 1987, p. 23.

23. *Ibid.*

24. *Ibid.*

25. *Ibid.*, p. 25.

26. John 4:22-24. *Ibid.*, p. 26.

27. **John Paul II, On the Holocaust**, *op. cit.*, p. 8.

28. *Ibid.*, p. 9. From a Letter to Archbishop John L. May, President, National Conference of Catholic Bishops.

29. At the panel discussion on interpreting Edith Stein's martyrdom, the opening session of the 21st Annual Scholars' Conference on the Holocaust and the Churches, we suggested a categorical recognition for Jews who left Judaism but remained loyal to the preservation of the Jewish people *as Jews*. In light of religious and secular Judaism, discussed in the context of this essay, they cannot be called Jews. Philo-Semites is a term appropriate for gentiles by birth who love Jews and Judaism. Perhaps the biblical terms Israelite or Hebrew would do; these titles encompass heritage by birth and include non-Jews in their biblicsal and modern usage. Of course, antisemitism and the impending Shoah reaffirmed Edith Stein's loyalty to the Jewish people; for others who have embraced faith in Christ while remaining a "Jew," the State of Israel, in addition to Shoah, plays a decisive role.

CHAPTER SIX

The 93 Beit Ya'akov Martyrs:
Towards the Making of a Historiosophy

By "historiosophy," I mean "mythicizing history," whose impor-
tance, for example, is demonstrated in biblical and rabbinical literature.
Though the celebrated suicide of the Ninety-Three Maidens, as conveyed
in the letter of Chaya Feldman, may not be an historical event (for most
historians of the Shoah), its importance, however, lies in the paradigmatic
value of its "faith knowledge." The objective of this essay is to explore the
sources of this famous letter (after analyzing the Yiddish-German of the
text), see what the author/redactor has in common with prior Jewish
genres of martydom, and determine what the letter reveals about tradi-
tional Jewish theology. The position taken is that responding to the Shoah
must move beyond historiography to historiosophy if it is to maintain a
commitment to life and memory and not a fixation on death and finality.
Portions of this essay were presented at the 20th Annual Scholars'
Conference, on the campus od Vanderbilt University, and at the 1990
Annual Meeting of the National Association of Professors of Hebrew in
Kansas City. The essay appeared in F.H. Littell, A.L. Berger, and H.G.
Locke (eds.), **What Have We Learned? Telling the Story and Teaching**
the Lessons of the Holocaust *(Lewiston/ Queenston/ Lampeter: The*
Edward Mellen Press, 1994). It also was published in **Shofar** *(Fall 1993).*
This piece was concluded with the death of my father, Morris Benjamin
Garber (25 Sivan 5741/ 7 June 1991, in Jerusalem). I dedicate it in his
memory.

I

On January 5, 1943, Mr. Meir Schenkolewsky of Brooklyn, New

York, handed the Annual Conference of the Jewish Orthodox Rescue Committee an unusual letter, forwarded to him through Zurich, Switzerland. The letter pertained to the martyrdom of 92 pupils and their teacher of a Beit Ya'akov school in Cracow, Poland, who chose mass suicide by poison rather than submission to forced prostitution demanded by German soldiers. The epistle, dated August 11, 1942, was composed by the teacher, Chaya Feldman, age 22. Deemed authentic by officials of the American Beit Ya'akov Committee in an emergency meeting held in their New York office, 131 West Eighty-Sixth Street, the letter was made public by Rabbi Leo Jung of the Jewish Center of New York City on January 7, 1942. The next day, the *New York Times* carried the story, in a singular column on page 8, and printed selections of the letter as translated by Rabbi Jung:

Dear Friend[1] in New York:

I do not know whether this letter will reach you. Do you still remember who I am? We met in the same house of (the late) Mrs. (Sarah) Schenirer (founder of the Beth Jacob movement) and afterward again in Marienbad.[2] When this letter will come into your hands, I shall not live anymore. With us are ninety-two Beth Jacob girls. Within a few hours everything will be over. Give our regards to Mr. (Jacob) Rosenheim (head of the world Beth Jacob movement) and our friend (Harry A.) Goodman (an English benefactor of the Beth Jacob movement), both in England. We all met in Warsaw at our friend's Y ..... [3] and Y .... 's son was also there.

We had four rooms. On July twenty-seventh we were taken out and thrown into a dark room, having only water. We studied the sacred works and got courage. In age we are from fourteen to twenty-two; the younger ones are afraid. I try to recall Mother Sarah's (Mrs. Schenirer's) teaching of the Torah.[4] It is good to live for God, but it is also good to die for Him.[5]

Yesterday and the day before we were given hot baths and we were told that German soldiers would come tonight to visit us. We yesterday swore to ourselves that we shall die together. Yesterday one sent us to a big house with bright rooms and nice beds. The Germans do not know that our last bath is our purification before death. Today, everything was taken from us, and we were each given one nightgown. All of us have poison. When the soldiers will come we shall drink it. Today we are together and all day we are saying our last confession. We have no fear.

We thank you, good friend, for everything. We have one request: Say Kaddish (the Hebrew prayer for the dead) for us, your ninety-three children. Soon we shall be with Mother Sarah.

Regards from .... [6] of Krakow

The terrifying matter of the Ninety-Three Maidens who said their last prayer (the *vidui*), took poison and died, "in order to sanctify the Name of God by their death as well as by their lives," elicited a plethora of cross denominational support. Rabbi Leo Jung saw the martyrdom of the Beit Ya'akov maidens in the noblest pattern of Kiddush Hashem. "It is unmatched in simplicity and sublimity, a living testimonial of Beth Jacob's service to Israel, indeed to all believers in the universal Father of man."[7]

Invited to comment on the letter of the Ninety-Three Maidens by the Editors of the *Reconstructionist*, Dr. Dora Edinger reflected, "I have met people that could not believe this sacrifice to have been offered in the way it has been reported. Since I have been in the Beth Jacob seminary, I am perfectly convinced that these Jewish girls proved in the last test, that they were true to the spirit of their education."[8] The "spirit" was forged against Orthodox educators, who opposed the teaching of Torah to girls, in the hundreds of Beth Jacob schools throughout Poland between the two great wars. It was inspired by the spell of Sarah Schenirer's personality: Love, respect, childlike devotion to God, Torah, Mitzvot, and *Ahavat Yisrael*, dedication and selfless sacrifice.

In a feature article, "in the Valley of Death," published in the *New York Times Magazine*,7 February 1943, Scholem Asch, the noted Yiddish novelist, analyzed the deeper meanings of the Ninety-Three Maidens in conjunction with the announced Nazi murders of the Jewish population in Poland. He concluded that Hitler would never have selected the extermination of the Jews if the road had not been prepared for him by all kinds and degrees of antisemites.

"It is a fact that all who have prepared the ground of hatred toward the Jews and other races are exactly as responsible for the bestial slaughter of the Jews in Poland, and others, as Hitler and his clique. Even if today they are frightened by the results of their hatred, they are as guilty as the Nazis. Hitler only gathers the fruit of their well-planted seed."[9]

Finally, the last will and testimony of the Ninety-Three Maidens have been immortalized by the Hebrew poet and professor of Hebrew literature at the Jewish Theological Seminary of America, Lithuanian-born Hillel Bavli (1892-1961):

The Letter of the Ninety-Three Maidens"[10]

> We have cleansed our bodies and purified our souls
> And now we are at peace.
> Death holds no terror; we go to meet it.
> We have served our God while alive;
> We know how to hallow Him in death.
> A deep covenant binds all ninety-three of us;
> Together we studied God's Torah; together we shall die.
> We have chanted Psalms, and are comforted.
> We have confessed our sins, and are strengthened.
> We are now prepared to take our leave.

Let the unclean come to afflict us; we fear them not.
We shall drink the poison and the, innocent and pure,
as befits the daughters of Jacob.
To our mother Sarah we pray: "Here we are!
We have met the test of Isaac's Binding[11]
Pray with us for the people Israel."
Compassionate Father!
Have mercy for Your people, who love you.
For there is no more mercy in man.[12]
Reveal Your lovingkindness.
Save your afflicted people.
Cleanse and preserve your world.
The hour of Ne'ilah approaches, Quiet grows our hearts.
One request we make of our brethren, wherever they may be.
Say Kaddish for us, for all ninety-three, say Kaddish.

Bavli's stark crossing of Mama Sarah (Schenirer) and Mother Sarah, the sacrifice of the Ninety-Three and the *Akedah*, and the implied *vidui* on approaching death[13] and the *Ne'ilah* service of Yom Kippur combine to make his poem a liturgical favorite for Conservative Jews, and others, during the solemn Yom Kippur *Eleh Ezkerah* service.

II

Few doubt the powerful cadences of Bavli's poem, read in Shoah memorial services, and the powerful values of observant Jews who died 'al Kiddush Hashem as suggested by the Letter of the Ninety-Three, but is the event a true (meaning, historical) account of the last daughters of Jacob, who studied in the Jewish quarters of Cracow, the Beit Ya'akov seminary on Stanislawa 10? The silence of historians on the Shoah, in contrast to pietists, to assess this letter suggests that the document is not to be taken seriously. One has spoken, however, the late Lucy S. Dawidowicz, author of **The War Against the Jews 1933-1945** (1975). **The Holocaust Reader** (1976), and **The Holocaust and the Historians** (1981), among other works, has dismissed it as a pious fraud.

A less pernicious form of historical falsification is the myth pretending to documentary veracity. In Holocaust history myths are especially abundant about the behavior of pious Jews in circumstances of extreme crisis; this is in fact a genere with many precedents in Jewish history. The most widespread such story is probably that of the ninety-three (more or less) devout girls of a Beth Jacob school in the Cracow ghetto who chose mass suicide over the degradation of a German brothel. It is a fanciful and moving tale of sacrificial piety, a lesson in religious morality, fashioned by people who knew nothing of the

Nuremberg Laws which made sexual relations between Germans and Jews illegal, criminal, and subject to severe punishment.[14]

The Nuremberg Laws referred to by historian Dawidowicz were promulgated on September 15, 1935. Paragraphs 1-3 speak against marriages between Jews and state members of German or cognate blood; extra-marital relations between Jews and state members of German or cognate blood are prohibited; and Jews must not engage female domestic help in their households among state members of German or cognate blood, who are under forty-five years old.[15]

Despite the Nazi fury against the Jews, the racist principles of the Nuremberg Laws were not always strictly applied by the Germans to the Jews of Poland. Shoah responsa literature deal with women prostituted by the Germans, and some were tatooed by the words, "prostitute for Hitler's soldiers."[16] Affidavits mentioned in **The Black Book of Polish Jewry**[17] convey, not infrequently, the humiliation of Jewish women: Random roundup (forced labor, rape), and forced entry into their homes where they were raped, 15-16 year olds among them, before parents and relatives. Regarding brothels, several eyewitness accounts will suffice. In January/February 1940, a session of the Health Department of the Warsaw municipality agreed to open a brothel in Warsaw for the German military forces: 50 Jewish girls were figured among the prostitutes.[18]

In an affidavit signed in New York City on January 14, 1940, Dr. Henry Szoszkies, a former member of the Executive of the Warsaw Jewish Community Council, declared, "I hereby affirm that to my knowledge proposals were made by Nazi officials to the Jewish Community Council to organize houses of prostitution in Nazi-occupied towns, and that Jewish girls be provided for use of the army."[19] He went on to describe a meeting at the central office of the Gestapo at 23 Szucha Street, room 37, on Saturday, November 4, 1939, which decreed "the need of two brothels; one for the officers and a separate one for the privates,"[20] to be supplied by the Jewish community. To Szoszkies' anguish cry that "nobody in our community will accept it — even if death is the penalty for all of us," Unit Leader Wende, speaking for the German Gestapo, replied: "Mr. Szoszkies, you take the matter much too tragically. After all you are a man and you can understand us; we need women and we believe that we are proposing a plan for the Jewish community from which it can profit. *Don't let race laws bother you* (italics added). War is war, and in such a situation all theories die out."[21] So also, *lehavdil*, Dawidowicz's objection to the Letter of the Ninety-Three Maidens based on prohibition of race mingling.

The events described in the letter appear to telescope incidents from July 27-August 11, 1942. But questions abound regarding content and several names. How did the maidens under the scrutiny of their German guards manage to find time for group study and therapy, communal prayers, and to provide for themselves poison? Who are the Ninety-Three Maidens and why has no family member stepped forward to claim knowledge of their being? There is no known burial spot or mass grave for the victims nor any supportive evidence, outside of Agudah Israel lore, that describes the terrifying ordeal.[22] Though the names Marienbad, Rosenehim, Goodman, and, of course, Sarah Schenirer, can be identified, the names "Sholemman" and "Sholemszon" appear contrived. Chaya Feldman from Cracow is known only from this document; there appears to be no collateral evidence of her person.

Among the living, Mr. Friedenzon from New York, Editor of *Dos Yiddishe Vort* (Yiddish), questioned the historicity of the account.[23] Rabbi Moshe Klotne, archivist of Agudah Israel Archives in New York, expressed reservations about its facticity but he strongly asserted that the girls' martyrdom has not become the central piece in Agudah teaching about Kiddush Hashem from the Shoah.[24] Rabbi Dr. Yitzchak Lewin of New York (former chairman of the American delegation to the World Agudah and professor emeritus at Yeshiva University in New York) denied any collaboration with the letter outside of an occasional public reading.[25] But his verbal testimony contradicted an article in *The Jewish Observer* (November-December 1974), which reported that Rabbi Lewin "is in possession of the (following) letter (i.e., of the Ninety-Three Maidens),"[26] and Mr. Schenkolewsky's retort that Lewin was intimately connected with the epistle from the start.[27] Interestingly, Lewin in his seven-volume **Eleh Ezkerah**, a record of righteous acts, individuals, and martyrdom during the Shoah, made no reference to the Ninety-Three.[28] Finally, Meir Schenkolewsky of Williamsburg (Brooklyn, New York) insisted that the letter is authentic and cited the Jung press release and the Asch piece as early supportive evidence. He observed, since the communication had been used only as a warning signal for the impending Judeocide and (later) conscious raising, and never for fund raising, then this, in his opinion, is (further) proof of the intent and sincerity of the document.

III.

Some impressions concerning the syntax of the letter by Chaya Feidman are in order.

The letter reflects the Judeo-German favored by Jews in Cracow, and elsewhere in Poland, at the time of the German occupation. Written basically in Latin 'antiqua,' it contains strong influences from German so-called 'gothic,' most strikingly in d,t,k,z,R,J,W,S and many more. This by itself is not surprising because in Germany, Austria and Switzerland, the 'gothic' gave way to 'antigua' in the schools in the early 1930s.

Complicated features of New High German syntax are featured. For example, mastery of "*kennenlernen*"(to meet, get to know), where "kennen," a verb, serves as a separable prefix to another verb, "lernen"(to learn), and uses it in the present perfect tense with the right word order. More complicated and properly used is "Den 27 Juli sind wir geholt worden..." First, it requires a good knowledge of German to write "den 27 Juli" instead of "der 27 Juli," using the accusative "den" (which is correct) to the more tempting "der." And then, this phrase is in the passive voice, requiring "sein" (to be) as the auxiliary instead of "haben" (to have). Also, the use of "worden," instead of the more logical "geworden," a word that has in this mutilated form no meaning except in the present perfect and past perfect tenses of the passive voice.

Knowledge of German syntax is indicated in the proper use of adjective endings which requires a knowledge of noun genders and cases. Examples (including so-called "der"-words and "ein"-words): dies*er* Brief/ das Land/der Brief; *aus dem* Rosch David (knowledge that 'aus' must be followed by the dative case) / die Jungen/;Deutsche Soldat*en* / in ein gros*zes* Haus (accusative neuter after the preposition "in," if the action implies change of location or condition) / *mit* haell*em* Zimer*n* and schoen*en* Bet*en* (haell*em* is dative singular and case required is dative plural, but the writer knew that *mit* requires the dative case; schoen*en* is correct dative plural) / *ein* Hemt.

Another refined use of syntax: "Wen Soldaten Kemen werden wir alle drincken "("When soldiers come, we will all drink"). It requires a good knowledge of German to know that if the subordinate clause (introduced by "wen") precedes the main clause, the verb of the main clause ("werden") precedes the subject: "When the soldiers come will we all drink." Also, the final greeting requires a knowledge of how to use the impersonal *es* in German, here: "It greets you," which is very idiomatic and very correct. It is a less formal substitute for the stiff: "Be greeted." And a bit less informal and personal than, "Ich grusse Sie."

The more or less good German syntax is punctuated by Cracow Yiddish: To write almost consistently *sz* for any *s* sound (s, ss, sz); to write final *t* instead of *d*; to write *ai* instead of *ei*; to replace umlaut with correct umlaut substitute *e* (ue/ae/oe); to write "nischt" and "gelaernt" instead of "nicht" and "gelernt"; and to consistently ignore double consonants that are so prevalent in German. Also, distinctive Yiddish words are utilized: *mairoh, taitsch, hachem, Rosch (posuk) Davit, tevele, Kadisch, jom, vidujoh (vidui), and schwio (shevuah).* Finally, the handwriting is from one older than age 22, who retained now and then an amazing elegance in a word here and there (e.g., the word "Marienbad," beginning, line 5; see Appendix A).

In summation, the Letter of the Ninety-Three Maidens does not meet the rigorous standard of a factual historical document. One can not say that it is *Historie*: Controlled objective facts, in keeping with the closed cause-effect continuum, and characteristic of a modern scientific understanding of history. But the letter can be seen as a true reflection of the nature and sentiments taught at the Beit Ya'akov seminary in Cracow, including the pious obligation of Kiddush Hashem. We suggest that the document be considered as *Geschichte*, above the historical but attached to it and in no way determined by it. Personal meaningful memory, whose events impinge on man's life in keeping with the nature of Shoah-related events. It is faith-history, existential and subjective. It represents paradigmatic and not pragmatic concern; it is historiosphy (a philosophy of history) and not historiograpy.

IV

The Ninety-Three Maidens are martyrs within a subliminal Kiddush Hashem universe, but they are not facts on the ground. The significance of their document does not depend exclusively upon historical information about them. What is clear is the assertion that thousands of European Beit Ya'akov girls were taught and lived by the strict obedient laws of traditional Judaism and a number of them, it can be assumed, would have acted in the way and fashion of the Ninety-Three Maidens.

There is continuity between Beit Ya'akov "Torah Judaism" and the Ninety-Three mentioned in the epistle and in contemporary Jewish liturgy and preaching. However, to write an "historical" account of their alleged suicide, separate from the faith-paradigm a post-Shoah age has placed in it, is not only impossible, but also illegitimate and useless.

The "historical Ninety-Three" is not a record of facts. The writer of the document presupposes that the maidens lived and died, since he sees in them an expression of genuine historical occurrence, e.g., the destruction of Cracow Orthodoxy. They are the symbolic flame of Sarah Schnenirer's Torah Judaism in the struggle for human dignity and Jewish piety; and the letter's importance is in its telling message of suicide, expressed in the categorical imperative of Kiddush Hashem.

The Written Torah contains no specific injunction against suicide. On the verse, "And surely your blood of your lives will I require it" (Gen 9:5a) — a thought contained in an expanded verse(s) on the prohibition of homicide—the Rabbis taught that suicide was wrong and punishable by divine decree, burial outside the sacred precincts of the cemetery, and suspension of mourning laws and customs. This stern decree, to discourage Jews who might surrender their lives in violation of Jewish law, caused additional grief and embarrassment for the family of the deceased. To mitigate this problem, the Sages ruled that suicide must be voluntary and premeditated, *meabbed azmo lada'at* ("one who destroys himself knowingly"). The rabbinic presumption is that a person who kills himself — axiomatic in cases of child suicide -does so without the necessary premeditation. The *locus classicus* is the suicide of King Saul, who was in great mental distress "... 'lest these uncircumcised (Philistines) come and thrust me through, and make a mock of me...' Therefore King Saul took his sword, and fell upon it."[29] His death, and the reasons for it, are used by many rabbis as a precedent for not stigmatizing a person who took his own life, if it was shown that he anguished under stress and despair (*onus k'shaul*).[30]

In normal times, acts of suicide are deemed blameworthy. In distressful times, such actions are considered praiseworthy, constituting a Kiddush Hashem, a sanctification of God's Name. In the turbulent period, following the ill-fated Bar-Kochba Rebellion (133-135 C.E.), the Sages sanctioned that a person must kill oneself or let oneself be killed if one is asked to violate cardinal sins against God and man: Idolatry (apostasy), unchastity (incest, adultery), and murder (Sanh 74a). Lore and law record countless instances of justifiable suicide, in the noblest tradition of the Sanctification of the Name, from the Maccabean revolt,[31] to the Roman occupation of Eretz Israel,[32] throughout the Middle Ages, during the Russian pogroms, and in the ghettos and murder camps of Nazi Europe.[33]

In one arresting paragraph in Rabbi H.J. Zimmels important work, **The Echo of the Nazi Holocaust in Rabbinic Literature**, he writes:

> A different outlook on suicide in general can be found in the era of the Nazi Holocaust. Humiliation, fear of torture and starvation produced two diametrically opposed feelings among the Jews living under the Nazi heel. These feelings had great consequences in their attitude to life.
>
> One was pessimism, resignation, despair and abandonment of any hope for the future, leading to suicide. The other was optimism, a strong will to survive and to bear patiently all sufferings and hope for a change for the better. The former view was shared mainly by the Jews of Germany and Austria, while the latter attitude can be found among Jews of Poland and other eastern territories.[34]

The divergence in attitudes may be explained thusly: Whereas the denationalized Jews of Berlin rejected the pillar of Orthodoxy, the Jews of

Kovno, Cracow, and other centers of commitment to traditional Judaism, chose the guidelines which instructed life under the most horrific circumstances, since their rabbis taught them that an action of suicide "is a hillul ha-Shem (profonation of the Name) because it shows that the Jews do not trust in God to save them..."[35]

Contra responsa from the Shoah and the ruling of m. Terumot 8.12, "If Gentiles said to many women, 'Give us one from among you that we may defile her, and if not we will defile you all,' let them defile them all, but let them not betray to them one soul from Israel,"[36] the Ninety-Three Maidens chose suicide rather than submit to a forced act of prostitution. On strict halachic terms, irrespective of historical validity, choosing death, in this case over prostitution, though emotionaly commendable, is an *'averah* (transgression) against the will of Heaven, which proclaims "Choose Life."[37]

In this regard, the Halachah is consistent with the view of post-70 C.E. Tannaim, who consciously avoided any written reference to the contemporary Masada suicide. Despite Josephus Flavius' portrayal of Masada as the final act of the Great Revolt against Rome in terms of horror and annihilation on the one hand and courage and heroism on the other,[38] these Rabbis of Yavneh and Usha saw in everyday acts of holiness expressed in the formula "Choose Life" to be more significant than catastrophic events, however heroic, as the lasting way for Jewry.

This may well explain why the Orthodox community which spun the tale of the Ninety-Three does not utilize it as a paragon of Jewish living.

V

Above we expressed that the value of the Ninety-Three lies not in historical and halachic evidence but in historiosophy, a kind of attitude which one internally makes in response to external facts, and which is enhanced in categories of the will, of action, and of creative imagination.

The nature of historiosophy, or faith-knowledge, makes its "factual distortion" irrelevant, since its message is not to assent to doctrine or mastery of historical information. Historiosophy is not validated by historical research; thus, the importance of the Ninety-Three is a contemporary existential encounter in which the listener, confronted by their suicide as a claim on life in a proclaimed death, decides to acknowledge (or not acknowledge) the Sanctification of the Name. This response of faith is itself a part of *Heilgeschichte* (salvation history), just as the proclamation of it is part of Kiddush Hashem. To seek historical validation behind the Ninety-Three is to deny its power in realized eschatology, which in turn denies the strong appeal of Kiddush Hashem itself.

The Ninety-Three is mythicizing history, i.e., it reflects the way tradition portrays heroism and martyrdom. On the one hand, ancient archetypes—for example, David's lament over Saul and Jonathan:

> Thy beauty, O'Israel, upon thy high places is slain!
> How are the mighty fallen!
> Tell it not in Gath,
> Publish it not in the streets of Ashkelon;
> Lest the daughters of the Philistines rejoice,
> Lest the daughters of the uncircumcised triumph.
>
> (2 Sam 1:19-20)

—reinforce and echo the story of the death of the Ninety-Three Maidens, whose suicide avoided the mockery of the German Philistines. Also, Jephthah's daughter, who dies childless, and the Ninety-Three Maidens share a similar fate of grief and reproach: Neither brought new life into being and nobody knows their grave.[39] On the other hand, the story of Ninety-Three adds to historiosphy by helping to shape the response of the Jew to the anguish of the European Jews. Take "Rachel weeping for her children," for example:

> Thus saith the Lord:
> A voice is heard in Ramah,
> Lamentation, and bitter weeping,
> Rachel weeping for her children:
> She refuseth to be comforted for Her children,
> Because they are not.
> Thus saith the Lord:
> Refrain thy voice from weeping,
> And thy eyes from tears;
> For thy work shall be rewarded,
> Saith the Lord;
> And they shall come back from the land of the enemy.
>
> (Jer 31:16-17)[40]

Are not the Ninety-Three Maidens, portrayed as pure in body and holy in soul, true daughters of Rachel our Mother? *Yehareg v'lo ya'avor*,[41] they are "killed and do not transgress" merits their plea on behalf of the murdered before the throne of God, who hears their just cry and declares: "Refrain from weeping ... for thy work shall be rewarded" (Jer 31, above). Alas, the heavenly proclamation descends as an imposing silence on earth.

Paradoxically, this abdication of traditional theology, that is, compensatory reward for sincere trial and tribulation, permits a more radical yearning, couched in a sacred archetype adapted to contemporary thoughts and feelings, to emerge, wherein one may find a sustaining challenge to the silence of God and the voice of man.

Gittin 57b reports the mass suicide by drowning of young boys and girls who had been taken captive and destined for a shameful life in Rome. The young children were convinced that suicide would not impede their voyage to the World-to-Come, when the oldest of them quoted Ps 68:23: "The Lord said: I will bring back from Bashan, [42] I will bring them back from the depths of the sea," and explained, *mibashan* (from Bashan) means *mibein shinei aryeh* (= from the teeth of the Lion/Rome), and "I will bring them back from the depths of the sea" suggest that "they who drowned in the sea" will share in the World- to-Come.[43] Lamenting the drowning suicide of the 400 children, an editorial note applies to them the verse from Ps 44:23: "It is for your sake that we are slain all day long, that we are regarded as sheep to be slaughtered."

The Letter of the Ninety-Three Maidens, knowingly or unknowingly, is anchored to this talmudic story. Both episodes speak of children, whose suicide is of the highest *madreiga* (level, standard) — no killing of reluctant victims nor is blood spilled. Each act of Kiddush Hashem is encouraged by the oldest child, who assures his/her eager and innocent followers that heavenly approval and reward await them. Alliteration of the word *bashan* connotes *boshna/bosnet* (shame, ill repute). Further, the prooftext from Ps 68:24 talks of righteous vengeance against the enemies of God (i.e., Rome, Nazis), "the dogs shall lick the blood of their slain."

However, there is a difference: God redeems from Bashan, but the maidens, by their suicide, acted in God's stead and redeemed from *boshet* (act of ill repute). May a passive God not be accountable? Are the innocent Ninty-Three Maidens — and by extension, all Shoah-Jews who have followed the Torah path — suffering and "killed all day long" for His sake? Unacceptable is the apologia, divine punishment for disloyalty, for they are virtuous, and their hard faith urgently requests divine intervention:

Awake, why sleepest Thou, O'Lord
Arouse Thyself, cast not off for ever
Wherefore hidest Thou Thy face,
 and forgettest our affliction and oppression?
 For our soul is bowed down to the dust;
Our belly cleaveth unto the earth
Arise for our help
And redeem us for Thy mercy's sake.
(Ps 44:24-27)

"The Keeper of Israel that neither slumbers or sleeps" (Ps 121:4) is implored to save Israel, and by so doing, "give glory unto Thy name" (Ps

115:1). He is inseparably linked with the destiny of Israel; and in the face of unremitting tragedy, when many nameless sanctify His name, He is besieged to manifest His name — holiness, righteousness, mercy — by demonstrating His saving power in behalf of Israel before all nations. What concerns the Psalmist is God's seeming indifference to His people's persecution, thereby leading to an uncertainty about a moral rule in the universe ("redeem us for Thy mercy's sake"). But the strength of man, implicit in the righteous deeds of the Ninety-Three Maidens, enables the opportunity for the saving power of God to be redeemed.

Historiosophically, this may explain the letter's crescendo, "Say the Kaddish for us." On the one hand, continue the work of Torah, which the maidens and a slaughtered Yeshiva world can never again do, thereby perpetuating their memory by contributing to *tikkun 'olam* (restoring the world) and the continuity of the Jewish people. But on the other hand, continuously praising God in the name of the innocent murdered victims, obligates Him for an eternity to remember the evil done;[44] reminds Him that He alone could have saved His faithful people from the slaughter which befell them; and challenges Him to permit never again the mockery of the Nazis and Nazi-like behavior.

A final observation. The Nazi terror campaign against European Jewry began in earnest in the summer of 1941, first in open shooting fields in areas within the Soviet Union and later in murder camps in Auschwitz and Chelmno. Verification of this systematic mass murder became known to the West, in June 1942, when the Jewish Bund in the Warsaw Ghetto reported up to 700,000 Polish Jews had been murdered. Governments-in-exile, press and radio responded quickly to these atrocities, and the American Jewish Congress organized a mass protest meeting in Madison Square Garden on July 22, 1942. In early August 1942, Gerhart Reigner, the World Jewish Congress representative in Switzerland, alerted the United States Consulate in Geneva and the British Foreign Office that he received an alarming report that Hitler's high command had discussed with favor a plan for the annihiliaton of 3.5 to 4 million Jews in countries occupied or controlled by Germany. Reigner's cable was considered too fantastic to be believed in seriously, and no direct action was taken by the allies.

Against the background of these terrible days in the summer of 1942, the Letter of the Ninety-Three Maidens was composed. May the letter not be seen as a protest of the Jewish spirit against a world that offered no hope for the Jews? Further, if the letter is a concoction, one wonders why the "trei wochen" leading to Tisha B'Av (9th of Av) were not intentionally chosen as the background for the maidens' ordeal. As it stands, the girls' wrenching decision occurred between 27 July and 11 August /13 Av- 28

Av, the start of the period of consolation; its sublime message may be interpreted as an encouragement to maintain hope in the face of Nazi bestiality.

VI

We have tried in this chapter to describe the dynamics of the Letter of the Ninety-Three Maidens in categories of historiography and historiosphy. The position of either historiography or historiosophy provides an agenda which exuberates an aura of certainty and absolutism. Historiosophy alone permits no final questions and historiography alone entertains no final answers. Historiography and historiosophy, in contrast, ask questions and attempt answers but leave many uncertainties unresolved. Yet uncertainty is truth in the making and the inevitable price of academic freedom. Since the Letter of the Ninety-Three Maidens is elusive and defies pigeonhole analysis, it is fitting to conclude by suggesting lessons learned from its spirit of *yir'at shamayim, chutzpah, and ahavat yisrael* — fear of Heaven, courage bordering on the reckless, and love of the Jewish people.

Yir'at shamayim

Do we state that there is no God and the Ninety-Three are witness to nothing?

Do we declare that the lesson is the question, if God lives and He is not indifferent, should He not go on living, He who has permitted the death of the Ninety-Three Maidens, symbol of the murdered righteous?

Do we follow Richard Rubenstein and let go of traditional Judaism's doctrine of God for a new symbol of God's reality conclusive with the slaughter of innocents?

Do we suggest Emil Fackenheim's 614th Commandment-no posthumous victory for Hitler- *keneged* ("equal to," but for many, "against") the 613 Commandments as the *raison d'etre* for Jewish living and existence?

Do we maintain Irving "Yitz" Greenberg's Voluntary Covenant and not tradition's Obligatory Covenant as a response to the shattered trust between God and Israel?

Do we follow Elie Wiesel's witness-story, promoting Jewish survival as the unshakable dogma after Auschwitz?[45]

Or is the response the purity of Orthodox Jewish faith: There are many thoughts in the heart of man, but only the counsel of the Lord prevails. Whatever the Merciful does, He does it for our good. May His great Name be blessed for His manifold blessings.

Chutzpah

The Beit Ya'akov movement is forged in the personality of its matriarch, Sarah Schenirer (1883-1935). In her own words, she entrusted her young charges, everyday after morning prayers, with these words of Torah *musar* (ethical instruction): "And now, O'Israel, what does the Lord, your God, ask of you, except to serve the Lord, your God, to walk in all his ways, to love Him and to serve the Lord, your God, with all your heart and soul."[46]

Sarah Schenirer knew that her seminary in Cracow could instruct to teach and to learn *yiddishkeit* and to establish a Jewish home in Israel, but she wondered if it could train Jewish souls. The severest test of soul-making, that of Kiddush Hashem, was not sought but came to the Ninety-Three Maidens, who did not avoid it. They thought of it as the holiest of God's commandments and met its challenge with reverence, love and service. From the circumstances of their suicide, we learn new words about martyrdom: When one is in danger of sin (the imposed rape), when one is in danger of weakening, then one has a right to destroy oneself. Death by one's own hand for the glory of Torah is considered by the Master of the Universe as a sanctification of His Name.

The enormity of the cruelty that the Nazis perpetrated upon the Jews of Cracow and Warsaw is arrested by the paradigm of the Daughters of Jacob; they fulfilled the supreme mitzvah of Kiddush Hashem, with love and without regret, in order that there shall be no blemish upon their souls when they come before the seat of the Holy to plead for Israel's complete redemption. The martyred children have met the "decree from Heaven," and this permits them to say before the Holy One, Blessed be He: In Your endless wisdom, You have decreed that our generation should experience the most terrible cruelties to sanctify Your Name. We have met your request and have bettered it;[47] now have mercy on the remnant of Israel, Guardian of Israel.

Ahavat Yisrael

In his preface to the volume, **Secretaries of Death**,[48] Harry James Cargas writes, "If our generation is to have meaning, it will be by the way of response to the Holocaust. If we ignore that mystery, we imperil our souls and the souls of our grandchildren yet unborn. That weight lies heavily upon us."

We who read and hear the Letter of the Ninety-Three Maidens are now accountable. We mock the memory of those who fought Hitler with weapons of Torah and were murdered, whose last plea was, "please say Kaddish for us," if we do not respond. But what is a proper response to their death?

Do we respond with clichéd sentimentality, or deafening silence? Do we etch their memories in stones and in monuments that mesmerize us into no actions? Do we let grass grow, birds sing, and children play on land where night and fog once prevailed? Do we encourage pilgrimages to crematoria, where the way-to-heaven was by smoke and ashes? Do we remember and not act?

For the writer of the Letter of the Ninety-Three Maidens, the response must be deed over creed but not in the expected judicial sense, e.g., let justice not be delayed, for it will be denied, or the metaphyiscal-theological sense, viz., confront Auschwitz and root out its causes from the world of God and man. Rather, to honor the memory of the saintly martyrs, is to never forget, and thereby to act Jewishly. The writer-mourner has been touched by the anti-life of the Nazi period and his/her letter reflects this sense of tragic loss and incompleteness. Paradoxically, in the face of violent interruption of self, community, and God relationship, the letter stresses the importance of life. Touched by the story of the suicide, the living is sensitized to the value and quality of religious life.[49] The salient message: Do not focus on tragic death (alone), but continue to live, exuberating dignity, morality, responsibility, and hope.[50]

The death-bed message of Sarah Schenirer, spoken in Cracow in 1935, conveys this thought:[51]

> My dear girls, you are going out into the great world. Your task is to plant the holy seed in the souls of pure children. In a sense, the destiny of Israel of old is in your hands.
>
> Be strong and of good courage. Don't tire. Don't slacken your efforts. You have heard of a Hasid who came to his rabbi and said joyfully, "Rabbi, I have finished the whole Talmud." "What has the Talmud taught you?," asked the rabbi. "Your learning is fine, but your practical task is the main thing."[52]

Let me complete these words with verses you all know so well.
Serve the Lord with joy.
I keep the Lord before me continuously.
The beginning of wisdom is the fear of the Lord.

Teach us to number our days
The Lord's Torah is perfect, it restoreth the soul. May the Lord guard your going out and your coming in now and forever more.
May He listen to our prayers and send us the true redeemer and true redemption.

The continuation of the Beit Ya'akov movement is Sara Schenirer's Kaddish; but her comforting words to live Jewishly (religiously) and not desparingly may well be taken as the proper Kaddish by the living for the brutally murdered Jewish nation. It is the charge of *ahavat yisrael*, this Letter of the Ninety-Three Maidens, which transcends time and clime, and confronts the generations after Auschwitz with the "living" message of the dead. Their Kaddish becomes an act of doing not just an exercise in remembering.[53]

Endnotes

1. Meir Schenkolewsky of Brooklyn, New York (Williamsburg section).

2. The Third Great Assembly of Agudah Israel was held in Marienbad (West Bohemia, Czechoslovakia). The first and second Great Assemblies were held in Vienna in 1923 and 1929 respectfully.

3. Scholemman and Scholemson.

4. Posuk David, i.e., Psalms (*tehilim*).

5. The line reads in the Agudah Israel of America archives: "I learn together Mamma Sarah's *taitsch* (torah-teaching) to live well on a higher (*madreigo*, spiritual level) but also to die well."

6. Chaya Feldman from Cracow.

7. Leo Jung, **The Path of a Pioneer** (London: Soncino Press, 1980), p. 148.

8. The *Reconstructionist*, ix.2, March 5, 1943, pp. 23-24.

9. Scholem Asch, "In the Valley of Death," The *New York Times Magazine*, 7 February 1943, p. 36. His "A Child Leads the Way," is a fictionalized account of the martyrdom of the Ninety-Three. See S. Asch, **Tales of My People**, tr. Meyer Levin (New York: Putnam's Sons, 1948), pp. 191-202.

10. **Mahzor for Rosh Hashanah and Yom Kippur,** edited by Rabbi Jules Harlow (New York: The Rabbinical Assembly, 1972), p. 561. "The Letter of the Ninety-Three Maidens," by Hillel Bavli was featured in the American Hebrew bi-weekly, *Hadoar*, vol. 23.12, and an English translation by Bertha-Badt Strauss appeared in The *Reconstructionist*, ix.2, March 5, 1943, p. 23.

11. Lines echo "The Binding of Isaac" (the Akedah), Gen 22 (especially sentences 1, 7, 11), the Torah reading for the second day of Rosh Hashanah, and part of the morning service everyday of the year.

12. A similar thought is conveyed by Haim Nahman Bialik (1873-1934) on the atrocities of the Kishinev Easter pogrom (April 6 and

7, 1903) in his poem, '"On the Slaughter" (Iyar, 1903).

13. *The vidui shekiv mera'* ("Confession on a Death Bed") and the *Ne'ilah* (concluding) service of Yom Kippur end with identical refrains:

> The Lord is King; the Lord was King; the Lord shall be King for ever and ever; Blessed be His Name, whose glorious kingdom is for ever and ever; The Lord He is God; Hear O' Israel: The Lord is our God, the Lord is one.

14. Lucy S. Dawidowicz, **A Holocaust Reader** (New York: Behrman House, 1976), p. 13.

15. Paul R. Mendes-Flohr and Jehuda Reinhartz, editors, **The Jew in the Modern World** (New York and Oxford: Oxford University Press, 1980), p. 492. The source is Bernard Dov Weinryb, **Jewish Emancipation Under Attack** (1942), p. 45.

16. Ephraim Oshry, **Responsa from the Holocaust Era** (New York: Judaica Press, 1983), pp. 193-194.

17. Jacob Apenszlak, ed. et al, **The Black Book of Polish Jewry**, New York: Roy Publishers, 1943.

18. **The Black Book of Polish Jewry**, p. 26.

19. *Op.cit.*, p. 26.

20. *Op.cit.*, p. 27.

21. *Op.cit.*, p. 27.

22. An early "witness" to the suicide is Hanah Weiss, "Kiddush Hashem: Heroic Death of the Ninety-Three Maidens in the Cracow Ghetto on 13 Av 5702" (Tel Aviv: Beit Ya'akov, 1947), pamphlet (Hebrew), 39 pages. See, by the same author, "Kiddush Hashem," **25th Year Jubilee Volume of High School and Seminary for Kindergartners (teachers) and Teachers, "Beit Ya'akov" in Tel Aviv, 1936-1961** (Tel Aviv: Beit Ya'akov, 1961), pp. 20-24 (Hebrew).

23. Per verbal (phone) communication, February 19, 1990.

24. Per verbal (phone) communication, February 19, 1990.

25. Per verbal (phone) communication, February 21, 1990.

26. Chaim Shapiro, "A Flame Called Sarah Schenirer," *The Jewish Observer,* November-December, 1974, p. 19.

27. Per verbal (phone) communication, February 20, 1990.

28. Yitzchak Lewin, editor, **Eleh Ezkerah** (New York: Shulsinger Bros., 1956-1972). Note, too, that there is no reference to the Ninety-Three in **The Black Book of Polish Jewry**, which lists Dr. Lewin as co-editor.

29. I Sam 31:4. Other cases of suicide recorded in the Bible are Samson (Judg 16:30), Ahitopel (2 Sam 17:23), and Zimri (1 Kgs 16:18). Another version on the death of King Saul is reported in 2 Sam 1:9, where we read that an Amalekite obeyed the words of a wounded Saul and slew him.

30. A brief summary of martyrdom for the Sanctification of the Name is found in H.J. Zimmels, **The Echo of the Nazi Holocaust in Rabbinic Literature** (printed In the Republic of Ireland, 1975), pp. 82-86; and Irving J. Rosenbaum, **The Holocaust and the Halakhah** (New York: Ktav, 1976), pp. 35-40.

31. A primary source is the Apocrypha books I, II Maccabees, which emphasize themes of religious persecution, loyalty of martyrs to tradition, and God's concern for His people. The story of the mother and her seven sons is illustrative (2 Macc 7).

32. The Yom Kipputr musaf service contains the *Eleh Ezkera* ("These I well remember") prayer in behalf of ten martyrs, including Rabbi Akiba and Rabbi Hananya ben Teradyon, whose martyrdoms are reported — contrary to talmudic sources — to have taken place on the same day. Though the prayer is post- talmudic, it properly portrays the harsh times for Jewish scholars between and after the revolts against Rome (first and second centuries).

33. A sampling of documents on the persecution of Jews in the medieval and modern periods are found in relevant sections of Jacob Marcus, **The Jew in the Medieval World** (Cleveland and New York: Meridian Books, 1961), and Paul R. Mendes-Flohr and Jehudah Reinharz, *op. cit.* Various literary responses to Jewish martyrdom and suffering, a veritable literary history of destruction, are presented in Alan Mintz, **Hurban: Responses to Catastrophe in Hebrew Literature** (New York: Columbia University Press, 1984); David Roskies, **Against the Apocalypse: Responses to Catastrophe in Modern Jewish Culture** (Cambridge: Harvard University Press, 1984); David Roskies, **The Literature of Destruction** (Philadelphia: Jewish Publication Society, 1988); and Pesach Schindler, **Hasidic Responses to the Holocaust in the Light of Hasidic Thought** (New Jersey: Ktav, 1990).

34. H.J. Zimmels, *op. cit.*, p. 83.

35. Rabbi Ephraim Oshry, **Sheilos Utshuvos Mimamakim**, vol. I, no. 6, cited in H.J. Zimmels, *op. cit.*, p. 85. Rabbi Oshry goes on to say with admiration that in the "Ghetto of Kovno there were no cases of suicide save in three instances. All the other inmates of the Ghetto believed with perfect faith that God would not forsake His people ..."

For a nationalist view on the assimilationist tendency of 19th century Jews of Berlin, see Peretz Smolenskin, "The Haskalah of Berlin (1883)," in Arthur Hertzberg, **The Zionist Idea** (New York: Althenum, 1975), pp. 154-157.

36. In a collection of responsa arranged according to the order of the Shulhan Aruk, **Mahaneh Hayyim** (1879-1885), section 2, no. 19, Rabbi Hayyim Ben Mordechai Ephraim Fischel Sofer (1821-1886) admonished a Jewish community's error in handing over Jewish girls by "cities in Galicia," during the German-Austrian war, in light of m. Terumot 8.12. The racial laws of the Germans prevented the violation of this mishnah from repeating multiple times over.

37. Deut 30:19; cf., also, Ezek 18:32.

38. Josephus Flavius, **Bellum Judaicum** (The Jewish War), VII. 6-11; Josephus, **The Jewish War**, trans. by G.A. Williamson (Baltimore: Penguin, 1959), pp. 352-370; Joseph Bentwich, **Josephus** (Philadelphia: Jewish Publication Society, 1914), pp. 108-135.

39. See Judg 11, and especially vv. 34-40.

40. These sentences are part of the Haftorah reading for the second day Rosh Hashanah (Jer 31: 2-20); the Torah reading on this day is the "Binding of Isaac," the Akedah (Gen 22: 1-24). In Jewish tradition, both readings are understood as patriarchial-matriarchal (parental) entreaty in behalf of the Children of Israel.

41. Pesahim 25b relates the narrative of a man who asked Rabba, what should he do if one in authority threatens to kill him unless he would kill another person. Rabba's answer, "Be killed and kill not. Who has told you that your blood is redder than his? Perhaps his blood is redder." Rabba's teaching is to honor the sixth injunction of the Decalogue, "You shall not murder" (Exod 20:13; Deut 5:17); however, the decision of the Ninety-Three Maidens to sacrifice their lives is viewed as a sacrificial intercession on behalf of innocent blood before divine justice.

42. The *aggadic* discourse speaks of saving the righteous martyred children; the *peshat* of "I will bring back," is God's resolve to seek, find and bring to justice those who rebel against Him, whether they hide among the hills of Bashan (the fertile tract of country in the East of Jordan, between Hermon in the North, Salchah in the East, Gilead in the South, Geshar and Ma'achah in the West) or in the depths of the sea. Cf. Ps 68:24.

43. Fascination about the 400 Children is well attested in Jewish lore and tradition: The Halachah of Rabbi Moshe Gaon b. Rav Hanoch,

an exile from Spain; the poetry of Y.L. Gordon; the rabbinic lore of H.N. Bialik and Y. Rawnitsky, **Sefer ha-Aggadah** (1908-1911); and Z. Kolitz's short story, "Yossel Rakover's Appeal to God," among disparate sources.

44. Ever since Sinai, the language of Jewish anthropomorphism has portrayed God as curtailing the evil decree against His people (Exod 32: 9-14), when warranted by a purposeful attitudinal change in the life of the people. If the character and conduct of the people are proper and righteous from the outset, and still they are murdered, shall not the "Lord repent of this evil to His people" (Exod 32:14)?

45. For theological thought on Rubenstein, Fackenheim, Greenberg and Weisel, see above, chapter two.

46. From the remarks of Rebetzin Judith Gruenfeld, London, co-worker of Sarah Schenirer, commemorating the 50th Yahrzeit of Sarah Schenirer, Sunday, 24 Adar 5745/March 17, 1985, Madison Square Garden, New York City.

47. Cf.2 Macc 7:33,37: "Be one with the servants (of the Lord in the World-to-Come) and may our sacrifice (not be in vain); God be merciful to our nation."

48. Lore Shelley, editor, **Secretaries of Death** (New York: Sheingold Publishers, 1986), p. xiv.

49. The significance of the Ninety-Three for religious life in Eretz Israel is voiced by several authors in a Hebrew publication, **93** (Tel Aviv, Iyar 1943), which sees in their martyrdom a negation of exile and a recommitment to love of Zion. The latter is directed to the Daughters of Israel and expressed in traditional categories of woman modesty and behavior. For more on the effect of the Ninety-Three on the *yishuv*, and questions on the letter's validity, see Judith Tydor Baumol essay on the story of the Ninety-Three Maidens (n.d.), obtainable from the Yaffa Eiach Collection of the Center for Holocaust Studies, Brooklyn, N.Y.

50. Cf. the remarks of Eli Wiesel before some 1600 survivors gathered at Manhattan's Marriot Marquis Hotel for the "First international Gathering of Children Hidden During World War II: "Continue not only to face (your past) and cope with it, but also share it. Because once you share it, it becomes an act of conscience, not just an act of consciousness." The *Jewish Journal of Greater Los Angeles*, June 7-June 13, 1991, p. 20.

51. From the remarks of Rebbetzin Judith Gruenfeld commemorating the 50th Yahrzeit of Sarah Schenirer. See note 46.

52. A hasidic version of how the excessive *pilpul* is counterproductive

to Mitzvah-doing is found in Abraham Joshua Heschel's "The Inner World of the Polish Jew," in Roman Vishnaic, **Polish Jews, A Pictorial Record** (New York: Schocken Books, 1947), p. 14. The unimpressed rebbe is identified as Rabbi Mendel of Kotzk in Heschel's **The Earth is the Lord's** (New York: Henry Schuman, Inc., 1950), p. 83.

53. In his phone conversation to me (February 20, 1990), Mr. Schenkolewsky emphatically insisted that he met Chaya Feldman and can recall her disposition but not her face. It is incumbent upon us, who cherish the sacrifice of the Six Million, to sketch the lines and contours of that memory for human dignity.

CHAPTER SEVEN
Deconstructing Theodicy and Amalekut
A Personal Apologia

At the 21st Annual Scholars' Conference, hosted by Stockton State College in New Jersey, I presented remarks on theodicy and Amalekut. I argued that the underpinnings of Amalek language disclose how defenders (and detractors) defined themselves within the holocaustal world and in the post-Shoah age. A preliminary draft was published in G. Jan Colijn and Marcia S. Littel (eds.), The Netherlands and Nazi Genocide (Lewiston/ Queenston/ Lampeter: The Edward Mellen Press, 1992).

The sections that follow have a twofold goal. First a partisan reflection on the language of theodicy and Amalekut in the making of today's post-Shoah Jew. Second, to suggest restraint in the modern-day popular rhetoric that flows from these categories.

I. Theodicy

In the theistic theology of Jews and Christians, God is seen as all powerful, all-wise, completely benevolent, all-caring, and all-love. But evil exists in His world created from nothingness and how to reconcile the goodness of God in spite of the presence of evil?

Three centuries before the Christian era, the Greek pagan philosopher Epicurus stated the problem of theodicy (from the two Greek words, god and justice) in terms that gods cannot or will not prevent evil. If the gods cannot prevent evil, they are not omnipotent. If the gods will not prevent evil, then they are not omnibenevolent. And if the gods are not limited in either power or benevolence, why is there evil in the world?

In a popular college text, *Exploring the Philosophy of Religion*,[1] editor David Stewart suggests that there are two types of evil in the world: natural and moral. Natural evil refers to those elements of nature which cause pain and suffering to human beings, such as natural disaster, disease and death. Moral evil is suffering brought about by human perversity, and history testifies that human beings are capable of causing great physical and psychological pain to their fellows, which makes natural evil pale in comparison.

Stewart further points out that these two kinds of evil challenge important theistic teachings on the nature of God's management of the world. Natural evil raises questions about the order of nature and moral evil raises questions about human nature. In both cases, the question for the Jew and Christian is why God allows a world such as ours to exist.

> Why does the natural order produce human suffering? Could God have created the world in such a way that it would not produce events that cause human suffering? If so, why did God not? The question posed by moral evil is why God allows us to inflict misery and suffering on others. Could God have created free beings who nonetheless would not produce misery and suffering for their fellow human beings?
>
> (cited in D. Stewart, *loc. cit.*, p. 246)

The fundamental evil of human nature permeates the novels of Fyodor Dostoevsky (**The Brothers Karamazov, Crime and Punishment**, and others), who asks why does God let children suffer? Rabbi Milton Steinberg in his classic, **Basic Judaism**[2] posits if God is why is the world not better? Why is it so marred and weighted down with disorder and suffering that it seems at times not the handiwork of a God of goodness but the contrivance of a fiend? Also, radical Christian theologian, A. Roy Eckardt, sensing the silence of God during the Shoah, questions if God is alive and not dead, then how can He live with Himself knowing that millions of Jews, including 1.5 million children, were murdered so cruelly in Hitler's inferno.

The attempts to answer the question of theodicy, in rabbinic terms, why the good suffer and the wicked prosper, match the moral and metaphysical nuances of the question itself. In the end, modernist Rabbi Steinberg comments, evil is inscrutable, an enigma, beyond unraveling, to which the answer, if any, is known to God Himself. This is the purport of the rabbinic epigram: "It is not in our power to explain the tranquility of the wicked or the suffering of the upright."

The traditionalist Jew, however, goes one epoch backward and thus one step further. For him, the question of theodicy is the question of anthropodicy (evil by man):

> The Rock, His work is perfect;
> For all His ways are justice;
> A God of faithfulness and without iniquity, just and right is He.

Is corruption His? No; His children's is the blemish;
A generation crooked and perverse.
Do you requite the Lord,
O foolish people and unwise?
Is He not thy father that has gotten thee?
Has He not made thee, and established thee?

(Deut 32:4-6)

Free will and man's ability to discern right from wrong are implicit in the doctrine of anthropodicy. Without this power, man cannot be responsible for his actions and the fabric of society will dissolve into chaos and anarchy.[3]

In Jewish theology, strict traditionalists believe that the dire effects of antisemitism and Shoah are caused by Israel's own backsliding:

> And the Lord said unto Moses: You are soon to lie with your fathers. This people will thereupon go astray after alien gods in their midst, in the land which they are about to enter; they will forsake Me and break My covenant which I made with them. Then My anger will flare up against them, and I will abandon them and hide My countenance from them. They shall be ready prey; and many evils and troubles shall befall them. And they shall say on that day, "Surely it is because our God is not in our midst that these evils have befallen us."

(Deut 31:16-17)

The antidote to "the lure of strange nations and trust in them" (Targum Onqelos for "go(ing) astray after alien gods in their midst") is strict adherence to the Torah, *teshuvah*-returning to its teachings, learning and passing on its moral precepts (Deut 31:19). For the righteous who follow the Torah way, the Deuteronomist proclaims:

> The secret things belong unto the Lord our God;
> but the things that are revealed belong unto *us*
> *and our children* (these words are dotted) forever,
> that we may do all the words of this Torah.

(Deut 29:28)

In discerning a suitable hermeneutic for the *puncta extraordinaria*, we suggest, why do the righteous suffer? Do we parse the verse and connect "revealed things' with God, thereby suggesting that He alone knows why mortality suffers?; or are the 'overt acts' doing Torah, which are not capable in preventing suffering by the righteous? On this verse, biblical exegesis and homiletical eisegesis interact and form a circle — a theodicy circle.

II. Jewish Theodicy

In recent years, a number of thinkers and politicians has suggested a variant to classical theodicy: *Jewish* theodicy. In their view, the problem of evil for Jews is group oriented; the paramount effect of antisemitism, the Shoah, and threats to the sovereignty of Israel. In this theodicy, Jews are always innocent victims of hatred and violence.

John Murray Cuddihy, Professor of Sociology at Hunter College of the City University of New York, comments that religious and secular Jews alike see themselves as a small, weak, good group dispersed among a large, strong, bad group (the nations), which consistently and persistently victimizes them. Further, the Jewish people considers itself blameless, and sinned against by other groups, itself not sinning against them.[4]

Thus, many liberation theologians[5] maintain that the Zionist actions in Palestine created a stateless people, who in turn, blame the Jews and the Israelis, and how does Jewish theodicy respond? They blame the victims, the Palestinians, and see nothing hypocritical or irrational in this.

Similarly, Black antisemitism is wrong but Jewish racism is equally repugnant. Also, Jews have an obligation to understand Christian categories of forgiveness (Waldheim affair; Auschwitz Convent) and theology of suffering (New York Cardinal John O'Connor's conviction that the Jewish suffering in the Shoah is seen as "gift" to humanity) before reacting to them with denunciations in the media. In short, Jewish theodicy is preventing many Jews from seeing their own faults and wrongly perceiving the Jews as blameless and benevolent as God Himself is supposed to be in the dilemma of classical theodicy.

Are the proponents of "Jewish theodicy" fair in their assessment of Jewish group behavior? We think not, and let us explain.

Jewish Racism. An enforced Jewish negativism against black people is not the problem; it has never been the problem. Afro-Americans have never suffered at the hands of Jews. Individuals, yes; but en masse, no. The issue is not Jewish racism. The issue is what it has always been racism.

And the oppression of black people by a racist system; a system which the Jews did not create and are themselves a perennial victim.

For example, the accusation heard at the NAACP Los Angeles Convention (Summer 1990), that Jewish racism limits the Afro-American in the film industry, is unfounded.

True, Jews built the "dream factory" and are well positioned behind the scenes. It was, however, in response to antisemitism in WASP America that immigrant Jews built an empire of their own. Likewise in the areas of banking, insurance, hospitals, higher education, private clubs, etc. Second class Jewish "greeners" came to America and proved that they are as able and capable as first class blue blooded aristocracy. Further, on the silver screen, proper Jewish types are minted as frequently as the buffalo nickel.

Some black leaders on the Mideast and Black-Jewish relations appear self-righteous and arrogant. From Bishop Tutu to Jesse Jackson, we hear that Jews must show more sensitivity and be prepared for more consultation before taking positions contrary to the best interests of the Afro-American community.

But American Jewish Black writer and educator, Jules Lester (previously, an accuser of Jewish racism and now a victim of black antisemitism[6]) writes:

> While I understand that such a statement (Jewish racism) comes from years of anger at active Jewish opposition to affirmative action, and how deeply Blacks were hurt by this opposition to what was in our "best interests," Black leadership still seems to be ignorant of the fact that Jews have been hurt by Black indifference to the fate of Israel.
>
> (*Jerusalem Post*, November 6, 1979)

Ethnocentric insensitivity knows no discrimination; it lives in everybody's neighborhood and traverses everyone's group line.

Christian Reconciliation. Jewish leadership welcomes the attempts at reapproachment made by the Church to the Jewish people. Recent pronouncements from the Vatican and the World Council of Churches (Protestant) condemn antisemitism from any source, person, and place; recognize the biblical source for Jewish attachment to Eretz Israel (but not necessarily the State of Israel); and confirm the "inextricable connection" between Israel and the Shoah.

These are among the first fruits of a fruitful dialogue between Jewish and Christian communities of faith. However, Christian protagonists of Jewish theodicy must understand that many Jews feel that these official announcements are from Christians "at their best."

Hear the perspective from respected Protestant theologian, Robert McAfee Brown, writing in *Christianity and Crisis* (October 23, 1989):

> But Christians are not usually "at their best," and so to Jews the cross almost immediately became a symbol not of divine love but of the very human hatred it was meant to overthrow. Ample historical evidence over two millenia confirms the tragic accuracy of their perception. Very early in its history, the Christian church, in the name of the one who died on the cross, took the cross and made it a symbol, in Christian hands, not of love but of conquest and terror — a symbol in the name of which Christians felt mandated to force "conversions" from Jews, subject them to ghettoization, bloody pogroms, and outright murder. With that record, Christians should not be surprised when the presence of a cross suggests to others, and particularly to Jews, a deity who is at least in complicity with human evil if not the direct inspirer of it.

The jury is out while Jewry waits and sees if the Church can match deeds with creeds, e.g., move the cross from the Carmelite convent at Auschwitz[7]; officially recognize the State of Israel and Jerusalem, its capital; and excommunicate Nazi murderers, alive and dead.

Jewish 'self-centeredness' is the right way when Christian divines advise Jews to practice a theology of forgiveness, and to forget the perpetrators of the Shoah.

For example, A.C.J. Phillips, Chaplain of St. John's College, Oxford, commented on the Jewish advocacy against Bitberg Sunday thus: "In remembering the Holocaust, Jews hope to prevent its recurrence; by declining to forgive, I fear that they unwittingly invite it."[8] This statement, typical of counsel from many Christian friends, occupies the moral high ground of which Jews are accused, and put frankly, it is obscene.

Palestinianism. The Israeli-Palestinian conflict is not only an issue of economics, politics and militarism. It is an ideological one as well. Jews have every right to question the tendency among Arab intellectuals, who accept unequivocally the adverse teachings against the Jews (Christian "teaching of contempt" literature; czarist **Protocols of Zion**; Hitler's

Mein Kampf, etc.), and then proceed to fabricate evidence in the **Qur'an** and **Shari'**a to support them.

Thus misanthropy, deicide, blood libel and other deep-rooted prejudicial fears and accusations are read into the **Qur'an**, the Tradition and the Commentaries by revisionist historians, theologians and politicians.

Anti-Jewish sentiments in Islam may be traced scripturally to Koranic injunctions which see the Jews as a people who do evil, and politically to the Pact of Omar issued in the seventh century, which recognizes freedom of religion of Jews, in exchange for high taxation and a host of discriminatory laws. These include a halt in synagogue building and the wearing of distinctive dress to ostracize the Jews from Islamic society. Yet the measures against the Jews were less extreme than in medieval Christian Europe because Judaism was portrayed as unimportant and Jews, who lacked political and military power, offered no threat to the Islamic state.

Historically, Jews were not forced to convert to Islam, nor is there any record of state-sponsored slavery and genocide of the Jews. Consequently, Jews felt more at ease under the Crescent than the Cross. Significantly, Jewish tribes aided Mohammed, assisted the Moslems in their wars against Christians, and were partners in a host of economic and learning adventures, particularly in Egypt, Tunisia and Spain during the High Middle Ages (900-1200 CE). Unfortunately, humanism and tolerance were replaced by rigidity and religiosity from the thirteenth century on, and Jews suffered from unfair political and antisocial laws and measures. They were prohibited from many trades and guilds, forced into hated professions, e.g., moneylending, and placed in *mellahs*, created ostensibly to protect Jews, but in reality self-contained ghettos which restricted them from social contact with Moslems.

In due time, Judaism became a despised faith, and Jews suffered from public humiliation. Norman A. Stillman reports in his history and source book, **The Jews of Arab Lands** (Jewish Publication Society of America, 1980), that in some communities Jews had to walk barefoot and in others they were required to wear metal rings around their necks so that they could be isolated at the public bathhouse. Turning inward to Jewish spiritual and messianic tendencies provided some relief, and when western secularism penetrated the Arab world in the nineteenth century, many Jews gladly followed its beacon of light. Arab Jews educated in western mores, languages, education, and mindsets were tolerated but seen as a third column in the reawakening of Arab values and nationalism beginning in the nineteenth century. The successful rise of modern-day political Zionism, advocating freedom, equality, independence and sovereignty of the Jewish people in its historic homeland of Eretz Israel, confronted the geographical dominance of pan-Arabism in all countries from the Mediterranean to the Indian Ocean.

The rise of the Jewish state in 1948 and the succession of Israeli victories in Arab-Israeli wars, including the Six Day War of 1967 which resulted in the establishment of Israeli/Jewish/Zionist authority over a significant Arab population, exacerbated Arab stereotype of the Jew. How so? The Jew is seen as greedy, cunning, cowardly — the trait goes back to **Qur'an** — and lacking in the basic Allah-given virtues of self-respect and self-defense. Then how to explain Israeli victories?

In his important work, **Semites and Anti-Semites: An Inquiry into Conflict and Prejudice**, Professor Bernard Lewis opines that the Arab views the Jews as "the sons of Satan, exercising demonic powers, engaged in a conspiracy against mankind extending through the millennia and across the world ... The struggle against such an adversary gives cosmic stature to those who engage in it, and lends some dignity even to these who suffer a defeat, which, they firmly believe, can only be temporary."[9] Shades indeed of vitriolic pagan, Christian and Nazi antisemitism.

In summation, we may say that the conflict of nationalisms is the contributing factor to today's animosity and strife between Israeli and Palestinian, and by extension, Jew and Moslem. The 1989-90 ballots for Allah in Algeria, Tunisia, Kuwait, Jordan, Egypt, and Iran have brought fundamentalists to the streets shouting, "Oh, Jews! The army of Mohammed will return!" But Islamic antisemitism ascribes to the Jews a quality of world-historical cosmic evil which zealously precipitates ugly fratrical features. Consider, too, the platforms of two vying factions of the Palestine National Movement, PLO and Hamas, expressing the eradication of the Jewish state by armed Palestinian struggle.[10]

The Israeli/Jew after Auschwitz reacts in brash, non-conforming terms because he knows well the long night's journey into hell. To defend oneself, honor and homeland when attacked is not wrong. It is the right thing to do. Are Palestinians choosing differently in their much publicized campaign of Intifada? 'Jewish theodicy' like the Shoah is not a Jewish problem. It is the mindset of genteel Gentile critics who cannot accept fully Jews as Jews.

If this fact cannot be faced, then there is little else to be said. It is this which Jewish people understand. If there are caring and empathetic criticism of the Jews, let the voices be heard. All we hear is silence, accusation, indifference and hypocrisy.

If that is all there is going to be, then Bilaam's words are starkly true: Israel "is a people that dwells apart, and not to be reckoned among the nations" (Num 23:9).

The Jews may not be blameless but they are certainly not guilty. Jews are not like most people: Good, yes but evil, no.

III. Genocide: Commandment 604

The Sabbath before Purim, designated as Shabbat *Zachor*, confronts the traditional Jew, who is committed to living within the bonds of Halachah (Jewish law), a system of divinely inspired biblical commandments, as well as rabbinic decrees and derivations, with a paradoxical dilemma. On the one hand, as a survivor of a state-sponsored policy of genocide, he is a strong supporter of the United Nations Genocide Convention. Also, moral and ethical concern for other families of man is demanded by the repeated biblical injunction: "Remember, you were slaves in the Land of Egypt" (Lev 19:34, and elsewhere).

On the other hand, this same Jew is confronted with an explicit Mitzvah the 604th — to commit genocide:

> Remember what Amalek did unto these by the way as
> you came forth out of Egypt: how he met you by the
> way, and smote the hindmost of you, all that were
> enfeebled in thy rear, when you were faint and weary;
> and he feared not God. Therefore, it shall be, when the
> Lord your God had given you rest from all your enemies
> round about, in the land which the Lord your God gives
> you for an inheritance to possess it, that you shall blot
> out the remembrance of Amalek from under heaven;
> you shall not forget.

> (Deut 25:17-19)

Other tribes have warred against Israel — Edomites, Moabites, Ammonites, Egyptians, and others — but none have been totally rejected or stigmatized by divine decree for eternal genocide and damnation.

Could it be because Amalek "feared not God" and could not be like others, who after a period of moral regeneration are accepted into the Household of Israel? Contrast Deuteronomy 25:19 and Deuteronomy 23:8-9.

In rabbinic literature, Amalek is shown as a paradigm of absolute wickedness and evil, destroyer and rejector of all that God and man have wrought.[11] Thus, the Halachic Jew, were he to be confronted with a bona fide descendant of Amalek, would be duty-bound to kill him/her forthwith without the necessity or requirement to obtain a mandate from any rabbinical court.

How does one balance Abraham's agonizing plea over the fate of Sodom and Gomorrah, "Shall not the Judge of all the earth do justly?" (Gen 18:25) and the divine injunction of the descendants of Abraham "to do righteousness and justice" (*loc. cit.*, verse 19), with this imperative:

> Write this for a memorial in the book, and rehearse it in the ears of Joshua: for I will utterly blot out the remembrance of Amalek from under heaven. And Moses built an altar, and called the name of it A-nai-nisi. And he said: "The hand upon the throne of the Lord: the Lord will have war with Amalek from generation to generation."

(Exod 17:14-16)

Any attempt at understanding this warrant for genocide against the Amalekites and their descendants must start with knowledge of the biblical texts, in conjunction with known historical data.

The Bible records the collective life of the Amalekites from the days of the Exodus (mid-thirteenth century BCE) till the time of King Saul (1020-1005). The tribe inhabited the Sinai peninsula in the region of Kadesh (Gen 14:2) as far to the south as Shur (I Sam 15:7; 27:18), from which they made raids on the settled population of southern Palestine (Num 13:29; 14:25,43; I Sam 27:8 ff.).

The Israelites first met with the Amalekites in the region near Sinai, when Amalek naturally tried to prevent the entrance of a new tribe into the region (cf. Exod 17:8-16). The battle which pursued left a powerful impression on Moses: "Then the Lord said to Moses, 'Inscribe this in a document as a reminder, and read it aloud to Joshua: I will utterly blot out the memory of Amalek from under the heaven'" (Exod 17:14).

Deut 25:17-19 (cited above) suggest that Amalek made other attacks on Israel, including "from the rear." On the southern border of Palestine, the Amalekites also helped at a later time to prevent Israel's entrance from Kadesh (Num 13:22; 14:25).

During the period of the Judges (1200-1000), Amalekites aided the Moabites in raiding Israel (Judg 3:13), and at a later time, they aided the Midianites to do the same thing (Judg 6:3,33; 7:12). This enmity kept alive the old hostility which continued in the days of Saul (see 1 Sam 15; the haftorah of *parshat Zachor*, which talks of the command to exterminate all Amalekites) and David (I Sam 27:8).

We read of the last of the Amalekites in I Chr. 4:42 ff. There a strange story is reported that 500 Simeonites attacked and smote a remnant of the Amalekites in Edom. Finally, Ps 83:8 refers to the Amalekites as aiding Israel's enemies; but this is probably a poetical imitation of ancient conditions.

In summation, the biblical material on Amalek notes:

• The hatred between the Israelites and the Amalekites is an expression of clan warfare and feudal conflict over territory.

• Amalek engaged in a war of killing non-combatants, and this has forfeited all claims of mercy ("smote all that were enfeebled in your rear, when you were faint and weary"; Deut 25:18).

• Amalek shared with other enemies of the Israelites in battles against the Jewish people. This is compatible to conventional warfare among belligerants,and when completed, it is normally forgotten and forgiven. However, the Jew is obligated to "remember," to "blot out," and "not to forget," since the unique evil of Amalek is his war against the Covenant, against Judaism ("he feared not God"; Deut 25:18).

The biblical record sees Amalek as the traditional enemy for primarily political-military-survival reasons. But how to explain the existential, *theological* input after the disappearance of Amalek as a recognizable entity?

Why the need to mold the Jewish character by means of genocide?; to wit, "The Lord will be at war with Amalek throughout the ages" (Exod 17:16).

IV. Amalekut: Seeds of Amalek

The Mitzvah of Genocide cannot be easily dismissed.

The Book of Esther, which is read twice on Purim day, claims that Haman is a direct descendant of Agag (Esth 3:1), the Amalekite king (I Sam 15:8), who from his authoritative position to the emperor of Persia and Media, attempted to eliminate all Jews.

His protaganist is Mordechai, the Jew, who, according to rabbinic tradition, is a descendant of Kish the Benjaminite (Esth 2:5). Kish is identified as the father of Saul, the first king of Israel. Biblical tradition maintains that Saul's downfall came about as a direct result of his failure to eradicate Amalek as commanded by divine decree through Samuel (I Sam 15).

I Sam 15:33 suggests that the Prophet Samuel "hewed Agag (= Amalek) in pieces before the Lord." His action is existentially imitated whenever and wherever Jews celebrate Purim.

How so? Each time Haman's name is read in the Synagogue on Purim, noisemakers, foot-stomping, and jeering uterably 'blot out' his name in the observance of the Mitzvah of 'remembering' what Amalek did and not 'forgetting.'

The biblical record on Amalek defends the genocide commandment by suggesting that this people "smote the hindmost of you, all that were enfeebled in your rear, when you were faint and weary; and he feared not God" (Deut 25:18). Thus, Amalek is a robber and outlaw tribe, which attacks a tired and defenseless people, and does not accept basic standards of morality and humanity.

Two biblical characters, Agag and Haman, represent the same characteristics. In contradiction to the Mitzvah, "And you shall love the stranger," stressed 36 times in Scripture, and the principle that "every man be put to death for his own sin" (Deut 24:16), Amalek represents evil in potential, if not in actuality.

He is to be eradicated in keeping with the often repeated Deuteronomic admonition: "And you shall eradicate the evil from the midst of you" (Deut 13, 17, 19, 22, and 24).

With recourse to biblical texts only, we read of the end of the Amalekite Reich: "... the sons of Simeon, 500 men ... smote the remnants of the Amalekites ..." (I Chr 4:42,43).

Rabbinic texts and commentaries abound with Amalekite references. But do we know how to read such texts?

In a paper presented before the National Association of Professors of Hebrew, meeting in Boston on December 6, 1987, we observed:

> Jews in pre-modern eras did not look backwards with the aim of discovering facts. They sought rather to derive paradigms from the sacred events of the past by which they could then interpret and respond to contemporary events. Paradigmatic and not pragmatic concern was the issue and emphasis. Jews dabbled in historiosophy (a philosophy of history) and not historiography.[12]

Rabbinic illusions to Amalek are not transmission of historical data, but of the Bible, and "historical facts" are not interesting as such, only as applications of the biblical texts. Present events for the Rabbis and Commentators (traditional) get their meaning when put into the biblical mindset: God now speaks through texts.

Furthermore, biblical Amalekite passages illustrate well the strong hermenuetical concern to be felt in the Rabbis' comments on Amalek in general. The rabbinic interpretations are coloured by the milieu in which they are used and for which they are intended.

Let us Illustrate.

Gen 36:8 states that Esau (brother of Jacob) is Edom, and "Timna was concubine to Eliphaz, Esau's son; and she bore to Eliphaz, Amalek" (Gen 36:12). Amalek was the illegitimate grandson of Esau.

The blessing of Isaac to his son, Esau, is that he will live by the sword (Gen 27:40), and the Torah records, "Esau hated Jacob because of the blessing wherewith his father blessed him (*loc. cit.*, verses 27-29). And Esau said in his heart: 'Let the days of mourning for my father be at hand; then will I slay my brother Jacob'" (Gen 27:41).

The medieval commentator, Nahmanides (1194-1270), understands the fear of Moses and his charge to Joshua to fight with Amalek (Exod 17:9), because the latter lives by the sword. Nahmanides teaches that the first and last wars against Israel come from this people.

First? Note the biblical verse, "Amalek was the first of the nations" (Num 24:20).

Last? The descendants of Edom-Amalek, viz., Rome and Christendom. The latter was particularly meaningful to Nahmanides, since he lived during height of the medieval Church's absolutist "teaching of contempt" and persecution of the Jewish people. Totalitarian ideology, political and economic antisemitism, and Christian anti-Judaism combined in the 20th century, and helped bring about the Great Catastrophe, the Shoah, in the lands of Christendom!

God speaks through texts. In destruction there is the seed of creation. Edom-Amalek in the classic rabbinic mentality become a synonym for treachery, violence, oppression, and injustice, which one day would be obliterated.

"But his end should come to destruction" (Num 24:20), said of biblical Amalek, and applied in talmudic-midrashic historiosophy to foreparent Edom and to posterity Rome.

Thus by associating in the rabbinic mind (Amalek-) Edom and Rome, a hope theology was born that was intended to ease the Jewish catastrophe of the first and second centuries by suggesting that a day of vengeance against the enemy was coming, and that the day of victory was at hand.

After the fall of Rome, medieval commentators read into Edom-Amaiek their contemporary sources of evil, such as, Christendom and the Great Exile. Again, the teaching of Nahmanides: Edom and associates would be discomfited, and Israel will be saved from exile. "And saviors shall march up to Mount Zion to wreak judgment on Mount Esau (=Edom-Amalek); and dominion shall be the Lord's" (Obad 1:21)

Now whatever Moses and Joshua did with Amalek at first (Exod 17), Nahmanides comments, Elijah and Messiah ben Joseph will do with their descendants. This was why Moses strained himself in this matter (Exod

17:9,12).

The Amalek *Zachor* commandment is not just academic, but a verbal remembrance. It is not only recalled on Shabbat *Zachor*; it is promulgated as obligatory Jewish law (see **Orach Hayim** 685:7). Its importance is to mold the Jewish character.

Tradition sees Amalek in metaphorical, metahistorical, and metaphysical categories:

• The Jews are to destroy the descendants of Amalek when those descendants follow in the Edom-Amalekite path of purposeless cruelty. Amalek represents cruelty and criminality for their own sake. And so do daily acts of terrorism, thousand years later.

• Amalek "did not fear God" (Deut 25:18). The crime of Amalek was an act of defiance, predicated on the denial of God's existence. The assumption that morality is neither universal nor important, and that chance and survival for their own sake dominate the universe. Amalek's perversity, therefore, derives from his nihilistic theological posture. And so does Nazism and other forms of extreme technological dehumanization current today.

• Amalek represents unredeemed evil; and Kabbalistic theology places its onus on the shoulders of man. The moral imperative of the *Zachor* commandment is for each individual to join together to eliminate evil, not by destroying the sinners, but by eliminating sins. "May sinners disappear from the earth, and the wicked be no more" (Ps 104:35). Read not *hattaim* (sinners) but *hataim* (sinful acts). This supports the rabbinic-halachic thought that teaches the rehabilitation of sinners. Condemn drugs, promiscuity, AIDS, for example, but show compassion to the victim, and certainly support sincere repentance.

In addition, we may add, the "Seeds of Amalek," dwell *within* the Jewish peoplehood.

In the Song of Deborah, we note:

"Out of Ephraim came they whose root is in Amalek; After you, Benjamin, among thy peoples" (Judg 5:14).

So rendered, the phrase can mean a) some of the Ephramites (= Joseph tribes of Israel) dwelt among the Amalekites; or b) some of the Amalekites were absorbed in Ephraim.

Rashi (1040-1105) and others translate "against" instead of "in," and explain: From Ephraim, the root (viz., Joshua, a scion of the tribe; see, Num 13:8) fought against Amalek (Exod 17:10,13), and after him, Benjamin (viz., Saul the Benjaminite; see, I Sam 15) will also fight against him.

But overinvolvement today with *external* powers to be the "war against Amalek" as a result of the Shoah and Arab terrorism is an

Amalekite-inspired red herring. This is *Amalekut*, which semi-paralyzes and deflects the Jew from going about his/her business, i.e., the redemption of the Jewish people from the "Seeds of Amalek" by doing what is right and nurturing a climate which would encourage others to do the same.

Because the Children of Israel strove with Moses and "tried the Lord, saying, 'Is the Lord among us, or not?' Then came Amalek and fought..." (Exod 17:7b-8a).

V. A Final Note on Amalekphobia

Many types of *Amalekut* exist in the Jewish world today. For example, extreme right-wing Zionists and anti-Zionist traditionalists' statements on the current Israeli-Palestinian impasse. However divergent their views, the former speaks of the expulsion of the Arabs from the Jewish state and the latter insists on Jewish national contrition and dismantling the (secular) Jewish state, they both claim to speak in the name of God and Jewry. Equally shortsighted and sinister is the oft-repeated slogan, "Saddam Hussein is worst than Hitler" –given prominence and notoriety by President George Bush — articulated in and out of the classroom during Operation Desert Storm (1991).

Many said that Iraq's declared policy of P.O.W. treatment, homocide and ecocide is equivalent to the ultimate sin of Nazi Germany: Evil acts done for thoroughly evil purposes, with no foreseeable nor fareseeable redeeming value.

But Hussein is not Hitler and the Iraquis are not Nazis. There is historical inaccuracy when we equalize the Shoah with any human disaster we wish to condemn. For all its moral odiousness, calling victims of conventional warfare (or non-conventional warfare) another Holocaust, betrays an effort to compromise the uniqueness of the Nazi brutality.

Likewise, it is thoroughly unsound and wrong headed to see Saddam Hussein as a modern-day Amalek and the current Middle East crisis as a prelude to a final Armageddon (Rev 16:16), for this carries the divine obligation to obliterate every man, woman, child of the Amalek/Iraq nation in the case of the former and million of innocence in the case of the latter. After Auschwitz, this is an unbearable notion and morally repugnant.

If the crimes of Hussein and his Baath regime are to be seen as horrendous, they are in this respect: Nuremberg-like war crimes: Rape, looting, murder of civilians; hostage-taking of thousands of reluctant 'guests'; unprovoked Scud missile attacks on Israeli and Saudi civilian centers; humiliating abuse of P.O.W.s; the threat and possible use of chemical-biological weapons; and the continual "war of aggression" fed by politics of hate and destruction against the Kurdish nation and others.

There is no need to add metaphorical allegations and biblical allusions to Iraq's dark record. Or contribute exaggerated atrocities regarding her occupation of Kuwait and her performance in the Gulf War (e.g., the number of Kuwaiti hostages taken back to Iraq is less than 3000 and not the reported 40,000).

To paraphrase Yehudah Bauer on the dangers of Shoah distortions: False history (also, false analogy) establishes false consciousness and creates false myths. What is needed in the fight against old world orders and establishing new world orders is truth not Amalekphobia.

And truth making is the stuff of scholarship, free from government intervention, ecclesiastical bias, and academic deconstruction.

Endnotes

1. David Stewart, ed., **Exploring the Philosophy of Religion** (New Jersey: Prentice Hall, 1988), pp. 254-261.
2. Milton Steinberg, **Basic Judaism** (New York: Harcourt, Brace and tiaid, 1947), pp. 53-57.
3. See Deut 30:15-20; and especially, verses 15 and 19.
4. John Murray Cuddiiy, 'The Elephant and the Angels: Or, The Uncivil Irritatingness of Jewish Theodicy,' in **Uncivil Religion: Interreligious Hostility in America**, edited by Robert N. Bellah and Frederick E. Greenspahn (New York: Crossroads, 1987), pp. 23-37.
5. Exempli gratia, Rosemary Radford Reuther and Herman J. Reuther, **The Wrath of Jonah** (Harper and Row, 1989) and Marc Ellis, **Beyond innocence and Redemption: Confronting the Holocaust and Israeli Power — Creating a Moral Future for the Jewish People** (Harper and Row, 1990). R. Reuther and Ellis strongly advocate Arab and Palestinian views in academic symposiums highly critical of Zionist respectability and Israeli responsibility. Cases in point, Liberation Theologies Group section of the AAR Annual Meeting (November 19, 1989) in Anaheim, CA, and Symposium on "The Role of America Religious Leaders in the Middle East Peace Process," held at Marquette University in Wisconsin (November 7, 1990). On the latter symposium, see **American-Arab Affairs**, Fall 1990, pp. 53-103.
6. As told in his autobiography, **Lovesong: Becoming a Jew** (New

York: Henry Holt and Company, 1988).

7. See above, chapter five, endnote 6

8. Cited in Alice L. Eckardt and A. Roy Eckardt, **Long Night's Journey into Day** (Detroit: Wayne State University Press, 1988), p. 173.

9. Bernard Lewis, **Semites and Anti-Semites** (New York: W.W. Norton, 1986), p. 191.

10. The Covenant of the Islamic Resistance Movement (Hamas) proclaims in part:

> Our struggle against the Jews is very great and very serious. It needs all sincere efforts. The Islamic Resistance Movement is but one squadron that should be supported... It strives to raise the banner of Allah over every inch of Palestine... It is one of the links in the chain of the struggle against the Zionist invaders...
> The prophet, Allah bless him and grant him salvation, has said:
> The Day of Judgement will not come about until Moslems fight the Jews (killing the Jews), when the Jew will hide behind stones and trees. The stones and trees will say, "there is a Jew behind me, come and kill him" .. There is no solution for the Palestine question except through Jihad. Initiatives, proposals and international conferences are all a waste of time and vain endeavors. Palestine is an Islamic land.

PLO Covenant Against Israel, Article 21, reads:

> The Palestinian Arab people, in expressing itself through the armed Palestinian revolution, rejects every solution that is a substitute for a complete liberation of Palestine, and rejects all plans that aim at the settlement of the Palestine issue or its internationalization.

In their mutual desire to liberate the "Islamic Homeland," PLO and Hamas are credited with at least two-thirds of the violent Palestinian deaths in the territories since the start of the Intifada. Among the victims, moderate Palestinians in favor of a peaceful resolution of the Israeli-Palestinian conflict.

11. Cf. Pesikta Rabbati 12:47; Pesikta de R. Kahana 27; Exodus Rabbah 26:2,3; Numbers Rabbah 13:3; Sifrei, Numbers 84, Lamentations Rabbah 3: 64,66; Mehilta, Amalek, etc.

12. Zev Garber, "Interpretation and the Passover Haggadah: An Invitation to Post-Biblical Historiosophy," *BHHE*, vol. 2.2 (Spring 1988), p. 27. The paper is reprinted in Duane L. Christensen, ed.,

Experiencing the Exodus from Egypt (Oakland: Bibal Press, 1988), pp. 51-60.

CHAPTER EIGHT

Disorder in Order: The Interlocution of Shoah in the Passover Haggadah and Seder

Passover commemorates the birth of the Jewish people and the Exodus from Egypt. Yet in telling the story of national freedom, many contemporary Jews add narrative and song to honor the memory of the Six Million who did not escape the slave and death camps of Nazi Europe built by the whims of tyrants worse than the Pharaoh. What does Passover inform about the Shoah, and what does the Shoah inform about the Passover was the focus of my address at the 23rd Annual Scholars' Conference, hosted by the University of Tulsa. This essay is dedicated to the blessed memory of my mother, Pearl Garber, who passed away in Jerusalem on Shabbat between Passover and Yom Hashoah 5753 (17 April 1993).

I. The Preliminary Order

The Festival of Passover (*Pesaḥ*) commemorates the deliverance from Egyptian bondage of Hebrews and a "mixed group"[1] who joined them and with it the birth of the Israelite nation. Classical rabbinic thinking understands the Exodus not as an event itself but as a prelude to a greater Event: The Revelation at Sinai.[2] Commenting on "the counting of the Omer," a levitical law governing the offering of an Omer (measure) of barley from the Spring produce,[3] Maimonodes states: "We count the days that pass since the preceding Festival (Passover), just as one who expects his most intimate friend on a certain day counts the days and even the hours. This is the reason why we count the days that pass since the offering of the Omer, between the anniversary of our departure from Egypt and the anniversary of the Law-giving. The latter was the aim and object of the Exodus from Egypt."[4] In other words, the deliverance from Egypt is directed to a spiritual purpose. Indeed, in the talmudic tradition, the Feast of Weeks (*Shavuot*),[5] so-called because a period of seven weeks is counted between the start of *Pesaḥ* to the "Festival of the Law-Giving,"[6] also known as the "Festival of the First Fruits,"[7] is often referred to as *Atzeret*, the "concluding festival" of the Passover. Thus, the oldest ongoing story of freedom in the Western world is interpreted in the Jewish tradition as two-fold: Physical (Passover) and spiritual (*Shavuot*).[8] The message is clear: Liberty without Law is anarchy; Law without freedom from external restraint or compulsion is fanaticism. Both are necessary if a moral society is to function and to flourish.

The transformation of the biblical paschal sacrifice, which became a Temple-based cult, into a family ritual, called the Seder (proper "order" of service), was part of the rabbinic response to the destruction of the Second Temple in 70 C.E. In his important study on the origins of the Seder, the late Baruch M. Bokser showed that the *Tannaim* salvaged the Passover by moving its communal celebration from the destroyed Temple precincts to home sacred space.[9] In responding to national catastrophy, the Rabbis democratized a biblical rite: They restructured the Passover from cultic act to religious ritual; they encouraged prayer, study and learning in lieu of animal offering; and they implored every Israelite — including, the commoner and the untutored — to participate in a liturgical ceremony so that all can derive new meaning from the Torah narrative of redemption from slavery, then associated with Roman occupation of the Land of Israel.

"In every generation let each individual see oneself as if s/he came forth out of Egypt" and "For it was not one individual only who stood against us to destroy us; in every generation they stand up against us to destroy us, and the Holy One, blessed be He, saves us from their hand," summarize well the rabbinic Tendenz: Make the biblical odyssey from slavery into freedom personally meaningful so that current crises can be faced. For example, by interlocking Rome and Egypt in the rabbinic Seder,[10] a hope theology was born that intended to ease the Jewish pain of the first and second centuries by suggesting a day of retribution against the enemy was coming, and that day of victory was at hand, as in the days of Egypt, so in the days of Rome.

The earliest full description of the Seder is found in the Tannatic collection of Mishnah Pesahim 10 (circa 200 C.E.) and Tosefta Pesahim (*Pisha*) 10, edited in the early third century C.E. Obligated by the biblical injunction, "When, in time to come, your child asks you, 'What mean the exhortations, laws, and rules which the Lord our God has enjoined upon you?' You shall say to your son, 'We were slaves to Pharaoh in Egypt and the Lord freed us from Egypt with a mighty hand',"[11] and ratified by the Mishnah's dictum, "According to the child's intelligence, his father instructs him,"[12] Jewish tradition over the centuries has augmented the narration of the Exodus well-beyond its biblical-rabbinic *loci classici*,[13] but in the full spirit of the Mishnaic mandate, "Begin with disgrace and end with glory."[14]

The manual incorporating the collection of teachings, which became the primary text of the Passover evening Seder, is ceremoniously titled, **Haggadah shel Pesah** ("Narration of Passover").[15] It contains biblical quotations, talmudic and midrashic explorations, prayers and benedictions, legends and table songs, and guidelines for the ritual performance. The narrative is told in a three-fold sequence: Past, present, future. The "past" comprises the manner of Israel's descent into Egypt, subjugation into slavery, divine deliverance, and chosen-choosing status of Israel to be bearers of God's moral teaching. The "future" praises God for having sustained Israel but it also petitions Him to bring about the rebuilding of the Third Temple in Jerusalem, the symbol of the ingathering of the exiles and a restored mankind. The "present" is blocs of thought patterns reflecting the fluid, constantly changing life of the Jewish society as it understands redemption in accordance with concessions to history.

The Passover in history has evolved from the essential meaning of freedom to the serious lesson of Jewish self-identity and survival. Passover night has become an open-ended forum in which participants anchored in literature, folklore, religion, history and current events contemplate contemporary reality and debate the merits of ideal redemption. By so doing, they enter into sacred tones and a timeless pathos that give meaning and value to past (temporal slavery) and future (eschatological redemption), while idealizing the present moment as both afflicted and hopeful. This paradox may explain why the antithesis of the Passover message, the Shoah, is for many a fundamental part of the post-World War II Seder and challenging the Jewish community to create, define and rethink itself.

II. The Pardigmatic Order

Our attempt to evaluate the place of Shoah memory within the Passover ritual is precluded on acquaintance with a number of Seder legalisms and customs.

The Four Cups
There are a number of rabbinical explanations to explain the obligatory Four Cups, which are imbibed interspersedly throughout the Seder, but the dominant one is that they symbolize the four verbs of freedom mentioned in Exod 6:6-7:

> Wherefore say unto the Children of Israel: I am the
> Lord, and I will *free* you from under the burdens of the
> Egyptians, and I will *deliver* you from their bondage,
> and I will *redeem* you with an outstretched arm, and

with great judgments; and I will *take* you to Me for a people, and I will be to you a God.

Yet a fifth verb is stated in verse 8: "I will *bring* you into the land which I swore to give to Abraham, Isaac, and Jacob, and I will give it to you for a possession (*morashah*), I the Lord." However, the presence of Rome in Eretz Israel, seen by the Rabbis to be a compromise of the divine promise of *morashah*, led to their decision to pour ceremoniously, but not to drink, the Fifth Cup. In the course of time, the Fifth Cup, symbol of the messianic redemption, and in rabbinical terms, no subjugation under foreign powers for the Jewish people in Eretz Israel, was named the Cup of Elijah, in honor of Elijah, the harbinger of messianic deliverance in Jewish folklore and tradition.

Night of Watching

"It was a Night of Watching unto the Lord for bringing them out from the land of Egypt; this same Night of Watching unto the Lord for all the Children of Israel throughout their generations" (Exod 12:42). This verse sums up the basic leitmotif of Passover: God alone redeemed Israel. The Sages interpreted the text in terms of *peshat* (exegesis) and midrash (eisegesis): By the former, the anniversary to remember the deliverance form Egypt is *Pesah* night, and, by the latter, many biblical miraculous events happened on Passover night and day.[16] Moreover, this night of vigil unto the Lord for all generations is understood in rabbinic lore to mean that the final redemption of the future will take place on this anniversary night. The old-new tradition of leaving the door unlocked on Passover night — a courageous action during the long night of exile in the lands of the Cross and Crescent — underscores surely that divine protection is strongly felt on this "Night of Watching."

Open Door

A number of suggestions have been offered to explain the "Open Door," following the Grace after Meals and before the recitation of the Hallel. Though reasonable, we find them non-persuasive.

1. An invitation to hospitality. An important Passover mitzvah since all Israelites are bidden to participate, remember and do. But hospitality is extended at the beginning of the Seder not at the end of the meal when all that remain on the table are the Fourth Cup and the Cup of Elijah.[17]

2. To discredit disinformation, viz., the blood of a Christian victim is used in the preparation of Passover foods (Matzah, wine) and ceremony. But surely in the Dark Ages, during periods of persecution, can the

powerless Jewish community shed light in an *open door* policy? Would not the claim of innocence become fodder for the mob and made mockery by Church-State authorities who delighted in teaching contempt about the Jewish Passover?[18] Besides, the proper moment to dispel this horrific charge is at the start of the service not after the meal when the culinary evidence is all gone.

3. Connecting Jewish households with one another. That is, the prophet Elijah, who travels from open door to open door and brings tidings from home to home, solidifies the world-wide Jewish community. Though this stance is romantically appealing, it suffers as an interpolation since the "Open Door" is very ancient but Elijah's travel is comparatively late. Further, Elijah (name, cup, voyage) is implied in the Seder ritual; he is not mentioned outright in many historical Haggadah editions.

The custom of the "Open Door"? Probably not for mundane reasons of generosity, antisemitism, nor unity but rather for the mystical exercise of experiencing God's presence and salvific role on this "Night of Watching."

Blood Libel

One of the most hideous slanders directed against the Jews by medieval Christians is the accusation that Jews kill Christian children and partake of their blood in the Passover holiday. First associated with the death of a boy, William of Norwich (1144),[19] during the decade of the Second Crusades, and connected with the Crusaders' cry, "Kill a Jew and save your soul," this myth was strengthened by numerous charges in the 13th century, and has continued down to this day, primarily in anti-Israel propaganda.

The prominent place given to blood in biblical covenantal,[20] paschal,[21] and atonement[22] law vanished in rabbinic Judaism with the destruction of the Second Temple but assumed new form in the Apostolic Writings, with Jesus as the sacrificial Lamb of God, whose pouring of blood is linked eternally to atonement for sin. This is suggested by the words of Jesus at the Last Supper, "This is my blood of the covenant which is poured out for many for the forgiveness of sins,"[23] words which have empowered Christian tradition to transform his passion into a redeeming sacrament of central importance.

To Jews, blood is the symbol for the veneration of life and because life resides in the blood, for that reason is its consumption prohibited:

> It shall be a perpetual statue throughout your
> generations in all your dwellings that you shall
> eat neither fat nor blood.

(Lev 3:17)

You shall eat no manner of blood, whether it be
fowl or of beast in any of your dwellings. Anyone
who eats blood shall be cut off from his kin.

(Lev 7: 26-27)

Therefore, I said unto the Children of Israel:
No soul of you shall eat blood, neither shall
any stranger that sojourns among you eat blood.

(Lev 17:12)

Make sure that you do not partake of the blood;
for the blood is the life, and you must not consume
the life with the flesh. You must not partake of it;
you must pour it out on the ground like water.

(Deut 12:23-24)

The act of draining the blood is a symbolic recognition that all life is
sacred, including the life of animals we kill for the sake of sustenance and
self-defence.[24]

The repulsion of Jews to drinking blood, for sacramental and/or
worldly reasons, was well known to medieval Christian authorities and
this explains the Papacy's frequent denunciation of this libel, even as ritual
murder accusations were vigorously supported by local church authorities.
Why then such a strong, persistent caricature?

In the literalist folk tradition of Christians, Jesus is seen as the
embodiment of the Jewish people; meaning, the commandments of God to
bibilical Israel are fulfilled in the acceptance of Christ by the "New Israel."
Accordingly, Jesus' words are perceived as Jewish words, and what they
say is what Jews believe. Thus,"Jesus said unto them (Jews), 'I tell you the
truth, unless you eat the flesh of the Son of Man and drink his blood, you
have no life in you,'"[25] suggest that Jews devour flesh and blood in their
attempt at divine reconciliation. By identifying the Crucifixion of Jesus
with Passover day, the potential for blood libel is born and made manifest
in historical Christian catechesis which teach the idea of collective Jewish
guilt in the death of Jesus.

The reversal of this misfortunate libel is exhibited in more recent
Church statements. When the Second Vatican Council repudiated the
charge of Jewish deicide (1964-1965), and advocated the excommunication of any Catholic prelate who continues to teach this falsity, the

Congregation of Rites issued its finding that Simon of Trent, allegedly murdered in 1475 for Passover celebration, was killed by non-Jews. It is to be hoped that the decree banning further veneration of young Simon be converted into compassion for all innocent victims of blood libel and that the thinking which lay behind these absurdities be lay to rest forever.

"Pour Out Thy Wrath"

One of the most enigmatic passages in the Passover Haggadah is the *Shefok Hamatka/* "Pour Out Thy Wrath."[26] It is recited immediately after the Grace after Meals and the blessing over the Third Cup, in the presence of the Cup of Elijah, and before the pouring of the Fourth Cup. Many Haggadot are incorrect in suggesting that its *Sitz-im-Leben* is an imprecation directed to the levelers of the blood libel, who smuggled dead children into Jewish homes at Passover time, and then "discovered" the crime when the door opened for Elijah's visit. Rather the original intent of this curse, as expressed in Jer 10:25, Ps 79:6-7 and linked to Ps 115, which follows it in the Passover service, is a polemic against heathen nations who insist that God's essence is diminished when Israel appears to be abandoned by Him (i.e., the destruction of the Temple and the Exile). The thought conveyed is that Israel, downtrodden and dispersed, put her trust in God, maker of heaven and earth. For He, not the helplessness of idols, upholds the righteous and "at His wrath the earth trembles, and the nations (who) are not able to abide His indignation" will proclaim "the Lord God (as) the true God . . . the living God, and the everlasting King."[27]

The medieval counterpart to the heathen who knew not God and destroyed His Temple are the civilizations which believe in Creation, and in the Exodus, and in the moral teachings of Sinai, and still "devour Jacob and lay waste his habitation." Under the stress of persecution by Christians and Moslems, during the period of the Crusades, the powerless, wandering Jew denied the rival monotheistic claims that he is cursed by God and man, and invoked the Judge-of-all-the-Earth to deal justly with the nations of the World as He continuously does with Israel (classical Jewish apologia for Jewish suffering), so that the complete messianic fulfillment of the future, a universal siblinghood inspired by the Torah way, be realized in our day.

This is not poor theology, as some have argued, but a significant Jewish understanding of *Heilsgeschichte*: Justice, righteousness, and mutual respect usher in the Great Redemption for Israel and the World.[28]

Elijah the Prophet

In the ninth pre-Christian century there walked in Israel an upright, fearless, uncompromising figure, zealous in the pursuit of righteousness and in the service of God. Scriptures identifies him as Elijah the Tishbite

(I Kgs 17:1) and Tradition calls him, Elijah Ha-Navi, Elijah *the* prophet.

The original traditions concerning Elijah are found in I Kings 17 to II Kings 2, interspersed with the story of his disciple, Elisha. The Elijah narrative is full of miraculous elements and this, coupled with signs of later editing, makes it difficult to be confident about the historical role of Elijah. Scholars, however, do not doubt that he was part of the ninth century prophetic activity which was constantly hostile to the kings of the northern kingdom of Israel, particularly when the latter attempted to set up dynastic succession or became involved in the religious idolatrous practices of the surrounding countries.

Periodic famines, brought on in part by the sins of Israel (I Kgs 17:1; 18:18), play a central role in the Elijah narrative. The food shortage of this period is indicated by Elijah being fed by ravens (I Kgs 17: 2-7); by the scanty oil and meat supply of the Zarephath widow (I Kgs 17: 8-16); and by King Ahab and his court official Obadiah looking for pasture land to keep horses and mules alive. Also, the dramatic context between Elijah and the prophets of Baal on Mt. Carmel to determine the true God (I Kgs 18:20-40), ended much theological uncertainty among the people (I Kgs 18: 24, 39) and the conclusion of the drought (I Kgs 18:41-45).

This checking of the Phoenician Baal worship in Israel was a blow to immorality, projected the priority of God over all the other gods, and was an important step to strengthening monotheism in Israel.

Around the drought sequence have been woven miraculous stories — the meal and oil which never diminished, the raising of the widow's son, the calling of fire from heaven, and the crossing of the Jordan dry-shod.

The historical value of these miracles will be differently assessed in accordance with one's presuppositions about the miraculous. Yet, Elijah emerges as the determination of the old order in Israel, loyal to its God and the traditions that it had received, not to give in to compromise, assimilation, and state absolutism. Here, above all, the Elijah tradition is in full harmony with that of the later "rational" and writing prophets of Israel.

Having said this, however, the Elijah character is sketched in larger than human terms. For example, at Mt. Horeb, Elijah relived some of the cosmic experiences which had attended the original theophany of Moses about four centuries earlier (Exod 3:1 ff.). To the mosaic Torah was added the still small voice that followed the storm, earthquake and fire (I Kgs 19:9-14). Thus the historic process of the revelation of God for matters of conduct was carried from fixed laws applicable to a simple agrarian state into the more complex forms of society through the direct revelation which the individual could receive from God.

Elijah's special role in Jewish law and lore is guaranteed by his Moses-like theophany at Horeb. And his later assumption into heaven (II

Kgs 2:1, 11) equally secures his place in Jewish legend.

Talmudic tradition continues the full-blown image of Elijah portrayed in the Book of Kings and further embellishes his role as wonder worker, faith healer, and spokesman of God. Some of the tales are stories of daring-do; some are humble, and homely tales. Other tales speak of Elijah as the saint of those in need and the nation's savior. It is he who visits at every circumcision, as he will at the end of days, and announce the Messiah.

The medieval Kabbalists of Eretz Israel, following rabbinic lore, believed that the Sabbath was a foretaste of the World to Come. Each Saturday night when the Sabbath was turning into secular time, they sought to summon Elijah that he might save them from the bitterness of daily life. Their song, *Elijah the Prophet*, like *Come, My Beloved*, sung at the inauguration of the Sabbath, became a mainstay in the liturgical folk song of Shabbat.

Elijah left no written record. His story represents popular oral tradition about him passed on for a few decades before being composed by a member of the prophetic school founded by him and Elisha (I Kgs 19:19; II Kgs 21:15). There is no biblical tradition connecting him to Passover. Yet on Seder night Jews prepare a place for Elijah and pour a Fifth Cup — the Cup of Elijah — in his behalf. But what is the connection between this prophet of unconventional appearance and dress (II Kgs 1:8), rugged constitution (I Kgs 19:8), cave dwelling habits (I Kgs 17:3; 19:9), and the warmth of a sit-down, home-oriented Seder meal and ritual? Here are some ideas:

1. Elijah is the patron saint of home and family (the Seder embraces both), and the harbinger of peace and good will; and he is so acknowledged in the Grace after Meals.[29]

2. Passover celebrates freedom from "the bread of affliction" and consecrates hope for "all who are hungry." Elijah personifies freedom and hope.

3. Elijah ever jealous for the Lord accused the Children of Israel of forsaking His covenant. By choosing to do Passover (and the other rites of Judaism properly), Jews show that they have been falsely accused (I Kgs 19:14). They invite Elijah into their homes to witness that they do the Commandments in order to understand the Commander (*na'aseh ve-nishma*'; Exod 24:7). They choose life and not death.[30]

4. Passover Week has evolved into a week of fatal memories caused by vicious past anti-Jewish violence: Blood Libels, Easter pogroms, Inquisition, Warsaw Ghetto. At the start of "Our Season of Freedom," Jews remember their martyrs and heroes, fallen victims of crescent, straight cross, and crooked cross.[31] They open the door to greet Elijah and recite the verses of "Pour Out Thy Wrath." Additionally, present-day

physical attacks and vitriolic antisemitism directed against Jews everywhere, salient by-product of rising nationalism in eastern and central Europe and religious fanaticism in East Jerusalem and Judea-Samaria, and coupled with United Nations charges that Israeli policy in the West Bank is "oppressive" and a major factor for a "justified" Palestinian uprising, beckons the Seder loyalist to recall the Naboth incident.

Naboth, a hard-working vintner, owned a fine orchard ("the inheritance of my fathers") next to the royal lands, which King Ahab and Queen Jezebel coveted (I Kgs 21). The royal couple falsely accused him of treason. He was convicted on perjured evidence and executed. The land of the rightful owner was then confiscated by the authority of the State. But an angry Elijah confronted the king and charged: *Haraṣahta ve-gam Yarashta?/"Has thou murdered and taken possession"?* (I Kgs 21:19)

The clear message of the Elijah ultimatum — hidden in the words, "Has thou murdered and taken possession" — within the Seder's empirical and symbolic forms, is the design of a future society, integrated and supported by the full power of justice. It is rooted in the bedrock of prophetic Judaism: "Nation shall not lift up sword against nation, neither shall they learn war no more" (Isa 2:4; Mic 4:3).

III. The Paradoxical Order

In the main, the pageantry of the Passover Seder focuses on two periods of Jewish history: The biblical Exodus from Egypt and the rabbinic retelling of the account. Through ritual food, drink and animated reading and interpretation, the participant travels with the Children of Israel as if "s/he came forth out of Egypt," and sits at the table of the Rabbis as they observe Passover in Jerusalem. Alas, the forty-year trek into freedom succumbed in Jewish history into a long night's journey into exile. "Begin with disgrace and end with glory."[32] That is to say, talk openly and informatively about exilic degradation and destruction, so that, in contrast, the moment of Jewish freedom and triumph are cherished and appreciated. Therefore, it is expected, nay mandated, that the greatest tragedy of the Jewish Night, the Shoah, be recounted on the night that accentuates Jewish being.

Having said this, several questions arise immediately. Where is the Shoah inserted, beginning, middle or end of the Seder ceremony? Does not the message of Hell on Earth compromise the theme of redemption from Heaven? By reading the Shoah into the Haggadah, are we not turning the Jewish genocide into a (paschal) sacrifice, making it a "biblical" event rather than an event of our own time? Further, does not the Shoah have its own process of memorialization; why recall it at a time when *Yom*

HaShoah is commemorated less than two weeks later?

In answer to these non-traditional Passover questions, we recognize that Jewish history is reflected in the Haggadah and that affliction and suffering are transmitted in past, present and future paradigms: Ten Plagues, "In every generation they stand up to destroy us," and "Pour Out Thy Wrath," respectfully. The Shoah is not counted in the Ten Plagues because they represent a fixed Pentateuchal event, which the Torah sees as a condemation of Pharaoh and his advisors, not the Egyptian people.[33] "Thou shall not abhor the Egyptian," [34] is the cause of the tempered joy on Passover evening, that is, sprinkling from the Second Cup when the Ten Plagues are computed, and by omitting Pss 115 and 116 from the "Egyptian Hallel" (Pss 113-118), during the last six days of Passover. In contrast, the Shoah was designed by the Nazi state, but its program of Judeocide was carried out willingly by ordinary men and women. Further, to paint the victimization of the Shoah like that of Egyptian slavery in compassionate hues is absurd and obscene.

Two notable places in the Haggadah are conducive for a homiletical commentary on the Shoah: "In every generation they stand up against us to destroy us," and "Go forth and learn" the evil ways of Laban, the Aramean, and Pharaoh. These two back-to-back paragraphs speak of death to the Jews in a world that Jews continue to inhabit. But what if that realized society is destroyed forever, memory of it no longer rational but mystical, its sharers no longer people but numbers and ashes? Unlike coeval genocidal ethnic cleansing, the events which form the subject matter of the Shoah defy philosophical and academic explanation of their causes.[35] "The witness feels . . . duty bound to declare: . . . You may think you know how the victims lived and died but you do not. Auschwitz cannot be explained nor can it be visualized. Whether culmination or aberration of history, the Holocaust transcends history. Everything about it inspires fear and leads to despair; the dead are in possession of a secret that we, the living, are neither worthy of recovering."[36] The survivor's sentiment is clear: Though the Shoah happened in history, the difficulties its legacy poses are not explainable by any past-present event, and it will take mankind centuries, if ever, to unravel its arresting message.

The idea of the Shoah as continuance may well explain why it is addressed in the second part ("future") of the service. Above, in reference to the Four Cups, we spoke about the midrashic understanding that the Cups represent acts of freedom. In the ritual arrangement of the Seder, therefore, the Cups are the matrix around which the redemptive memories are spun: Cup One, the *Kiddush*, festival benediction of blessing and joy; Cup Two, in honor of God, the Redeemer of Jewish history; Cup Three, an abbreviated *Kiddush* for the benefit of latecomers, at the transition between the first and second part of the service; Cup Four, the acknowledgment of the Passover of the Future. The Third Cup follows the Grace after Meals sans narrative accompaniment. Then a special cup, the Cup of Elijah, is filled to overflowing and the door is opened and the "Pour Out Thy Wrath" passage is recited. After the door is closed, the Fourth Cup is filled, and the "Egyptian Hallel,"[37] "The Great Hallel,"[38] and the "Benediction of Song"[39] are chanted. Finally, the Fourth Cup is drunk at the close of the Passover Seder.

At many Seders, at the point of the Open Door and the Cup of Elijah, when the malediction against idolatry and antisemitism is pronounced, a requiem for the Six Million who perished in the Shoah is added. Its designation here is noteworthy: The Shoah is grounded in the antisemetic history of Church and State, which gave it birth, and its *sui generis* must be taken as emblematic. If the Shoah is seen as the unbearable past that bears inexplicably in the living then it must be made explicable how the enslavement of the powerless came about, how this functioned into the murder of the innocents, so that all can learn the universal message of the Shoah, that is, what all people are capable of doing and what all people are capable of suffering. Then can we speak of the end of maledictory history and the dawning of the messianic epoch.

This message cannot be overstated. The world must never forget the murdered Jewish people and that active participants and bystanders alike contributed to the Final Solution. Though killing fields may never cease in the land, we must never again tolerate genocidal activity towards any group in any place at any time. The Third Cup is history, and the Fourth Cup illuminates a revolutionary age of crumbling differences and indifference and of identifying the interdependence of mankind based on the belief in the oneness of God and acting morally as one humanity.

The discerning reader will observe that the addendum of the Shoah produces no formidable content change neither in the Seder nor in the traditional Haggadah. No additional food, drink or halachic reading. Maybe a short reading or song in association with the medieval "Pour Out Thy Wrath," but the Open Door refers to the "Night of Watching" and the Cup of Elijah signifies the ingathering of the exiles.[40] We suggest that the reasons for the lacuna are paradoxical and pragmatic:

• The message of Passover is Liberation and the medium for conveying that message is the Written and Oral Torah from Sinai; the message of Shoah is Annihilation carried away in the fumes of cyanide.

• Passover represents providential design in history but Shoah evolved from history. In Jewish Halachah, the latter, however meaningful, may not trample on the former. To challenge, yes; but to obliterate, no.

• God as Deliverer of the Passover is overpowering, and messengers, such as, Moses and Elijah, are implied and anticipated but never made full-blown. In contrast, God's presence during the Shoah is disturbingly silent, but may this not suggest that surviving *di milhomeh yohrn* requires more than God and Tradition; the Jews themselves have to want it. If they do not permit the memory of the Judeocide to destroy their morals or their own sense of destiny, then they, like Elijah the prophet, can traverse past and future, temporal and eternal, and bring Heaven down to Earth:

> Behold I am sending My messenger (*malachi*) to clear the way before Me, and the Lord whom you seek shall come to His Temple suddenly. As for the angel of the covenant[41] that you desire, he is already coming...
> Be mindful of the Teaching of my servant Moses, whom I charged at Horeb (Sinai) with laws and rules for all Israel. Lo I will send the Prophet Elijah to you before the coming of the awesome, fearful day of the Lord. He shall reconcile fathers with sons and sons with fathers
> (Mal 3:1, 22-24a)

The failure not to act and take responsibility for their own actions and ultimate redemption — i.e., "lest I come and smite the land with utter destruction"[42] — is unthinkable.

• Indeed the agenda to act Jewishly is contained in the Haggadah. According to the tradition of Rabbi Judah ben Bezalel, the Maharal of Prague (c. 1525-1609),[43] one reads the "Great Hallel" with the Fifth Cup in hand, and in testimony to the passage, "Who remembered us in our low estate and has delivered us from our adversaries,"[44] one drinks from it. So, in our day, drinking from the Cup of Elijah testifies to "the land (He gave) for a heritage unto Israel."[45] By filling the Cup of Elijah and then opening the door for the curse against destroyers of Jews, are Jews not linking Auschwitz to Jerusalem? Not in terms of cause and effect but in the proposition that rebuilding Zion sustains Jews in their anguished lost of a vanished Jewry and also sends forth a clear "Never Again" to a recurrence of the European *Churban*.

Why Shoah on Passover night? Some argue because on the eve of Passover 5703 (April 19, 1943), the Warsaw Ghetto uprising began. Others suggest that the Shoah is part of the malediction against antisemitism. And some challenge God, on this Night of Vigil, to make expiation for the massacred innocent millions. But, it can also be said that Passover, concerned with the eternal idea of Liberation, cannot ignore the threat posed to that ideal: The Shoah.

As a religious institution, Passover crosses generation, gender and cultural lines and invites all to participate in its narrative of freedom and its act of liberation. Its table drama, the Seder, has evolved into a forum on right and wrong, enslavement and empowerment, equality and inequality. Passover is thus both a feast of redemption and a memorial; its intrinsic value system provides an excellent pedagogic tool in teaching basic values and recording the sacrifice made and the vigilance necessary in the triumph of moral victory.

Shoah on Passover? Because the legacy of remembrance is the underbelly of Freedom.

Endnotes

1. *Erev rav*. Exod 12:38, but Neh 13:3, speaks of the separation of the alien admixture from Israel.
2. Exod 19-20; Deut 5.
3. Lev 23: 10-15.
4. Cited in Joseph H. Hertz, Editor, **The Pentateuch and Haftorahs With Hebrew Text, English Translation, and Commentary** (London: Soncino Press, 1966, Second Edition), p. 521.
5. Exod 34:22; Num 28:26; Deut 16: 9-10, 16; 2 Chr 8:13. Also, in the Apocrypha book, Tobit 2:1, "... in the feast of Pentecost, which is the holy feast of the seven weeks."
6. The phrase in rabbinic tradition, *Zeman Matan Torahteinu* ("The Season of the Law-Giving"). In accordance with the tradition of the "Seven Weeks," the Israelites assembled at the foot of Mount Sinai, when the Ten Words (Decalogue) were proclaimed by God, on *Sivan 6*.
7. Num 28:26; the feast is called "Feast of Harvest" (*Hag ha-Kazir*) in Exod 23:16. On the offering of Pentecostal first fruits, see, Exod 23:19, 34: 22, 26; Lev 23: 17, 20; Num 18:13; Deut 26:2; Ezek 44:30; Neh 10:36, 13:31.
8. Likewise in Christain tradition. Easter Sunday celebrates the Resurrection of the Body, and seven weeks later on the fiftieth day, the Descent of the Holy Ghost upon the Apostles is reported (Acts 2:1). In the Nicene cannons (can. 20), the Paschal time between Easter and Whitsunday is called "Pentecost." The Jewish religious influence on the Easter faith is uncontested.
9. Baruch M. Bokser, **The Origins of the Seder: The Passover Rite and Early Rabbinic Judaism** (Berkely, Los Angeles, London: University of California Press, 1984).
10. Zev Garber, "Interpretation and the Passover Haggadah; An Invitation to Post-Biblical Historiosophy," *BHHE*, Vol. 2.2 (Spring 1988),

pp. 27-28. The article is reprinted in Duane L. Christensen, ed., **Experiencing the Exodus form Egypt** (Oakland: Bibal Press, 1988), pp. 51-60.

11. Deut 6:20-21. Cf. Exod 12: 26f., 13: 8, 14.

12. m. Pesahim 10.4.

13. Exod 12, m. Pesahim 10, Tosefta Pesahim (*Pisha*) 10.

14. m. Pesahim 10.4.

15. For a full bibliography of the printed Haggadah, see A. Yaari, **Bibliography of the Passover Haggadah from the Earliest Printed Editions to 1960** (Hebrew; Jerusalem, 1960), and the Addenta by N. Ben-Menahem, A.M. Habermann and T. Wiener, cited in Yosef Hayim Yerushalmi, **Haggadah and History** (Philadelphia: JPSA, 1975), p. 489. Yerushalmi's volume is a wonderful, aesthetically pleasant examination of the Haggadah as a reflection of Jewish history, from the end of the fifteenth century to the present. Two hundred facsimile plates and description accompany the text.

16. This thought is emphasized in the supplementary hymns of the Seder service: On the first night, "And it Came to Pass at Midnight" (*va-Yehi ba-Hazot ha-Laylah*) and on the seond night, "It is the Sacrifice of the Passover" (*Zevah Pesah*).

17. Recited by the Maggid (narrator) in the vernacular (Aramaic): "Let all who are hungry enter and eat; let all who are needy come to our Passover feast."

18. Consider, for example, the Council of Nicaea (325 C.E.), which established the date of Easter to fall on the first Sunday following the first full moon of the Spring season, and not by the date of the Jewish Passover (the traditional Last Supper): " ... it appears an unworthy thing that in the celebration of this most holy feast (Easter) we should follow the practice of the Jews, who have impiously defiled the hands with enormous sins (the killing of Christ), and are, therefore, deservedly afflicted with blindness of the soul. For we have it in our power, if we abandon their custom, to prolong the due observance of this ordinance to future ages, by a truer order, which we have preserved from the very day of the Passion until the present time... Let us then have nothing in common with the detestable Jewish crowd." Cited in Jacob R. Marcus, ed., **The Jew in the Medieval World** (Cleveland, New York, Philadelphia: Meridian Books and JPSA, 1961), p. 105.

19. The alleged crime is reported in **The Life and Miracles of St. William of Norwich**, written by a Benedictine Monk, Thomas of Monmouth, circa 1173.

20. "And he (Moses) took the book of the covenant, and read it in the

hearing of the people; and they said: 'All that the Lord has spoken we will do and obey.' And Moses took the blood, and sprinkled it on the people, and said: 'Behold the blood of the covenant, which the Lord had made with you in agreement with all these words'" (Exod 24:8-9). Consider, too, the "blood of circumcision" required by native born (Josh 5:1-11) and stranger (Exod 12:43-51) alike in the fulfillment of the Passover.

21. Exod 12:13, 22-23.

22. "For the life of the flesh is in the blood; and I have given it to you upon the altar to make atonement for your souls; for it is the blood that makes atonement by reason of the life" (Lev 17:11).

23. Matt 26:28; Mark 14:24. An earlier account records, "This cup is the new covenant in my blood" (Cor 11:25).

24. Judaism's first negative commandment, viz., the prohibition against murder and suicide, is linked with the dietary restriction of not consuming the blood of an animal (Gen 9:4-6). These sentences have become the basis of the ritual slaughter of animals (*Shechita*) and the core of the rabbinic eisegesis of God's covenant with Noah (gentile nations). On the latter, see D. Novak, **The Image of the Non-Jew in Judaism: An Historical and Constructive Study of the Noahide Laws** (New York and Toronto: The Edward Mellen Press, 1973).

25. Repeated four times in John 6:53-56. It is a key biblical sentence in the Lateran Council of 1215 doctrine of Transubstantiation, the Catholic theology of the Eucharist, which affirms the conversion of the breadness and wineness into the Body and Blood of Christ, with only the accidents (appearance) of the bread and wine remaining.

26. In various Haggadot, many different sentences, particularly from Psalms, comprise the *Shefok Hamatka* paragraph. However, in the course of time, three biblical verses previaled: Ps 79:6-7 (equals Jer 10:25, with a slight variation), Ps 69:25 and Lam 3:66. On the differences among Ashkenazim and Sepharadim in the liturgical use of *Shefok Hamatka*, see E.D. Goldschmidt, **The Passover Haggadah, Its Sources and History** (Jerusalem: Bialik Institute, 1969), pp. 61-64 (Hebrew).

27. Jer 10:10b-a.

28. This paragraph and the preceding one are taken from my paper, "Night Encounters: Theologizing Dialogue," presented at the 23rd Annual Scholars' Conference on the Holocaust and German Church Struggle (University of Tulsa, March 1993). See further, pp. 155-169.

29. "May the All-merciful send us Elijah the prophet (let him be remembered for good), who shall bring us good tidings, salvation and consolation."

30. Dramatically demonstrated at the birth of a male child: Elijah is sponsor of the child at circumcision, and he is honored by a precedng *Sholem Zokher*, a traditional home or synagogue ritual held on the first Friday evening after the birth of a boy. The origin of the *Sholem Zokher* is probably the talmudic dictate, "If a boy is born, peace comes to the world" (Nid 31b), but in folklore, this custom is seen as a consolation to the Torah taught in heaven and now lost at the child's birth. In some communities, this ceremony is also called *Yeshu'at ha-Ben*, *Shevu'at ha-Ben*, or *Ben Zakhar*. Regarding the latter, the *Ben Zakhar* is a rejection of the Prophet Jeremiah's vehement regret that he was ever born: "Cursed be the day that I was born! Let not the day be blessed when my mother bore me! Cursed be the man who brought my father the news, and said, 'a man-child (*Ben Zakhar*) is born unto you,' and gave him such joy" (Jer 20:14-15; see also, Jer 15:10).

31. Characteristic of modern Haggadot instruction and readings. Traditional biblical verses of mourning, readings from the elegies of Kalonymous ben Judah (11th century), the Zionide poems of Judah Halevi (c. 1075-1141), and the songs of H.N. Bialik and Shaul Tschernichowsky, pertaining to 20th century pogroms and destruction, are common fare in Haggadot published by the (secular) Kibbutz movement. On this, see A. Reich, **Changes and Developments in the Passover Haggadot of the Kibbutz Movement** (Unpublished Ph.D., University of Texas at Austin, 1972).

32. m. Pesahim 10.4.

33. Exod 3:22a, 12:36b: "You shall save the Egyptians," meaning, individual acts of Egyptian kindness and reparations clear the Egyptian name and vindicate their humanity.

34. Deut 23:8.

35. Adroitly argued by Charles Krauthammer, "Holocaust: Memory And Rescue," *Time*, May 3, 1993, p. 84.

36. Elie Wiesel, *New York Times*, April 16, 1978, from his review of the T.V. mini-series, *Holocaust*, presented on NBC television in April 1978.

37. Hymns of praise consisting of Pss 113-118, which sing of the greatness of God, His deliverance, and the ultimate hope that all nations will be united in the pure worship of God. The name, "Egyptian Hallel," is associated with Ps 114, which speaks of the marvels of the Exodus. Pss 113 and 114 are recited before the meal and Pss 114-118 are chanted after the Fourth Cup is poured.

38. The talmudic term for Ps 136 (Ber. 4b; Pesah. 118a; m. Ta'anit 3.9). This Psalm is called "the Great Hallel" because its opening line, "O

give thanks unto the Lord," is implied before most of the stanzas and "For His mercy endureth for ever," concludes all the strophes.

39. m. Pesahim 10.7 states: "The Fourth Cup is poured — (he) finishes the Hallel and says over it the *Birkat ha-Shir* ("The Blessing of the Song")." The Haggadah preserves several versions of the *Birkat ha-Shir*: R. Yehuda's choice, "Praise Thee , O Lord our God, Shall All Thy Works," which is recited at the conclusion of the "Egyptian Hallel," and the selection of R. Yohanan (Pesah 118a),"The Breath of Every Living Thing Shall Bless Thy Name, O Lord Our God," which immediately follows the chanting of "The Great Hallel." This prayer also concludes the Sabbath and festival *Pesukei de-Zimra* (Psalms and adorations before the"*Shema*' and its Blessings" section of the morning service).

40. The theme is well established in rabbinic lore:
    Cup One - "I will free - Egypt
    Cup Two - "I will deliver - Babylonia
    Cup Three - "I will redeem - Persia
    Cup Four - "I will take - Greece
    Cup Five - "I will bring - Rome (ongoing).

41. Or,"Messenger of the Covenant." A response to the previous sentence,"You have wearied the Lord with your words ...'Where is the God of Justice?'" (Mal 2:17). The generation of the Shoah can identify with this Malachian query when they see Evil seemingly prosper and aided by divine non-intervention.

42. Mal 3:24b.

43. Cf. Rabbi Menachem M. Kasher, **Israel Passover Haggadah** (New York: Sheingold Publishers, 1983), pp. 192, 204-205.

44. Ps 136:23-24.

45. Ps 136:21-22.

CHAPTER NINE

Night Encounters:
Theologizing Dialogue

At the Scholars' Conference, hosted by the University of Tulsa, my colleagues (Steven L. Jacobs, Henry F. Knight and James F. Moore) and I participated in a Conference first: We Jews and Christians read Scriptures together by the light of Shoah. My reading of Jacob at Jabbok (Gen 32:22-32) and Jesus at Gethsemane (Matt 26:36-46) is infused by the Hitlerian principle that Nazism is antisemitism and that antisemitism is anti-Christian and that supersessionist Christianity is anti-Judaism.

Our inquiry into Gen 32: 22-32 and Matt 26: 36-46 considers the methodology of the Old Rabbis as it was practiced during and shortly after the formative period of rabbinic Judaism. With humility bordering on *chutzpah*, we venture into the *PaRDeS* (paradise): *Peshat*, meaning of text as received; *Remez*, scriptural understanding bordering on the allegorical and philosophical; *Derash*, homiletic approach characterized by reading into the text; and *Sod*, esoteric inner and mystical meaning, existentially understood and applied.

GENESIS 32: 22-32

I. By Way of Introduction

More than the obedient Abraham and the frail Isaac, the figure of Jacob dominates Jewish ancestral traditions throughout the ages. History and fancy blend together in projecting Jacob as the patriarchal body and soul of the Jewish people, in whose personality and image the failures and successes, the dreams and reality, the curses and blessings of a parochial culture are portrayed in microcosm. To understand the Jewish people at any given juncture is to demythologize Jacob in accordance with the historical process and *Zeitgeist* of a given age and place. However, the timelessness of Jacob is anchored to personalities and events — sibling rivalry, flight, dream, theophanies, reconciliation, Laban, Esau, etc., are all part and parcel of imagining the historical Jacob and living his promise.

Among the events in Jacob's life that tradition assigns an influential role is the patriarch's wrestle with the "angel" at Peniel. The composite picture of Godwrestle at the ford of Jabbok suggested in Torah and *aggadah* involves little historical objectivity and much subjectivity. Overwhelmingly, the wrestle is portrayed in mythical categories, the role of which is to allow one to think constructively and imaginatively about what is not spelled out in history. Of course, the mythicization of history is found in all cultures and traditions. The American cowboy is a contemporary case in point.[1] By demythologizing the divine-human combat, one catches a glimpse of the biblical-rabbinic view of the Jew as victim-fighter-survivor. The historical imagination couched for the most part in symbolic allegory and metaphor can benefit contemporary discussion on the faults and merits of Christian-Jewish memory and responsibility after the Shoah. For it assumes an approach to group and individual feelings suggested in paradigms where the subjective spirit of the interpreter-transmitter is basic to the questions asked and the answers given by historians, theologians, and philosophers.

Aggadic sources embellish the theme of Jacob's encounter with man and Other presented in Genesis 32, 33. The Sages reflect their contemporary history and feelings into the figures of Jacob, Esau, and the unnamed combatant, and draw analogies between the biblical texts and current events, which set forth the agenda for Jewish survival after catastrophe.

Responding to the destruction of Jerusalem and the dispersion of the Jewish people during the Roman occupation of Eretz Israel, the Rabbis salvaged Judaism by placing it beyond time and history. They elevated Jewish values, practices and thought beyond the daily course of events — determined by Gentiles — to a timeless plane. After 70 C.E., in the rabbinic mind, Jews lived between the glories of the past and the messianic restoration to come — the future *Pardes*/Paradise, if you will. Contemporary events were noteworthy only insofar as they were foretold by past generations and/or gave clues about the coming redemption.

More specifically, the midrashic eisegesis on the Jabbok incident brings forth a rabbinic worldview of the non-Jewish world in successive periods: Rome's dominant presence in Eretz Israel followed by the Church's determined and dominant role in the Jewish Diaspora. The ahistorical response of the Sages: Survival with dignity now, survival with dignity then, with little change from the rabbinich epoch to the biblical period, and we may add, likewise to the post-Shoah age.

II. Biblical Exegesis and Rabbinical Eisegesis

Gen 32:25. "And Jacob was left alone (*levado*) ... until the breaking of the day." This is seen in conjunction with "There is none like God, O Jeshurun" (Deut 33:26). Read, "There is none like God *but* Jeshurun," which stands for the Patriarch Jacob and his descendants. In history, Israel dwells apart (*levadad*), not reckoned among the nations (Num 23:9), and God alone (*badad*) did guide him (Deut 33:12). And none but the Lord (*levado*) shall be exalted (Isa 2:11) in that "break of dawn" when Israel's subjugation to the Nations of the World will end.

Gen 32:26. "And when he saw that he prevailed not against him, he touched the hollow of his thigh; and the hollow of Jacob's thigh (*yerek*) was stained as he wrestled with him." Jacob is defeated at his thigh, the word can also mean "loins" (see Exod 1:15), the root of his enmity with his brother (Gen 25:26) and sisters-wives (Lev 18:18).

In rabbinic context, these sentiments are interpreted as the angel of Esau/Edom[2] (Peniel, the place of the wrestle — "for I have seen God face to face" [Gen 32:31] — is connected to Jacob being favorably received by his brother as "One (who) sees the face of God" [Gen 33:10]), that is to say, Esau/Edom which is Rome was unable to slay Jacob totally but managed "to touch" the righteous men, women, and children during the insurrection of the first and second centuries, and particularly, the Hadrianic persecution, 135-138, which followed the ill-fated Bar-Kochba rebellion, 133-135. In the fire of the Shoah, the "strained thigh" represents the murdered Six Million and their unborn generations and thousands of survivors who betray their ancestral faith and/or chose not to procreate future children of the covenant (*yerek*, a phallic symbol, is the site of the *Brit Milah*, Covenant of the Circumcision) due to the holocaustal experience. On the other hand, those who survived this great Kiddush Hashem and chose to live openly as Jews merit the reward of the lamed Jacob.

Gen 32:27. "And he said, 'let me go, for dawn is breaking.' But he answered, 'I will not let you go, unless you bless me.'" Since Jacob is asked to release his celestial opponent, it follows that the righteous are greater than angels. But Jacob demands a blessing as the price of release. Yet what blessing can Jacob demand from Esau/Edom, who in the rabbinic mind is a synonym for treachery, violence, oppression and injustice? The blessing, therefore, is a reconsideration of a past malediction: "(Esau) said, 'was he, then, named Jacob that he might supplant me (*'aqav*) these two times? First he took away my birthright and now he has taken away my blessing!'" (Gen 27:36). In light of history and the Shoah, when one-third of the Jewish people were murdered in the *Endlösung* by the Children of Edom, Jacob's Children have every reason to fear Esau, but they must also learn the *raison d'etre* of being Israel, to eternally hope and not to fear.

Gen 32:29. "And he said: 'Your name shall be called no more Jacob, but Israel; for you have striven with God and with men, and have prevailed.'"

No longer will Jacob attain the blessing by "supplanting" but as "fighter (*sarita*, connected with the first part of Israel) - with-God (*Elokim*, connected with second part of Israel)," who has earned the divine recognition to become the third patriarch of a people destined to fight "the battles of the Lord" (Num 21:14). In biblical idiom, *shem*/"name" means essence, and the new name removes the stain (curse) of Gen 27:36 (see above). This is a prologue to the incident at Beth-El, where God appeared to Jacob and blessed him and said: "'You whose name is Jacob, you shall be called Jacob no more, but Israel shall be your name.' Thus He named him Israel ... 'A nation, yea an assembly of nations, shall descend from you. Kings shall issue from your loins'" (Gen 35:10-11). Tradition understands this to be the kings of Judah and Israel, exilarchs in Babylonia, patriarchs in the Land of Israel, and the King Messiah.

Gen 32:30. "Jacob asked, 'Pray tell me your name.' But he said, 'You must not ask my name!' And he took leave of him there."[3] Angels have no set names; names change with the missions entrusted upon them (Rashi). Similarly, forces of destruction and antisemitism are everywhere and any where, and they are named only in the eye of the storm. Besides, the death of Jews in Nazi Europe are beyond human terminology and the power to recover from out of the whirlwind (Job 38:1, 40:6) resides in man and God and not in angels.

Gen 32: 32. "And the sun rose upon him." In the rabbinic mind, this is seen as an omen for the Children of Israel. Just as the sun has healed Jacob and burned Esau and his chiefs,[4] so will the sun heal the descendants of Jacob and scorch the Nations of the World. It will heal Israel in accordance with the verse, "unto you that bear My Name shall the sun of righteousness arise with healings in its wings" (Mal 3:20), but it will ignite the nations, as the verse states, "The day is at hand, it burns as a furnace. All the arrogant and all the doers of evil shall be straw, and the day that is coming — said the Lord of Hosts — shall burn them to ashes and leave them neither root nor branch" (Mal 3:19). Also, in Obadiah, we read, "And the house of Jacob a flame, and the house of Esau for stubble, and they shall kindle them, and devour them; And there shall not be any remaining of the house of Esau; for the Lord has spoken" (Obad v. 18).

By associating Edom with the teachings of *contra-Judaeos* found in Christendom, and evident in the *Voelkische Kulturreligion*, both Protestant and Roman Catholic of Nazi Europe, a post-Shoah theology is born that is intended to ease the Jewish holocaustal pain by suggesting that a day of vengeance exposing the sources of Nazi antisemitism and the Final Solution is at hand. And Christians and Jews in reconciliatory dialogue can ensure that victory is inevitable.

III. Angelophany: Three Faces

Michael

A number of midrashim[5] identify the combatant who injured Jacob as Michael, chief heavenly priest; he did the act voluntarily for the glory of God. The Lord reproached Michael for inflicting harm on "My first born son" (see Exod 4:22, "Israel is My son, my first born") by appointing him as the eternal guardian angel of Jacob and his seed unto the end of history.[6] On the other hand, Michael entreated with Jacob to let him go (Gen 32:27) since he feared the Angels of 'Arabot; they would consume him with fire if he did not start heavenly songs of praise at the proper time — day break. Jacob replied that Michael who blessed his father and grandfather should bless him too was met with a curt rejection: The servant, who was *not* sent by God, is subservient to the son. Under pressure, however, Michael conceded and took comfort in the thought if God yields to the wishes of Jacob's heirs, how then can he leave Jacob's wish unfulfilled. And he blessed him by saying, may the entire House of Israel be a pious as you are and may their contributions and choicest offerings of sacred things be accepted by the Lord God (see Ezek 20:40).

Jesus

What Jewish tradition ascribes to Michael is often transferred in the writings of the early Church Fathers to Jesus. It follows then that the struggle between the messenger and Jacob at Jabbok makes no sense unless it is seen as the future struggle between Christ and the Jews, which is said to reach its classic typology in the gospels. The fight at the river is seen as the contest in which the non-baptized Jews are forever lost in the ignorance of the night. The angel lost the wrestling bout voluntarily to signify the passion of Christ wherein the Jews overpowered him. Likewise, the nameless angel (Gen 32:30) — the name is not revealed since Jesus was not yet born in the flesh — gave a blessing, so also Jesus prayed for his executioners. Also, Jacob limped, and the Children of Israel do not cut the sinew of the thigh vein (Gen 32:33). This ritualistic act, which in the Jewish tradition is seen as a constant reminder of a people's providential origins, symbolizes in the Christian tradition eternal providential rejection. Another interpretation of Jacob's limping is that his two legs represent Jews and Christians, and the former will have a numbness concerning the grace of salvation. Finally, for others, the lamed Jacob represents the unbelieving Jews and the Jacob who sees "God face to face" (Gen 32:31) represents the true believers, Jews and Christians alike.

Combining the antiquity of Christian and Jewish views that the *'ish* who wrestled Jacob is Michael-Jesus, we are presented with several reinterpretations. First, Michael set out to destroy Jacob but in the end, he harmed and wounded him. Similarly, the Church, the Body of Christ, set out to tarnish the body of Jacob, which in the long nocturnal process has rendered immeasurably to the pain of the Jews as it lessened the value of Judaism in the theology of grace. Yet Michael was *not* charged by God to impair Jacob, and correspondingly, the Church's negative theologizing hermeneutic against the Jews is without a firm divine mandate. Second, Michael is viewed as the celestial choir master who cannot do his appointed task unless Jacob releases him and this is conditioned by the blessing offered. In like manner, can the Church continue in good conscience liturgy-as-usual without coming face-to-face with its participatory role (mainly as victimizer) in the genocidal night? The blessing requested is two-fold (in the spirit of Gen 32: 27, 30): Recognition and affirmation that the Chosen People has not been supplanted by the Chosen Church and knowledge that God's truth can never be tied to an eschatology of exclusive salvation. Renouncing supersessionism and antisemitism alike, and critically supporting Jewish survival, this sends forth a powerful stimulus for bringing on the Kingdom of Dawn.

In a post-Shoah age, the exigency of an injured Jacob to survive physically is an alliance with a supportive and protective Christianity; and the need of the Church to rectify morally bankrupt "truth-claims" is to connect Christocentrism with the historical development of Judaism, then and now.

Israel

The mystics of the geonic period speak of a *hayyah* (heavenly being) whose name is "Israel." This *hayyah's* function is to call the hosts of heaven to praise God's Name. He chants: "Blessed You the Lord who is to be blessed," and they reply, "Blessed is the Lord who is to be blessed for ever and ever."[7] In midrashic etymology, the name *Yisrael* in the text of Gen 32 posits four possibilities. The first affirms *'ish ra'ah El/* "one who sees God." The second states *yashir El/* "singing like angels." The third declares *shear El/* "the remnant of God," and the fourth proclaims *yashar El/* "he who walks straight with God." In calling the patriarch "Israel," may this not reflect the identity (*shem*) of the *'ish* (Yisrael= "warrior at the bequest of God") transferred now to Jacob? So interpreted, then Jacob's Godwrestling is in reality, self-wrestling.

In assessing the guilt of the Nazis, and the role of the Church and the nations in the most horrific crime directed against the Jewish people in history, the Jew must ask what role — or lack of role — did he play in the atrocities. What sin done, what punishment overturned, what signals ignored, what obligations unfulfilled?

In confronting the fire and sacrifice, one senses two faces of the victim of the Night struggle: *Yeshurun*, who walks straight, and *Ya'akov*, who walks crookedly. But the one named *Yeshurun* is "fat and gross and coarse — he forsook the God who made him and spurned the Rock of his support" (Deut 32: 15). Ingratitude to the Source of life and not caring or learning the lessons of annihilation will contribute to ongoing acts of perfidy. However, the one born *Ya'akov* earned the title "Israel" and his limp implies not lacking firmness or strength but represents that Jew who has confronted the holocaustal evil decrees of God and man and has prevailed (Gen 32:29). He is the true surviving remnant who knows that the Teaching given at Sinai, as "the heritage of the congregation of Jacob,"[8] to "choose life,"[9] is the antidote to the fumes of cyanide. This is the Jacob who can sing, "There is none like God, O Jeshurun, riding through the heavens to protect you, through the skies in His majesty" (Deut 33:26).

Jacob, weakened and yet made stronger in the crucible of the Shoah, is psychologically prepared to meet at the River the other streams of the Abrahamic faith in mutual dialogue and respect. Only the Jacob who can wrestle unabashedly with the curse of the Shoah can hope to emerge with the blessing of *Shalem* (Gen 33:7), totally whole and at peace with the struggle. He has seen the dark face of God and yet he walks upright, refusing to be downtrodden. He is the moral linchpin of Israel's great messianic hope — the dawning of God's kingdom over *Yeshurun*: "Then He became King in Jeshurun, when the heads of the people assembled, the tribes of Israel together" (Deut 33:5).

MATTHEW 26: 36-46

IV. Unending Seder

The encounter of the Patriarch Jacob and the *'ish* at the ford of Jabbok is often compared to the account about Jesus in Gethsemane (Matt 26: 36-46; and parallels in Mark 14: 32-42 and Luke 22: 40-46). The Night Words in both accounts are riddled with mystery, anxiety and ambiguity. Jesus, like Jacob, struggles on the eve of a dreadful crisis in solitude and pensive fear; and he is unsure what the dawn would bring. This uncertainty provides fertile ground for scriptural retrospection. How to respond to the indeterminate anguish of Jesus on the night that he was betrayed within a framework of Christian-Jewish dialogue after the Shoah is the intent of this section. What follows is a partisan view of Jesus in the garden read as part of the passion narrative according to the school of Matthew and qualified by the four cubits of the Halachah (Ber. 8a) — so justified since Matthew, unlike the other Synoptic Gospels, is recognized as a thoroughly Jewish account.

In context, the agony of Jesus is an extension of the narrative of the Last Supper, a Passover Seder meal, involving Jesus and his disciples (Matt 26: 26-29). Though there are halachic disparities with the Matthean Seder (e.g., Jesus blessing first the bread and then wine; at a festive meal, such as Passover, the rabbinic order is *Kiddush* [wine] and *Motzi* [bread]), especially, the Christological insertion, it is, however, traditionally informed with questions, interpretations and a concluding hymn. It is not clear from the text whether the hymn is one, several or all of Psalms 113-118 ("The Hallel [Praise] of Egypt"), which the Levites chanted during the offering of the paschal lamb (m. Pesah. V. 7) or Psalm 136 ("The Great Hallel"; Ber. 4b, Pesah. 118a, m. Ta'an. III. 9) is meant.

The formal Seder is extended to the Mount of Olives. "Then Jesus said to them, 'You will all fall away because of me this night; for it is written, 'I will strike the shepherd, and the sheep of the flock will be scattered'" (Zech 13:7).

Like the double-visaged god Janus, a Christological reading of Zech 13: 7,8 is not only concerned with the realized eschatology expressed at the ceremonial meal (Matt 26:29) and the agony of Jesus at Gethsemane (Matt 26: 36-46) but looks as well to the Shoah. Meaning, the shepherd, for Matthew, is Jesus, and the people who had rejected him will be scattered and will suffer the consequences.[10] And what may they be:

> I will turn My hand upon the little ones
> Throughout the land — declares the Lord —
> Two thirds therein shall perish, shall die,
> And one third of it shall survive.
> That third I will put into fire ...
>
> (Zech 13: 7b,8,9a)

Jewish commentators, however, view the shepherd as the perennial tyrannical antisemite, who will be punished for his oppression of Israel by the dispersion of his people. And the Jewish survivalist views the Shoah simile in terms of a purified surviving remnant:

> I will bring the third part through the fire,
> And will refine them as silver is refined,
> And will try them as gold is tried;
> They shall call on My Name,
> And I will answer them;
> I will say: 'It is My people,'
> And they shall say: 'The Lord is my God.'
> (Zech 13:9)

The anguish of spirit in the Gethsemane narrative implies images from the Hebrew Bible. The cup of suffering, for example, in Matt 26:30 recalls a charge to Jerusalem to awaken from the stupor of her cup of affliction and degradation (Isa 51:17,22); suggests that God doles out fire, brimstone and burning wind as the portion of the evil-doer's cup, i.e., they are instruments to demolish evil (Ps 11:6); and invokes God's cup of vengeance on Edom, who sided with Babylonia when Judah was conquered in 586 B.C.E. (Lam 4:21).

However, it is Jesus yearning for communion with God (Matt 26:39, 42,44) that is most inspired by a biblical prototype: The lament by one who is excluded from the Temple in Jerusalem. In Psalm 42, we read:

> My soul cries for You, O God (v. 2b)
> My soul thirsts for God, the living God;
> O when will I come to appear before God! (v.3).
> My tears have been my food day and night;
> I am even taunted with, "Where is your God?" (v.4).
> When I think of this, I pour out my soul (v. 5a)
> Why so downcast, my soul,
> Why disquieted within me (v. 6a)
> O my God, my soul is downcast (v. 7a)
> I say to God, my rock,
> "Why have you forgotten me,
> Why must I walk in gloom,
> Oppressed by my enemy?" (v. 10)
> Crushing my bones
> My foes revile me
> Taunting me always with, "Where is your God?" (v. 11)
> Why so downcast, my soul,
> Why disquieted within me? (v. 12a)

This is not merely a lament of levitical choristers cut off from divine service,[11] but a profound and striking image to Shoah theodicy: The predicament of the anathematized victim who feels further distressed when there is perceived divine silence to the enemy's taunt, "Where is thy God?"

If God is not limited in either power or benevolence, then why? Why the seeming apathy on the part of God, which gives succor to the destroyer. The meditative plaint of the Psalmist is the shattered faith of the survivor; "the unbearable reality that haunts sleep and destroys wakefulness."[12]

Yet festival sleep and not dreadful wakefulness overcame the disciples. On this "Night of Watching" (*Leyl Shemurin*),[13] Jesus' question to Peter, "Could you not watch with me one hour?" (Matt 26:40), a poignant concern which is also suggested in verses 43 and 45, graphically describes his state of abandonment. However, it is the seemingly silence of God (Matt 26:39, 42, 44) that affects Jesus so deeply that he feels emotional pain: "And being in agony, he prayed more earnestly; and his sweat became like great drops of blood falling down upon the ground" (Luke 22:44).[14] The strong language of sorrow is explained in Christian tradition as the recognition that physical death awaited Jesus and his bearing of human sins as well. Substitute the "Six Million" for "Jesus" and you have a core Christian and Jewish apology for the Shoah: "Theology of suffering" on the one hand and "birth pains of the Messiah" on the other explain why the crucifixion of the Jews[15] for the saving of humanity.

If the *Sitz-im-Leben* of the abandonment of Jesus is an extended Seder meal, as we argued, then the above apologia would not do. The proper parallel to his suffering and forsakeness is the *hopeful* refrain recited by Jews after the meal in expectation of deliverance. A closer look at the retelling of Passover in rabbinic tradition may explain why. In the biblical institution of the Passover, we read:

> It was for the Lord a Night of Watching
> to bring them (Israelites) out of the
> Land of Egypt; this same night is a
> Night of Watching unto the Lord for
> all the Children of Israel throughout
> their generations.
>
> (Exod 12:42)

The Rabbis interpreted this text and "It came to pass at midnight" (Exod 12:29) historiosophically, as was their custom. "Throughout their generations" marked the deliverance of their ancestors from the dangers that beseiged them. By microscopical examination of the biblical text, they found midrashic authority for suggesting that the whole succession of miraculous deliverances mentioned in the Bible, from the time of Laban

to that of Sennacherib occurred on Passover night (Num. Rab. XX.12).[16]
Similarly, the final deliverance of all generations, is to take place on
Passover eve, which is a true *Leyl Shemurin* unto the Lord for all
generations. Thus, the great tribulation of Jesus on that night of Passover
vigil when abandoned by his disciples, he experienced Godforsakeness,[17]
and this is echoed in the words at the cross: *"Eli, Eli lamah sabachtani,"*
meaning, "My God, my God, why has Thou forsaken me?" (Matt 27:46).

Yet one is saved from despair by placing invisible trust in the
Watchman of the Night. Consider the suffering Psalmist who rebukes his
moribund soul with the charge to trust the Lord:

> Why so downcast, my soul,
> Why disquieted within me?
> Have hope in God;
> I will yet praise Him
> for his saving presence
> > (Ps 42:6; repeated with
> > slight alteration in v. 12).

In like manner, Psalm 115, recited immediately after the Grace and
part of the "Hallel of Egypt" (Pss 113-118 which mirror future deliverance), is a call for national trust in God against the heathen who did not
believe in the wonders which God performed in Egypt and at Sinai. The
medieval counterpart to the heathen who knew not God and destroyed His
Temple are the civilizations who believe in Creation, and in the Exodus,
and in the moral teachings of Sinai, and still "devour Jacob and lay waste
his habitation." Under the stress of persecution by Christians and Moslems
during the period of the Crusades, the powerless, wandering Jew denied
the rival monotheistic claims that he is cursed by God and man, and
invoked the Deliverer to:

> Pour out Thy wrath upon the nations
> (Christianity, Islam) that know Thee not
> And upon the kingdoms that call not upon Thy Name
> For they have devoured Jacob (people), And
> Laid waste his habitation (Jerusalem).
> > (Ps 79: 6,7)

> Pour out Thine indignation upon them
> And let the fierceness of Thine anger
> Overtake them.
> > (Ps 69:25)

> Thou will pursue them in anger and
> Destroy them
> From Under the Heavens of the Lord.[18]
>
> (Lam 3:66)

The above reading should not be understood as an expression of vindictiveness toward the non-Jew — the Halachah instructs the Jew to pray continually for the welfare and success of kingdoms and ministers, and for all states and places in which he resides[19] — but should rather be interpreted as involking the Judge-of-all-the-Earth to deal justly with the Nations of the World as He continuously does with Israel (classical Jewish apologia for why Jewish suffering), so that the complete messianic fulfillment of the future, a universal siblinghood inspired by the Torah way, can be realized swiftly in our day. This is not poor theology, as some have argued, but an authentic Jewish understanding of *Heilsgeschichte*, as seen, for example, in Gen 17, Deut 32, Isa 2 and Micah 4.

The significance of the Seder message, retributive not vindictive justice ushers in the Great Redemption, should not be misconstrued by the post-Shoah Christian. It is a necessary wake-up call to the slumbering Christian to rediscover the Jewish roots of his/her faith, which are deep and far reaching, and to live with the *imitatio Christi* without antisemitism. It is an invitation to Christian preaching and catechism to understand Jewish belief and practice without polemics, politics and paternalism. It is a calling to see the Jew not as fossil or ashes but as God's first love in His salvific plan ("As far as election is concerned, they (Jews) are loved on account of the patriarchs. For God's gift and his call are irreversible."[20]). And by encouraging lessons learned from Darkness to Rebirth, Shoah and the State of Israel, it is hoped that the Church can correct an ambivalent triumphalist teaching about the Jews:

> For he (Christ) himself is our peace, who has
> made the two (Jew and Gentile) one and has
> destroyed the barrier, the dividing wall of
> hostility, *by abolishing in his flesh the*
> *law with its commandments and regulations*
> (italics added). His purpose was to create
> in himself one new man out of the two, thus
> making peace, and in this one body to reconcile
> both of them to God through the cross, by
> which he put to death their hostility.[21]
>
> (Eph 2: 14-16)

Then, and only then, can the Church ascend Jesus' conditional query (add, about the state of Christian belief) and proclaim: "My Father, it is possible that the cup passeth, as I will and as You will."[22] This is Christian redemption after Shoah, any alternative is Christian suicide.

V. Conclusion: The Snake in the Pardes

The Shoah has destroyed Christian and Jewish innocence in reading scriptures. Whether or not there is a direct link between two thousand years of Christian supersession teaching and the Shoah, the murder of millions of Jews in the heart of Christendom cannot be denied. The culpability of Christian teaching in fostering cultural and religious antisemitism in doctrine and dogma must be eliminated. To love the Lord Jesus Christ and to walk in his footsteps cannot be out of step to the Jewish, Christian and non-Christian victims of the Austrian Catholic, Adolph Hitler, and his co-religionist (Catholic and Protestant) murderers.

To say that not all Jews of Europe were murdered and that there is life affirmation among the *She'erith ha-Pleita* (saved remnant of Israel), and then invoke Torah as the panacea is naive and misleading. Torah is what it is and not what we make it out to be.

Torah is not the all perfect absolute of the true believers, nor does it provide an instant blueprint to rescue upon distress or demand. In God's creation, there is *tohu vavohu* ("unformed and void"),[23] so that man can redeem an imperfect world. God purposefully hides His face so that man can be free and choose the right ethical action.

God did His job and gave Torah at Sinai so that the Jew and mankind can learn and do. But can the Jew today read the Torah intact? Is he able, does he care? Pogroms, expulsions, crematoria have blackened and scourged its words. Memory of its content is filled with corpses and broken promises. To seek the seer and scribe is to find ashes, shoes and mattresses of hair.

But the Voice of Torah stubbornly refuses to be silent and its deafening words demand a hearing: God and Shoah. Do we read an evil demiurge capable of willing a universe in which Auschwitz can fit or do we say, the horrific Event is less severe by the presence of the Creator? In re-reading the Holy Scriptures after Shoah, do we encounter God and not Auschwitz, Auschwitz and not God, neither God nor Auschwitz, or God and Auschwitz?

In reading Jacob at Jabbok and Jesus at Gethsemane, the fourth option, for me, seems the most probable starting point for post-Shoah ecumenical dialogue. To wrestle with the Night Words of Jacob and Jesus is to confront the snake in the *Pardes*: A continuous *Din Torah* (disputation based on

Torah-judgment) with God, self and other, which instead of diminishing the paradox makes the problem more significant and more troubling and thus, more full of hope. It presents a challenge to Christians and Jews towards a true reconciliation accountable to scriptures and responsible to a post-Shoah world. Let the re-thinking on self and reciprocal discovery begin!

Endnotes

1. These words are being written as the 65th annual Academy Awards has voted an American western as the best film of 1992. In the literate, tasteful production of "Unforgiven," the myth of the American cowboy has passed from being lionized, to being derided to being revered.

2. Esau is identified as Edom in Gen 36:1.

3. Hebrew, "And he blessed him there." Midrash (Lekah Tob) understands the blessing to be longevity (Job 5:25), priestly (Num 6:24-26), progeny (Ezek 20:40), and messianic (Ps 132:17).

4. Gen 36 (all) and especially vv 31-43. "These are the kings who reigned in the Land of Edom before any king reigned over the Israelites" (v 31) is inspirational, i.e., when wickedness falls, triumphant good prevails.

5. Tanhuma Yelemmedenu Vayishlah 7, Midrash Avkir in Yalkut I, 132.

6. A biblical example of eternal vigil is provided to a non-bethrothed virgin who is taken by force. See Deut 22:28-29.

7. See Hekalot 4, 29; Zohar II, 4b. The *Borechu* is the ancient invocation to public prayer for the *Shema*, and the blessings before and after, in the morning and evening services.

8. Deut 33:4.

9. Deut 30:19.

10. Compare "the sheep of the flock will be scattered" (Zech 13:7b) and Jesus' charge in sending out of the twelve, "Go to the lost sheep of Israel" (Matt 10:6).

11. The heading of Ps 42 is "For the leader, a maskil of the Korahites." Korah was the leader who perished in the abortive revolt against Moses (Num 16), but the sons of Korah did not (Num 26:11) and they were part of the Levites who "extol the Lord God of Israel at the top of their voices" (2 Chr 20:19).

12. Robert McAfee Brown, **Elie Wiesel, Messenger to All Humanity**,

(Notre Dame, Indiana: University of Notre Dame Press, 1989[2]),
p. 54.

13. Cf. Exod 12:42.

14. This sentence is wanting in Matthew.

15. This phrase was first used by Abba Hillel Silver (1893-1963) in
addresses before the National Conference on Palestine (May 2, 1943)
and the American Jewish Conference, NYC (August 29 - September
5, 1943). But there is little doubt that the one man who has done most
to establish "The Crucifixion of the Jews" in the modern Christian
consciousness is Franklin H. Littell. Cf. **The Crucifixion of the Jews**
by Franklin H. Littell (New York: Harper and Row, 1975; reprinted
by Mercer University Press, 1986) for his impacting view on
Christianity and the Shoah.

16. A supplementary hymn in the Ashkenazi ritual on the first night of
Passover, "And So It Came to Pass inthe Middle of the Night," is
influenced by this midrash. It is said to be composed by Yannai, one
of the principal liturgists of the old Palestinian *piyyut*.

17. In Hebrew, *Hester Panim*("The Hidden Face of God").

18. See Zev Garber, "Interpretation and the Passover Haggadah: An
Invitation to Post-Biblical Historiosophy," *BHHE*, vol. 2.2 (Spring
1984), p. 27. The paper is reprinted in Duane L. Christensen, ed.,
Experiencing the Exodus from Egypt, (Oakland: Bibal Press,
1988), pp. 51-60. Connecting the "Pour Out Thy wrath" paragraph
with the Shoah is developed in chapter 8.

19. Jewish loyalty to ruler and country has its roots in Jeremiah's letter to
the exiles: "Seek the welfare of the city to which I have exiled you and
pray to the Lord in its behalf; for in its prosperity you shall prosper"
(Jer 29:7). Fear of Lord and king is expressed in Prov 24:21 and Ezra
6:10. Mishna Abot 3.2 reports in the name of R. Hanina, the Vice-
High Priest, "Pray for the peace of the ruling power (Rome), since but
for fear of it men would have swallowed up each other alive." The
fourth century amora, Mar Samuel of Nehardea, laid down the biding
principle, *Dina deMalkuta Dina*; in civil matters, the law of the land
is as binding on Jews as the commandments of the Torah. "Prayers
for the Government" are featured in the *Musaf* ("additional") liturgy
for Sabbath and festivals by all Jews today.

20. Rom 11:28b, 29.

21. Other noteworthy examples of supersessionist eschatology are John
4: 21-26 and Gal 3:26-29.

22. A post-Shoah re-reading of Matt 26:42b.

23. Gen 1:2a.

CHAPTER TEN

Gastgeschenk: Panim B'Fanim

On the fifty-third anniversary of the Reichspogromnacht — and the second anniversary of a reunited Germany — November 7-10, 1991, a number of scholars, survivors, and children of survivors joined Christian, Jewish, Senti-Romani, and Turkish citizens of Germany in a landmark meeting entitled, "Addressing the Cycle of Pain." I served as program coordinator and I gave the preliminary address on the eve of the conference. This landmark ecumenical event was noted in the Journal of Ecumenical Studies, vol. 28, no. 4 (Fall 1991) and my talk was printed in Shofar, vol. 10, no. 4 (Summer 1992).

Prologue

A landmark founder's meeting between Jews and Christians from America, Germany, and Israel, with representatives from the German Sinti and Roma and Turkish communities, took place November 7-10, 1991, in Berlin. Underscoring the historic significance of the conference ("Addressing the Cycle of Pain") is the fact that it took place on the fifty-third anniversary of the Reichspogromnacht–and the second anniversary of reunited Germany–in an atmosphere of existing tendencies of antisemitism and racism in Germany. Organized by *International Jewish News* publisher Phil Blazer and Prof. Zev Garber, the conference attracted about 150 people, including scholars, Shoah survivors, clergy, and Germans from the business and professional communities. Presentations ranged from religious, intellectual, and scientific topics to how antisemitism was used in the Nazi regime. Simultaneous group discussions involved hidden children, children of survivors and rescuers, and new-generation Germans, as well as practical options for the future.

Conference presenters included Beate Klarsfeld, the German Nazi hunter who apprehended war criminal Klaus Barbie (who murdered thousands of Jews and French freedom-fighters in Lyon, France); Franklin

H. Littell, president of the Philadelphia Institute on the Holocaust, Genocide, and Human Rights; and Dennis Prager, publisher of *Ultimate Issues*, a quarterly about religious values in modern society. Several persons from the Annual Scholars' Conference on the Holocaust and Church Struggle presented remarks, including Hubert Locke (University of Washington, Seattle), Harry James Cargas (Webster University), Alan L. Berger (Syracuse University) , Richard Libowitz (St. Jospehs University), and Marcia Sachs Littell (Director of the Annual Scholars' Conference). Among other presenters were Jacob Neusner (University of Southern Florida), Maurice Lamm (Yeshiva University), Pierre Sauvage (director of the film, "Weapons of the Spirit"), Mel Mermelstein (anti-"historical revisionism" activist), Christiane Schuetz (art historian, Berlin), Annegret Ehmann (Wansee-villa project and Atonement Action), Franz Mueller (a surviving member of the White Rose), Horst Roegner-Franche (founder, Berlin Free University), Stem Ete (leader, German Turkish community), and Romani Rose (leader, German Sinti and Romani community)

In the shadow of the Kaiser memorial church left in ruins since World War II, conference participants joined thousands in a Berlin *Kristallnacht* rally toward immigrant laborers and students. Littell pointed out the danger of "losing the uniqueness and specificity of the Shoah in vague and moralistic generalization about every kind of intolerance, bigotry, racism, persecution, and genocide." While Jewish opponents to holding the conference on German soil have claimed that the encounter was an act of gross irreverance to the insensitivities of survivors, this claim can, nevertheless, have a subtle effect of desensitizing the Jewish community to the suffering of others if, when Jews urge each other, "Never again!" the subtext is really "Never again *for us!*" The fact is that the Berlin *Kristallnacht* conference sympathized with the feelings of survivors and paid heed to the warning of the biblical prophets that society cannot endure without justice–even as people wrestle with the exigencies of survival in an increasingly ethnic and unpredictable world order.

I.

Fashionable though it is these days to invoke the Bitberg spirit of "storycide" among revisionist historians and Third World liberation theologians, workers in the cemetery of the Shoah testify to the stubborn persistence of the Shoah to "the past that weighs like a nightmare on the brain of the living," as French philosopher Jean-Paul Sartre once described history. It is the "deadly weight" of the Shoah—the horrific tradition of state-sponsored victimization and murder, and the unaccountable human, spiritual, and material loss that follow in its smoke—that has aroused many to discuss antisemitism, past, present, and future. Also it is the reason why a number of us came to Berlin on the eve *of Kristallnacht* to "address the cycle of pain": in order to learn how the lessons learned from the Shoah might help prevent future genocide.

The purpose of the Berlin encounter between concerned Jews, Christians, and Germans is threefold: first, we will explore the underpinnings of German thought and action, then and now, that are related to Jewish pain, suffering, and the Shoah; second, we will work at an agenda, considering Jewish dignity and self-respect and imploring German accountability and responsibility, in the fight against Shoah revisionism and worldwide antisemitism; and finally, we will study the atrocities of the Shoah not only to preserve their historicity but also to see signs of warning to prevent the atrocities from ever happening again to any people, at any time, in any place.

II.

Go back with me in time, in this land of Luther, when a monk gathered around him a circle of like-minded anti-Catholic protesters who initiated the Protestant Reformation in 1517. Believing that Jews would flock to the new Christian movement, now ex-monk Martin Luther (1483-1546) published a sympathetic book for the conversion of the Jews in 1523, **That Jesus Christ Was Born a Jew**. Alas, Luther's missionary zeal was not successful, and the Jews who did convert chose the Catholic variety, thus implying the superiority of Catholicism over Protestantism. Luther's growing bitterness against the Jews—e.g., he vehemently opposed the Book of Esther, which celebrates Jewish unity and victory over the enemy and contains no Christological reference, for inclusion in the Protestant German Bible—and sense of frustration finally vented in a notorious anti-Jewish tractate, **Concerning the Jews and Their Lies** (1543).

Luther's diabolic tirade against the Jews—the most infamous of any medieval anti-Jewish sentiment—is summed up in his words:

> Dear princes and nobles who have Jews in our domain, if this advice of mine (house arrest, taxing, flogging, extorting, expelling, restricting the Jews and their leaders. and burning their books) does not suit you, then find a better one so that you and we may all be free of this insufferable devilish burden—the Jews.

Elsewhere in the booklet he refers to the Jews as "poisonous bitter worms (who) are not accustomed to any work." It is shocking, but not surprising, that the Nuremberg laws accepted the spirit of Luther's antisemitic agenda and added the *Führers Wünsch* (Hitler's wish), the legitimate murder of the Jewish people.

III.

In this land of Luther and Hitler, Jews settled and sought emancipation and citizenship. To help facilitate the process, Moses Mendelssohn (1729-1786), the central personality of the German Jewish Enlightenment, supervised the translation of the Hebrew Scriptures into German in Hebrew letters and called it **Netivot HaShalom** (Pathways of Peace). This translation, which began in the 1770s, better known as the *Biur* (Commentary), because it includes a Hebrew commentary which combines the traditional rabbinic readings with the insight of the Enlightenment movement, remained the standard one for German-speaking Jewry.

Almost a century and a half later, in 1924/25, two important German Jewish philosophers, Martin Buber and Franz Rosenzweig, decided to translate the German Bible anew. Rosenzweig died in 1929 after a prolonged illness, but Buber, whose **Ich und Du** (1923) established him as one of the world's most influential thinkers, continued **Die Schrift und ihre Verdeutschung** (The Holy Scriptures and Its Germanization). He completed the project in February 1961.

At the completion of Buber's translation of the Bible, his colleague at the Hebrew University and rival in interpreting the meaning of Hasidism, Gershom Scholem, had this to say:

> Buber had a definite conception of the rough-hewn structure of the Hebrew language and sought to express it in his translation. No fill-in words, no transitions where none exist in Hebrew. No trifling with the sublime but letting it stand in its own rough greatness. Buber's method was to strive for the utmost literality, a literality that seemed at times to go to the limits and beyond.[1]

In addition, Buber produces, as Sholem correctly points out, a translation which in the final analysis renders the Bible as the word of God in which the name of God as such does not appear. The Name is replaced by the emphatic and prominent use of the subject pronouns I, Thou, He. This is consistent with Buber's existentialist "I and Thou" philosophy, namely that without meaningful relations to other persons, no one can have a meaningful relation to God. Buber's emphasis on personal encounter underscores the interpersonal aspect of religion. For Buber, the point of departure for life's ultimate issues is the question what it means to be an existing human being, and central to this question is our relationship to other persons.

We wish to point out that Buber's innovative and imaginative translation is rooted in the tradition of biblical and rabbinical exegesis. His substitution of pronouns for the Name suggests the people asking Moses: "What is His Name (meaning essence)? What shall I say to them? And God said unto Moses: 'I Am that I Am'; and He said, 'Thus shall you say unto the children of Israel: I Am has sent me unto you'" (Exod 13b-14). A sentence later, we read, "this is my Name forever" (Exod 3:15). In text, the consonantal Hebrew spelling "for ever" (l'olam) can also be read "to be hidden" (l'alem). In philosophical terms, then, Buber may well understand these excerpts from Exodus 3 to imply that God can be properly addressed but not adequately described.

Further, Buber's translation is an example of Sprachdenken, thinking in terms of language. Scholem points out that a unique feature of the Buber-Rosenzweig translation is that it uses every linguistic means and word sophistication to force the reader to read the text aloud. In other words, for the biblical word to be readable, it must be made audible. Similarly, the rabbinic choice word for the Bible is miqra', whose root letters mean to read and to call. suggesting an active. moral response to understanding the word of God.

Buber's intent in continuing the translation after the death of Rosenzweig was to elevate German Jewish literacy and to leave a "gift of thanks" to the German nation upon departure to Eretz Israel. Alas, the horrific events of the war years and the Shoah, conducted by the Nazis and their allies and supported by rank and file Germans, have altered the Gastgeschenk to a sefer zikaron, a memorial book to remember and to honor the murdered Jews of Europe.

IV.

We come to Berlin on the anniversary of Krislallnacht to address the Shoah as living history: Humanizing and remembering the event in terms of activism and not quietism. Thus, it is clear that the organizers and participants are not accepting (cornpromising) "the cycle of pain" but confronting it in the spirit or dialogue.[2]

Now the Torah speaks of two types of "Face to Face" encounter. Panim el panim, direct, logical, clear, as when God spoke to Moses, panim el panim (cf. Exod 33:11 and Deut 34: 10). The idiomatic expression, panim b'fanim is found in Deuteronomy 5: 1-4:

And Moses called unto all Israel, and said unto them. Hear, 0 Israel, the statutes and ordinances which I speak in your ears this day, that you may learn them, and observe to do them. The Lord our God made a covenant with us in Horeb. The Lord made not this covenant with our fathers, but with us, even us, who are all of us here alive this day. The Lord spoke with you face to face *(panim b'fanim)* in the mount out of the midst of fire.

The experience of Horeb is *panim b'fanim*, "face into face" or "face after face," teaching that the revelation at Horeb/Sinai was experienced by all but interpreted differently by each and every Israelite based on individual experience with the sacred. At Horeb, the Covenant proclaimed "out of the midst of fire" emphasized the present and not the past, but here in Berlin, we understand the words ("not with our fathers") to mean that the Six Million Jewish victims of Hitler's wholesale incineration are with us today. Their message of survival with dignity and morality must become the binding force upon all future generations (see, too, "I make this covenant and this oath with him that stands here with us this day before the Lord our God, and also with him that is not here with us this day" [Deut 29:13b-141]).

When Auschwitz (survival at any price) contends with Sinai (a moral standard), Sinai must prevail. Fascism, neo-Nazism, violent hate and bias are examples of what can happen when Auschwitz prevails. Sinai and not cyanide, Horeb and not *hereb* (sword; destruction).

This, then, is our message on Shabbat *Toledot* (Gen 25:19-28:9), which talks of the birthright of Isaac and the blessings of Isaac, *the first* survivor of a holocaust (see Gen 22, "The Binding of Isaac"), November 9, 1991, two years to the day when divided Germany is no longer and 53 years after *Kristallnacht:* Seek out with respect and sensitivity the holocaust of every survivor and penetrate the satanic edifice of Hitlerism, then, now, and in the future. Let our dialogue be conducted without politics, condescending politeness, and paternalism in the full spirit of *panim b'fanim.* And may we all discover the Thou in each I, and proclaim that mankind is improvable. We must all be reminded of this, and victimizers and victims of the Shoah, above all, must believe it.

Only then can we realize the inspirational prophetic message of Shabbat *Toledot:*

> From where the sun rises to where it sets, My Name is honored among the nations, and everywhere incense and pure oblation are offered to my Name; for my Name is honored among the nations, said the Lord of Hosts.
>
> (Mal 1:11)

Endnotes

1. Gershon Scholem, **The Messianic Idea in Judaism** (New York: Schocken, 1971), p. 315. The original German appeared in *Neue Zürcher Zeitung* (March 31, 1963) and *Judaica* (Frankfurt am Main, 1963).
2. The Newsletter of theAmerican Gathering/Federation of Jewish Holocaust Survivors (November 11, 1991) falsely charges that the Berlin gathering is political and bent to "close the cycle of pain."

Appendix A: The Letter of the 93 Maidens

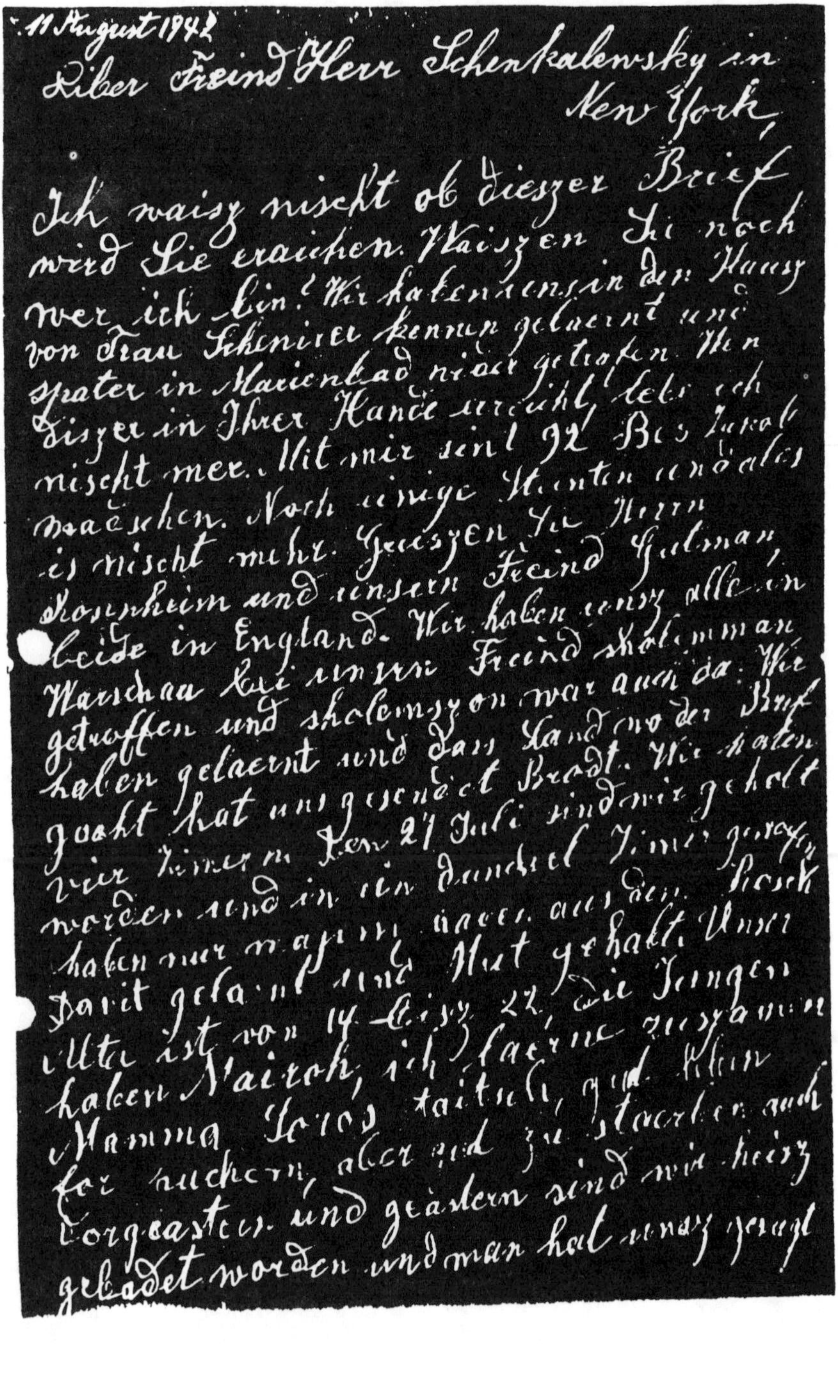

heute nacht werden kimen deutsch Soldaten
uns besuchen. Wir haben geastern die
schwie gethan zusamen zu sterben. Man
hat uns geastern in ein grozes Hausz
mit lachßen Zimern und schoenen Beten
gesaendet. Deutsche wizen nisht, das
Bad ist unszere levile vor den Todt.
Man hat uns haint alles genomen
und nur ein Hemt geschenket. Wir
haben all Giut. Wen Soldaten
komen werden wir alle dирeken.
Haint sind wir zuszamen lernen
zansen zom viduzoh. Wir haben
kaine moiroh. Danken guter
Freind vuer ales. Wir haben eine
Biti sagen Sie Kadich vuer uns
93 ihre Kinder. Baelde sind wir
bei mama Sore. Es gruszt sie

        Chaja Feldman von

    Kroko.

BIBLIOGRAPHY

Abrahamson, I. (ed.). **Against Silence: The Voice and Vision of Elie Wiesel.** 3 vols. (New York: Holocaust Library, 1983).

Alter, Y. L. "Teshuvah," in Holtz, B.W. (ed.), **Back to the Sources: Reading the Classic Jewish Text** (New York, Summit Books, 1984).

Anonymous. "The Last Song of the Jewish Community of Lublin," in Blumenthal, D.R., **Understanding Jewish Mysticism,** vol. 2 (New York: Ktav Publishing House, 1982), pp. 104-107.

Apenszlak, J. et al (eds.). **The Black Book of Polish Jewry** (New York: Roy Publishers, 1943).

Baeck, L. **This People Israel** (New York, Holt and Winston, 1964; Philadelphia: Jewish Publication Society of America, 1965).

Bartoszewski, W.T. **The Convent at Auschwitz** (London, Bowerdean Press, 1990).

Bauer, Y. **The Holocaust in Historical Perspective** (Seattle: University of Washington Press, 1978).

_____. **The Jewish Emergence from Powerlessness** (Toronto: University Toronto Press, 1979).

_____. "Whose Holocaust?" *Midstream* (November 1980), pp. 42-46.

_____. **American Jewry and the Holocaust: The American Jewish Joint Distribution Committee 1939-1945** (Detroit: Wayne State University Press,1981).

Baumol, J.T. "On Legends, Symbols and Reality: The Story of the 93 Maidens from the Beith Jacob Seminary in Cracow Who Died on the Sanctification of the Name" (Hebrew) (Unpublished paper, N.d.).

Bavli, H. "The Letter of the Ninety-Three Maidens," in Harlow, J. (ed.), **Mahzor for Rosh Hashanah and Yom Kippur** (New York, The Rabbinical Assembly, 1972).

Bentwich, J., **Josephus** (Philadelphia: Jewish Publication Society of America, 1914).

Benzaquin, P. **Holocaust!** (New York, 1959).

Berger, A.L. **Crisis and Covenant: The Holocaust in American Jewish Fiction** (Albany: SUNY Press, 1985).

_____(ed.). **Bearing Witness to the Holocaust 1939-1989** (Lewiston, N.Y.: Edward Mellen Press, 1991).

Berkovits, E. **Faith After the Holocaust** (New York, Ktav Publishing House, 1973)

_____. **With God in Hell: Judaism in the Ghettos and Death Camps** (New York: Sanhedrin Press, 1979).

Bialik, H.N. "On the Slaughter," in Bialik, H.N., **Kol Shirei H.N. Bialik** (Hebrew) (Tel Aviv: Dvir Co., 1961).

Blumenthal, D.R. **Understanding Jewish Mysticism: The Merkabah Tradition and the Zoharic Tradition** (New York: Ktav Publishing House, 1978).

Bokser, B.M. **The Origins of the Seder: The Passover Rite and Early Rabbinic Judaism** (Berkely, Los Angeles, London: University of California Press, 1984).

Borowitz, E.B. **Choices in Modern Jewish Thought** (New York: Behrman House, 1983).

Braham, R.L. "What Did They Know and When?" in Bauer, Y. and Rotenstreich, N. (eds.), **The Holocaust as Historical Experience**

(New York: Holmes and Meier, 1981).

Brenner, R.F. "Edith Stein: The Phenomenological Ethics in Her Religion" (Paper presented at Vanderbilt University, 5 March 1990).

Broszat, M. "Plädoyer für eine Historisierung des Nationlsozialismus," **Merkur** 39 (1985), pp. 373-385.

_____. **The Hitler State** (London and New York: Longman, 1991). German original (**Der Statt Hitlers**) published in 1969.

Brown, R.M. **Elie Wiesel: Messenger to All Humanity** (Notre Dame: University of Notre Dame Press, 1989²).

_____. "A Symbol Is a Symbol Is a Symbol," *Christianity and Crisis* (23 October 1989).

Van Buren, P.M. **Discerning the Way**, Part I of **A Theology of the Jewish Christian Reality** (New York: Seabury, 1980).

_____. **A Christian Theology of the People Israel**, Part II of **A Theology of the Jewish Christian Reality** (New York: Seabury, 1983).

_____. "Ecclesia Semper Reformanda: The Challenge of Israel," in Libowitz, R. (ed.), **Faith and Freedom: A Tribute to Franklin H. Littell** (Oxford: Pergamon Press, 1987).

Cargas, H.J. "Preface," in Shelley, L. (ed.), **Secretaries of Death** (New York: Sheingold Publishers, 1986).

_____. **Reflections of a Post-Auschwitz Christian** (Detroit: Wayne State University Press, 1989).

Colijn, G.J. and Littell, M.S. (eds.). **The Netherlands and Nazi Genocide** (Lewiston, N.Y.: Edward Mellen Press, 1992).

Cuddily, J.M. "The Elephant and the Angels: Or, The Incivil Irritatingness of Jewish Theodicy," in Bellah, R.N. and Greenspahn, F.E. (eds.), **Uncivil Religion: Interreligious Hostility in America** (New York: Crossroads, 1987).

Dawidowicz, L. **The War Against the Jews 1933-1945** (New York: Holt, Rinehart and Winston, 1975).

_____. **A Holocaust Reader** (New York: Behrman House, 1976).

_____. **The Holocaust and the Historians** (Cambridge, MA: Harvard University Press, 1986).

Doneson, J.E. **The Holocaust and the American Film** (Philadelphia: Jewish Publication Society of America, 1987).

Eckardt, A.L. "Post-Holocaust Theology: A Journey Out of the Kingdom of Night," *Holocaust and Genocide Studies*, vol. 1, no.2 (1986), pp. 229-240.

Eckardt, A.R. **Reclaiming the Jesus of History, Christology Today** (Minneapolis: Fortress Press, 1992).

_____ & Eckardt, A.L. **Long Night's Journey into Day** (Detroit:Wayne State University Press, 1988; 2nd ed. rev. 1988).

Edinger, D. "A Foot-Note To the Letter of the Ninety-Three Maidens," *The Reconstructionist* (5 March 1943).

Eliach, Y., **Hasidic Tales of the Holocaust: The First Original Tales in a Century** (New York: Oxford University Press, 1982).

Ettinger, S. "The Origins of Modern Anti-Semitism," in Gutman, Y. and Rothkirchen, L. (eds.), **The Catastrophe of European Jewry: Antecedents, History, Reflections: Selected Papers** (Jerusalem: Yad Vashem, 1976).

Ezrahi, S. **By Words Alone: The Holocaust in Literature** (Chicago: University Press, 1980).

Fackenheim, E. **Quest for Past and Future** (Boston: Beacon Press, 1970).

_____. **God's Presence in History. Jewish Affirmations and Philosophical Reflections** (New York: Harper and Row, 1970).

_____. **The Jewish Return into History: Reflections in the Age**

of Auschwitz and a New Jerusalem (New York: Schocken Books, 1978)..

_____. "Foreward," in Bauer, Y., **The Jewish Emergence from Powerlessness** (Toronto: University of Toronto Press, 1979).

_____. **To Mend the World: Foundations of Future Jewish Thought** (New York: Schocken Books, 1982).

_____. **What Is Judaism?** (New York: Summit Books, 1987).

_____. "Holocaust and Weltanschauung. Philosophical Reflections on Why They Did It," *Holocaust and Genocide Studies*, vol. 3, no. 2 (1988), pp. 191-208.

Feingold, H.L. **Did American Jewry Do Enough During the Holocaust?** (New York: Syracuse University Press, 1985).

Fisher, E. "Theological Education and Christian- Jewish Relations," in Garber, Z. (ed.), **Methodology in the Academic Teaching of Judaism** (Lanham.. University Press of America, 1986/87).

_____. "A Response to Daniel Polish," *Ecumenical Trends* (October 1987), pp. 24-27.

_____. "The'Jewishness' of Our Spiritual Heritage," *Our Sunday Visitor* (22 May 1988).

Fleischner, E. (ed.). **Auschwitz. Beginning of a New Era?** (New York: Ktav Publishing House, 1977).

Fleming, G. **Hitler and the Final Solution** (Berkeley: University of California Press, 1984). German original (**Hitler und die Endlosung:"Es ist des Führers Wunsch ..."**) published in 1982.

Fox, J. "The Holocaust: A Non-Unique Event for All Humanity," in Bauer, Y.et al (eds.), **Remembering for the Future**, vol. 2 (Oxford: Pergamon Press, 1988).

Friedlander, S. "From Antisemitism to Extermination: A Historigraphical Study of Nazi Policies Toward the Jews and an Essay in Interpretation,"**Yad Vashem Studies** XVI (1984), pp. 1-50.

Friedman, P. **Bibliography of Books in Hebrew on the Jewish Catastrophe and Heroism in Europe** (Jerusalem: Yad Vashem - YIVO, 1960).

Garber, Z. "Sinai and not Cyanide: Witness and not Survivor." remarks given at the Utah State Capitol Rotunda on 19 April 1985, in conjunction with the Governor's proclomation of Holocaust Memorial Week 1983.

_____. (ed.). **Methodology in the Academic Teaching of Judaism** (Lanham: University Press of America, 1986/87).

_____. "Triumph on the Gallows," *Israel Today* (August 1987).

_____. "Auschwitz: The Real Problem," *Israel Today* (April 1988).

_____, Berger, A.L. and Libowitz, R. (eds.). **Methodology in the Academic Teaching of the Holocaust** (Lanham: University Press of America, 1988).

_____. "Interpretation and the Passover Haggadah: An Invitation to Post-Biblical Historiosophy," *Bulletin Hebrew Higher Education*, vol.2, no. 2 (1988), pp. 24-29. Reprinted in Christensen, D.L. (ed.), **Experiencing the Exodus from Egypt** (Oakland: Bibal Press, 1988).

_____. "Blood and Thunder: Israel Under Siege," *Israel Today* (March 1988).

_____. and Zuckerman, B. "Why Do We Call the Holocaust 'The.Holocaust"? An Inquiry into the Psychology of Labels," in Bauer, Y. et al (eds.), **Remembering for the Future**, vol. 2 (Oxford: Pergamon Press, 1988).

_____. "*Reichspogromnacht*: First Berlin International Conference," *Journal of Ecumenical Studies*, vol. 28, no. 4 (Fall 1991), pp. 677-678.

_____. "*Gastgeschenk: Panim B'Fanim*," *Shofar*, vol. 10, no. 4 (Summer 1992), pp. 76-80.

Goldman, S. (ed.). **The Five Megiloth** (London: Soncino Press, 1961).

Goldschmidt, E.D. **The Passover Haggadah, Its Sources and History**
(Hebrew) (Jerusalem: Bialik Institute, 1969).

Greenberg, I. "Cloud of Smoke, Pillar of Fire: Judaism, Christianity
and Modernity After the Holocaust," in Fleischner, E. (ed.),
Auschwitz: Beginning of a New Era? (New York: Ktav Publishing
House, 1977). .

_____. "Religious Values After the Holocaust," in Peck, A.J.(ed.),
Jews and Christians After the Holocaust (Philadelphia: Fortress,
1982).

_____. **The Jewish Way** (New York: Summit Books, 1988).

Grondelski, J. "Theological Literature in Poland on Catholic-Jewish
Relations Since the Auschwitz Convent Controversy: A Survey," *The
Polish Review*, vol. 37, no. 3 (1992), pp. 285-296.

Gutferstein, J. "The Indestructable Dignity of Man," *Judaism*, vol. 19,
no. 3 (1970), pp. 262-263.

Halpern, B. "What is Anti-Semitism?" *Modern Judaism*, vol. 1, no. 3
(1981), pp. 251-262.

Hatch, E. and Redpath, H. **Concordance to the Septuagint** (Oxford,1897).

Hertz, J.H. (ed.). **The Pentateuch and Haftorahs With Hebrew Text,
English Translation, and Commentary** (London: Soncino Press,
1966²).

Heschel, A.J. "The Inner World of the Polish Jew," in Vishnaic, R.,
Polish Jews, A Pictorial Record (New York: Schocken Books, 1947).

_____. **The Earth is the Lord's** (New York: Henry Schuman, Inc.,
1950).

Hilberg, R. **The Destruction of European Jews**, 3 vols,, rev edn.
(New York: Holmes and Meier, 1985).

Hildebrand, K. "Wer dem Abgrund entrinnen will, muss ihn aufs genaueste auslaten. Ist die neue deutsche Geschichtsschreibung revisionistich ?," *Die Welt* (22 November 1986).

Hillgruber, A. **Zweieriei Untergang. Die Zerschlagung des deutschen Reiches und das End des europäischen Judentums** (Berlin: Corso bei Seidler, 1986).

Horowitz, I.L. "Many Genocides, One Holocaust?" *Modern Judaism*, vol. 1, no.1 (1981), pp. 74-89.

Insdorf, I. **Shadows: Films and the Holocaust,** 2nd ed. (Cambridge: Cambridge University Press, 1989).

Jaeckel, E. **Hitler's Weltanschauung: A Blueprint for Power** (Middletown, Conn.: Wesleyan University Press, 1972). German original (**Hitlers Weltanschauung**) published in 1969.

Joachmann, W. and Nellesson, B. **Adolf Hitler: Personlichkeit-Ideologie-Taktik** (Pederborne, 1960).

John Paul II. "Homily for the Beatification of Edith Stein," **NC News Service** (4 May 1987), pp. 22-26.

_____. **On the Holocaust** (Washington, D.C.: National Conference of Catholic Bishops, 1988).

Josephus. **The Jewish War** (G.A. Williamson trans.) (Baltimore: Penquin, 1959).

"Kahan Commission Report," *Jerusalem Post* (9 November 1983).

Kasher, M.M. **Israel Passover Haggadah** (New York: Sheingold Publishers, 1983).

Katz, J. **From Prejudice to Destruction: Antisemitism 1700-1933** (Cambridge, Harvard University Press, 1983[2]). Hebrew original (**Mi-Sin'at Israel La-Shelat Ha-Geza**) published in 1979.

_____. "Was the Holocaust Predictable?" in Bauer, Y. and Rotenstreich, N. (eds.), **The Holocaust as Historical Experience**

(New York: Holmes and Meier, 1981), pp. 23-41.

Katz, S. "The Unique Intentionality of the Holocaust," *Modern Judaism*, vol. 1, no. 1 (1981), pp. 161-183.

Kermisz, J. and Kiakowski, S. **Polish-Jewish Relations during the Second World War** (Jerusalem: Yad Vashem, 1974).

Kirschner, R. (ed). **Rabbinic Responsa of the Holocaust Era** (New York: Schocken Books, 1985).

Kolitz, Z. "Yossel Rakover's Appeal to God," in Friedlander, A.H. (ed.), **Out of the Whirlwind** (New York: Schocken Books, 1968).

Korman, G. (ed.). **Hunter and Hunted: Human History of the Holocaust** (New York: Viking Press, 1973).

Kosinski, J. **The Painted Bird** (London: Corgi, 1972).

Krauthammer, C. "Holocaust. Memory and Rescue," *Time* (3 May 1993).

Lanzmann, C. **Shoah** (New York: Pantheon Books, 1985).

Laquer, W. **The Terrible Secret: Suppression of the Truth about Hitler's Final Solution** (London: Weidenfeld and Nicholson, 1980).

Lester, J. "The Uses of Suffering," *Jerusalem Post* (6 November 1979).

_____. **Lovesong: Becoming a Jew** (New York: Henry Holt and Co., 1988).

Lewin, Y. (ed.). **Eleh Ezkerah** (New York: Shulsinger Bros., 1956-1972).

Lewis, B. **Semites and Anti-Semites: An Inquiry into Conflict and Prejudice** (New York: W.W. Norton, 1986).

Lewis, C.T. and Short, C. **A Latin Dictionary** (Oxford, 1879; rept. 1969).

Liddell, R.G. and Scott, R. **A Greek English Lexicon**, rev. Jones, H.S.

(Oxford, 1968).

Littell, F.H. **The Crucifixion of the Jews: A Failure of Christianity to Understand the Jewish Experience** (New York: Harper and Row, 1975; Mercer University Press, 1986).

_____. "Basic Lessons of the Holocaust," **N.I.H. Notebook** (November 1983).

Maier, C.S. **The Unmasterable Past: History, Holocaust, and German National Identity** (Cambridge, MA. Harvard University Press, 1988).

Maimonides. **Guide to the Perplexed**, 2 vols. (S. Pines, transl.) (Chicago: University of Chicago Press, 1975).

Marcus, J. (ed.). **The Jew in the Medieval World** (Cleveland and New York: Meridian Books and Jewish Publication Society of America, 1961).

Marrus, M.R. "The Theory and Practice of Antisemitism," *Commentary*, vol. 74, no. 2 (1982), pp. 38-42.

Marty, M. "The Convent at Auschwitz Recalls a Polish Past Most Want to Forget," *LA Times* (17 September 1989).

Mayer, A.J. **Why Did the Heavans Not Darken? The "Final Solution" in History** (New York. Pantheon Books, 1988).

Mendes-Flohr, P.R. and Reinhartz, J. (eds.). **The Jew in the Modern World** (New York and Oxford: Oxford University Press, 1980).

Mintz, A. **Hurban: Responses to Catastrophe in Hebrew Literature** (New York: Columbia University Press, 1984).

Mommsen, H. "Stehen wir von einer neuen Polarisierung des Geschichtsbildes in der Bundesrepublik?" in Miller, S. (ed.), **Geschichte in der demokratischen Gesellschaft. Eine Dokumentation** (Düsseldorf: Schwann-Begel, 1975), pp. 71-82.

Modras, R. "Jews and Poles: A Relationship Reconsidered," *America* 146 (January 2-9, 1982), pp. 5-8.

93 (Hebrew) (Tel Aviv: Office of the Chief Rabbinate for Tel Aviv and its Surroundings, 1943).

Nolte, E. "Vergangenheit die nicht vergehen will," *Frankfurther Allgemeine Zeitung* (6 June 1986).

_____. **Der europäische Burgerkrieg Nationalsozialismus und Bolschewismus** (Frankfurt am Main: Propylaen, 1987).

Novak, D. **The Image of the Non-Jew in Judaism, An Historical and Constructive Study of the Noahide Laws** (New York and Toronto: The Edward Mellen Press, 1973).

Oshry, E. **Responsa from the Holocaust** (New York, Judaica Press, 1983).

Patai, R. **The Jewish Mind** (New York: Charles Scribner's Sons, 1977).

_____ and Patai Wing, J. **The Myth of the Jewish Race** (New York: Charles Scribners Sons, 1975).

Presser, J. **Ashes in the Wind: The Destruction of Dutch Jewry** (Detroit, Wayne State University Press, 1968).

Ravitch, N. "The Problems of Christian Anti-Semitism," *Commentary*, vol.73, no. 4 (1982), pp. 41-52.

Reich, A. **Changes and Developments in the Passover Haggadot of the Kibbutz Movement** (Unpublished Ph.D., University of Texas at Austin, 1972).

Reuther, R.R. "Anti-Semitism and Christian Theology," in Fleischner, E. (ed.), **Auschwitz: Beginning of a New Era?** (New York: Ktav Publishing House, 1974)

_____. **Faith and Fratricide: The Theological Roots of Anti-Semitism** (New York: Seabury, 1974).

_____ and Reuther, H.J. **The Wrath of Jonah: The Crisis of Religious Nationalism in the Israeli-Palestinian Conflict** (San

Francisco: Harper and Row, 1989).

Rittner, C. and Roth, J. (eds.). **Memory, Offended: The Auschwitz Convent Controversy** (New York: Praeger, 1991).

Rosenbaum, I.J. **The Holocaust and the Halkhah** (New York: Ktav Publishing House, 1976).

Roskies, D. **Against the Apocalypse: Responses to Catastrophe in Modern Jewish Culture** (Cambridge, MA and London: Harvard University Press, 1984).

_____. **Literature of Destruction** (Philadelphia: Jewish Publication of America, 1988).

Rubenstein, R.L. **After Auschwitz: Radical Theology and Contemporary Judaism** (Indianopolis. Bobbs-Merrill, 1966; 2nd. ed. rev., Baltimore and London: The John Hopkins University Press, 1992).

_____. **Morality and Eros** (New York: McGraw-Hill, 1970).

_____. **The Cunning of History: The Holocaust and the American Future** (New York: Harper and Row, 1975).

Rudavsky, D. **Modern Jewish Religious Movements** (New York: Behrman House, 1979²).

Schindler, P. **Hasidic Responses to the Holocaust in Light of Hasidic Thought** (New Jersey: Ktav Publishing House, 1990).

Schwarz-Bart, A. **The Last of the Just** (New York: Bantam, 1977).

Secretariat for Catholic-Jewish Relations, National Conference of Catholic Bishops. **Guidelines for Catholic-Jewish Relations** (Washington, D.C., 1985).

Sherrard, G. **The Holocaust: Poems to the Children of England That They Might be Spared** (London, 1944).

Smølenskin, P. "The Haskalah of Berlin (1883)," in Hertzberg, A. (ed.), **The Zionist Idea** (New York: Althenum, 1975).

Sorer, H.B.M.E.F. **Mahaneh Hayyim** (Hungary, 1879-1885).

Stein, E. **Life in a Jewish Family: Her Unfinished Autobiographical Account** (J. Koeppel transl.) (Washington, D.C., 1986).

Steinberg, M. **Basic Judaism** (New York: Harcourt, Brace and World, 1947).

Stillman, N. **The Jews of Arab Lands: A History and Source Book** (Philadelphia: Jewish Publication Society of America, 1980).

Talmon, J. "European History as the Seedbed of the Holocaust," *Midstream* XIX (May 1973), pp. 3-25.

Thoma, C. **A Christian Theology of Judaism** (New York: Paulist Press, 1980).

Thomas of Monmouth. **The Life and Miracles of St. William of Norwich** (circa 1173).

Timmerman, J. **The Longest War: Israel in Lebanon** (New York: Vintage Books, 1982).

Vatican Commission for Religious Relations with the Jews. **Notes on the Correct Way to Present Jews and Judaism in Preaching and Catechesis of the Roman Catholic Church, With a Note on the Preperation of the Document** (Vatican, 1985).

Weinryb, B.D. **Jewish Emancipation Under Attack** (New York: The American Jewish Committee, 1942).

Weiss, H. **Kiddush Hashem: The Heroic Death of the Ninety-Three Maidens in the Cracow Ghetto on 13 Av 5702** (Hebrew) (Tel Aviv: Beit Ya'akov, 1947).

_____. "Kiddush Hashem," in **25th Year Jubilee Volume of High School and Seminary for Kindergartners (teachers) and Teachers, Beit Ya'akov in Tel Aviv, 1936-1961** (Hebrew) (Tel Aviv, 1961).

Wiesel, E. Review of J. Bor, **The Terezen Requiem**, *New York Times Book Review* (27 October 1967).

_____. **Night** (New York: Avon, 1970).

_____. **One Generation After** (New York: Avon, 1970).

_____. **The Oath** (New York: Random House, 1973).

_____. Review of "Holocaust," *New York Times* (16 April 1978).

_____. **Dawn** (Toronto. Bantam Books, 1982).

Wiesenthal, S. **The Sunflower** (New York: Schocken Books, 1978).

Wyman, D. **The Abandonment of the Jews: America and the Holocaust 1941-1945** (New York: Pantheon, 1984).

Yaari, Y. **Bibligraph.y of the Passover Haggadah from the Earliest Printed Editions** (Hebrew) (Jerusalem, 1960).

Yerushalmi, Y.H. **Haggadah and History** (Philadelphia: Jewish Publication Society of America, 1975).

Zimmels, H.J. **The Echo of the Nazi Holocaust in Rabbinic Literature** (Republic of Ireland, 1975).

Index

Source Index

About the Author

Zev Garber is Professor of Jewish Studies, Los Angeles Valley College, and Visiting Professor of Religious Studies, University of California at Riverside. The author of more than 325 scholarly articles and book reviews, he is the editor of **Methodology in the Academic Teaching of Judaism** (1986), **Methodology in the Academic Teaching of the Holocaust** (with A. Berger and R. Libowitz, 1988), **Teaching Hebrew Language and Literature at the College Level** (Shofar 9.3, Spring 1991), and **Perspectives on Zionism** (Shofar 13.1, Fall 1994). He is editor of *Iggeret* (Newsletter of the National Association of Professors of Hebrew), contributing editor of the *LA Jewish News* (formerly, *Israel Today*), and contributor to *Chasm Andaaz* (Persian monthly), where he has contributed hundreds of journalistic pieces and editorial columns on facets of Hebraica and Judaica. He is on the editorial board of *Shofar*; is a member of the Conference Committee for the Annual Scholar's Conference on the Holocaust and Church struggle and an educational consultant to the Philadelphia Center for the Holocaust, Genocide and Human Rights. He has also served as President of the National Association of Professors of Hebrew. Finally, he is the Editor-in-Chief of the **Studies in the Shoah** series from the University Press of America.